RETHINKING AMERICAN DISASTERS

RETHINKING AMERICAN DISASTERS

EDITED BY CYNTHIA A. KIERNER
MATTHEW MULCAHY & LIZ SKILTON

LOUISIANA STATE UNIVERSITY PRESS
BATON ROUGE

Published by Louisiana State University Press
lsupress.org

LSU Press Paperback Original
Manufactured in the United States of America
First printing

DESIGNER: Michelle A. Neustrom
TYPEFACE: Whitman
PRINTER AND BINDER: Sheridan Books, Inc.

COVER PHOTOGRAPH: Flooding in Baton Rouge, Louisiana, in 2016. Photo courtesy of Louisiana Department of Transportation and Development.

Cataloging-in-Publication Data are available from the Library of Congress.

ISBN 978-0-8071-7993-2 (pbk.: alk. paper) — ISBN 978-0-8071-7984-0 (pdf) — ISBN 978-0-8071-7983-3 (epub)

CONTENTS

RETHINKING AMERICAN DISASTERS

INTRODUCTION

CYNTHIA A. KIERNER, MATTHEW MULCAHY, AND LIZ SKILTON

In 1964, an Ohio State University historian named John C. Burnham was invited by a group of researchers at the university's Disaster Research Center to travel to Alaska to examine the aftermath of the devastating 1964 earthquake. "The sociologists on the team," Burnham recalled, "thought that it might be useful to have a historian's perspective as they studied the disaster." Burnham headed off to the library to read up on disasters but quickly discovered that historians had written very little on the topic. Journalists and other popular writers had chronicled well-known disasters like the Chicago Fire or San Francisco Earthquake, often focusing on the drama and destruction of such events, but with the exception of a study of the Great Lisbon Earthquake of 1755, Burnham found no serious historical accounts of disasters. Feeling he had little to offer the group, Burnham stayed home while the sociologists traveled to Alaska.[1]

Burnham's colleagues at the Disaster Research Center at Ohio State (now located at the University of Delaware) were at the forefront of academic research on disasters that first emerged in the wake of World War II. Although a few older studies existed—sociologist Samuel Prince's 1920 study of a dynamite explosion in Halifax a few years earlier is often seen as the first academic investigation of a disaster—the topic did not generate much interest until the 1940s and 1950s. Then, as tensions with the Soviet Union shifted into the Cold War, US military and government officials became concerned about how populations would respond to a possible nuclear attack. Would they panic and riot? Could any social order be maintained? What kind of aid would be available and how quickly? Seeking answers to these questions without dropping bombs, officials saw large-scale natural hazards like hurricanes, earthquakes, and floods as the closest equivalent, and they began to fund research by social scientists to explore how people responded to the chaos, disruption, and stress accompanying disasters.[2]

Over the next several decades, disaster studies emerged as an important subfield in sociology, political science, economics, and psychology. Historians, as Burnham discovered, were slower to get involved. But Burnham's forays into the stacks at the Ohio State library had "alerted" (his word) him to the possibilities that existed for historians to examine disasters as a means of exploring the "social fabric" of past societies. The history of disasters was, he wrote in a short essay in 1988, a "neglected field," and he urged his colleagues to build on the insights gained from other disciplines to ask questions about historical disasters. He included a short account of a successful graduate seminar he had taught on the topic, highlighting a pioneering study of the 1811 earthquakes in New Madrid, Missouri, by James Lal Penick Jr.[3]

Fast-forward thirty-five years, and historians have more than answered Burnham's call. The 2001 publication of a collection of interdisciplinary essays on American disasters, edited by Steven Biel—the first of its kind—was particularly noteworthy as a showcase for new scholarship in the field. Biel's collection, *American Disasters*, featured innovative work on hurricanes, fires, and environmental calamities, most of which occurred in the late nineteenth and twentieth centuries.[4] The two decades since then have witnessed an outpouring of more books and articles analyzing a range of disasters that have occurred in the territory that became the United States, before and after independence. A quick subject search in the *America: History and Life* database reveals that hundreds of articles on American "disasters" alone have appeared in academic journals since 2001. Panels exploring floods, earthquakes, hurricanes, and the like routinely appear at annual meetings of the American Historical Association, the American Society for Environmental History, as well as a variety of specialty conferences. Courses with such titles as "Disasters in American History" have become common at many colleges and universities. As Burnham foresaw, many of these studies and courses build on broad interdisciplinary foundations, drawing insights from the social sciences, literary studies, and, of course, a variety of environmental science disciplines.

There are several reasons for the rise of disaster studies in history. One is that historians came to recognize, as Burnham had suggested, that disasters offer a unique lens through which to explore past societies. Historians began to ask questions about the social and economic impact of calamities, how people made sense of such events, and how they responded to and recovered from the devastation. They found that disasters provide an opportunity to think about familiar issues like religion, politics, economics, and culture in new ways. Another factor is that disasters began to occupy an ever-more-prominent place in the collective consciousness of the nation, especially in the first decades of the twenty-first century. Hurricane Katrina (2005) in particular brought forth not only questions about the immediate suffering so vividly displayed on American television screens but also deeper questions about race and class and American society, past and present. Subsequent events such as Superstorm Sandy (2012), recurrent wildfires in the West, major ice storms, and other disasters have only reinforced such questions. Still another, related factor is the rising concern about the environment and climate change and the potential for even more, and increasingly more devastating, disasters in the future.

Heightened attention to disasters, both in popular media and among scholars, raises questions about definitions and about what constitutes a disaster. The answer to that seemingly simple question is actually rather complicated. A "disaster" can be any incident that negatively impacts a group of individuals. The term "disaster" is often used interchangeably with phrases like catastrophe, calamity, act of God, tragedy, crisis, or cataclysm.[5] The effects of disasters can include the loss of life, property, or disruption to existing political, social, economic, and environmental conditions. Disasters can be "rapid-onset incidents," with the majority of the damage taking place within a few minutes, hours, or days (a hurricane or a hard freeze), or "slow disasters," events that evolve over months, years, or centuries (such as pandemics or climatic change) and whose "slow violence" against people and environments often goes unrecognized due to its prolonged nature.[6] They can be isolated incidents (a building fire) or a series of events that become a larger, complex disaster (a hurricane followed by flooding and landslides). They can be incidents that garner considerable media and popular attention, resulting in quick responses and relief efforts; or incidents that evolve so slowly or affect populations so historically plagued with neglect or inequalities as to remain mostly invisible in the public consciousness.

Popular culture often defines disasters by their causal factors, commonly distinguishing between "natural" and "non-natural," or "human-caused," disasters. Such distinctions emerged during the seventeenth and eighteenth centuries as people increasingly distinguished phenomena like hurricanes and earthquakes, over which they seemingly had no control, from events like wars and fires, which resulted from human actions or errors. More recently, scholars have discouraged such binary definitions, arguing that there is "no such thing as a natural disaster." For some, this argument builds from the insight that while natural hazards such as earthquakes would exist under any circumstances, such hazards only become disasters when they adversely impact human populations. As a result, preexisting social, political, economic, and cultural forces are key to understanding the impact of any hazard on a particular society.[7] Others argue that in the current geological age (what is often termed the Anthropocene) humans have so irrevocably altered the physical world that nothing is left untouched by human influence.[8] In both cases, scholars highlight the need to think about disasters as reflecting complex interactions between various natural and human forces.

Most recently, scholars have proposed that there might also be "no such thing as a disaster" of any sort, as disasters are socially constructed events, influenced in definition and popular thought by the politics, timing, and conditions surrounding their occurrence. "To name something a disaster is to decry its outcomes as illegitimate, and to call for a restoration of the status quo," one historian has suggested, "instead of suggesting that the status quo may have been illegitimate in the first place."[9] While this observation rings true for some of the case studies presented in this volume, we nonetheless believe that "disaster" is a meaningful descriptor for phenomena that disturb the status quo—culturally, politically, environmentally—and are seen as disruptive by the people who experienced them regardless of whether that status quo is perceived as legitimate.

While scholars avoid talking about "natural disasters," they do distinguish events that arise from natural hazards from those caused by human action or inaction (also referred to as "anthropogenic hazards"). The Centre for Research on the Epidemiology of Disasters, for example, divides natural hazards into five primary categories: (1) *geophysical* (earthquakes, landslides, tsunamis, volcanic eruptions); (2) *hydrological* (avalanches and floods); (3) *climatological* (extreme temperatures, drought, wildfires); (4) *meteorological* (hurricanes, typhoons, storms, wave surges, derechos, tornadoes, hail storms); and (5) *biological* (epidemics/diseases and insect/animal plagues).[10] The United States Federal Emergency Management Agency (FEMA) divides human-caused, or anthropogenic, hazards into two primary categories—nonintentional hazards and intentional hazards. Nonintentional hazards include the *technological* (transportation hazards like roadway/aviation/nautical/railway accidents); *infrastructural* (power, telecommunications, computer network, water, sewer, gas, dam/levee, food systems, public health, and economic failures); *industrial* (hazardous and raw materials extraction accidents, structural failures including fire); *environmental* (pollution, deforestation, chemical contamination, climatic change); and *nuclear* (power plants, industrial use accidents, medical use failures). Intentional hazards encompass mass shootings, terrorism, and complex emergencies/conflicts (such as war, famine, and displaced populations).[11]

In some cases, a single disaster might be caused by, or worsen into, a combination of different types of hazards (both natural and human influenced). For example, drought conditions resulting from climate change may render forests vulnerable to a wildfire started by a lightning strike, and the loss of the forest may in turn contribute to landslides or floods in subsequent rainstorms. Scholars refer to the combination of these incidents as a "cascading disaster" and recognize the unintentional, intentional, and natural or human factors at play in their causes and effects.[12]

Whereas in the past, individuals, groups of people, or members of the media labeled particular incidents as "disasters," in recent years, the formal declaration of disaster status is given by a governmental entity. In the United States, disasters are officially recognized through declarations made by state governors and approved by the president, a process outlined in the Disaster Relief Act of 1950, the subsequent Stafford Act of 1988, and its updated iterations.[13] As new types of disasters have emerged (such as terrorist attacks like that of September 11, 2001), new categories of disasters have been added to qualified disaster declarations. This formal declaration of disaster status, which sets in motion federal disaster relief efforts, recognizes that disasters impact not only at the moment of occurrence but also during the period of recovery, long after the incident has passed. Disasters are both singular events and part of longer-term processes. How a disaster is defined thus reflects our past as well as our present. The types of disasters historians choose to focus on at particular moments in time indicate larger trends in historical studies, scientific understanding of hazards, and the political, social, and economic forces shaping the definition of and reactions to disasters at particular moments in time.

The essays in this collection both build on and contribute to the richly interdisciplinary work of historians and other scholars who study disasters, both as historical events and cultural constructions. Our emphasis on rethinking American disasters reflects the argument that disasters, like other historical phenomena, make sense only when they are situated in their specific historical contexts. Cultural, political, and environmental factors peculiar to colonial British North America, and later to the American republic, shaped not only the sorts of calamities that occurred in this geographical area but also how different individuals or social groups understood, prepared for, and responded to them, and how their understanding, preparation, and responses to disasters have changed over time. Even when hurricanes, earthquakes, floods, or fires become national—or even global—events and subjects of wide-ranging policy debates and news coverage, situating them in their particular physical and cultural contexts remains essential, both to understand the specific episode and to inform comparative analysis of disasters across both space and time. *Rethinking American Disasters* thus is not an endorsement of an outdated and xenophobic notion of American exceptionalism but rather an attempt to explore the place of disasters in the American past and to examine larger developments in American history through the lens of disasters.

Of the three overlapping approaches identified in our book—cultural, political, and environmental—environmental factors are often the most localized, though some environmental conditions (most notably climate change) are increasingly universal. One key theme in the history of American disasters from an environmental standpoint is the adaptation of first Indigenous peoples and then European colonizers to climatic conditions, such as hurricanes and other forms of extreme or unfamiliar weather they encountered in the Americas, which varied from region to region. Another is the way human interventions over centuries of settlement and agricultural and industrial development have altered physical landscapes and thereby shaped the impact of particular disasters, sometimes with grave or even deadly consequences. Yet another recurring theme is the sheer expanse of the North American continent, which contains an abundant diversity of climates and ecosystems, whose degradation, in turn, gave rise to an array of increasingly routine, and increasingly devastating, environmental catastrophes, such as hurricanes, floods, and wildfires. As the essays in this collection repeatedly show, the origins of so-called "natural disasters" were (and are) never entirely "natural."

The political context of American disasters has historically blended the local and the national. For most of American history, disasters occurred in a political environment in which safety-promoting (and hence lifesaving) government regulation was at best suspect, the prevailing capitalist ethos valued property over people, and disaster relief and other sorts of humanitarian aid were the domain of ad hoc local committees or, after 1881, of the Red Cross. Although the federal role in policy making and disaster relief became paramount in the second half of the twentieth century, that significant change followed nearly two centuries of general inaction on the part of American governments at every level. Even after the federal government became involved in disaster relief and prevention, moreover, partisan and regional divisions within the United States determined both the form and substance of disaster relief, as well as who got help when they needed it. For instance, as several essays in this volume demonstrate, even after the formal dissolution of the American apartheid known as Jim Crow, white power created and profited from environmental blight in majority Black areas and gave rise to inequitable disaster relief efforts, perhaps most vividly in New Orleans in 2005 in the aftermath of Hurricane Katrina.

Anyone who follows media coverage of contemporary disasters knows that the conversations surrounding them are always contentious, and that was equally true for hurricanes, fires, epidemics, and other calamities that occurred in earlier eras. Four sites of cultural contestation are particularly prominent in the essays in this volume. One is the changing role of religion, as Americans generally became more scientifically astute and secular-minded but as some nonetheless persisted in seeing disasters as punishment inflicted on sinners by an angry God and still others looked to religion mainly as a source of consolation and comfort. Another is the role of the press (and eventually other media) in creating and spreading information—and sometimes misinformation—and in crafting affecting and culturally resonant narratives that influenced both popular culture and public policy. The impact of racial (and to a lesser extent class) hostilities is another persistent theme, as social divisions informed vastly divergent understandings of the causes of disasters and dramatically different ways of experiencing calamity and crisis, especially in terms of access to physical relief and material compensation after the hurricane, earthquake, or other cataclysmic event was technically over. Finally, how people remember disasters—their causes and consequences, heroes and villains—has been, and will continue to be, widely contested and controversial. Will Donald Trump, Anthony Fauci, Joe Biden, essential health-care workers, research scientists, or corporate vaccine makers be remembered as the heroes of the COVID-19 pandemic? As its story is remembered, reinterpreted, and retold, likely each will have their advocates.

More than a half century ago, in calling for more research on historical disasters, John Burnham observed that because disasters were "the products of historical as well as natural processes . . . historians are obliged to help furnish [their] historical meaning."[14] Bringing together essays that engage big issues and themes with others that draw illuminating insights from specific case studies, the essays in this volume are one more step in that direction. Some provide a macrolevel view of disaster history. They emphasize theoretical approaches and explore continuity and change over lengthy chronological periods, often privileging the perspectives of governments, pundits, newspaper readers, and other outsiders who did not experience the disasters directly. Others are microhistories of particular calamities that offer historians and students a point of entry into the lives of individuals and communities as they endured disaster-related hardships that both revealed and exacerbated cultural tensions and social conflicts. Taken together, these two approaches go a long way toward helping to rethink both people's lived experiences and the larger historical significance of American disasters.

NOTES

1. John C. Burnham, "A Neglected Field: The History of Natural Disasters," *Perspectives* (April 1988): 22–24.

2. Jonathan Bergman, "Disaster: A Useful Category of Historical Analysis," *History Compass* (2008): 934–46; Cécile Stephanie Stehrenberger, "Disasters Studies as Politics with Other Means: COVID-19 and the Legacies of Cold War Disaster Research," *Items: Insights from the Social Sciences* (December 3, 2020), Social Science Research Council, https://items.ssrc.org/covid-19-and-the-social-sciences/disaster-studies/disaster-studies-as-politics-with-other-means-covid-19-and-the-legacies-of-cold-war-disaster-research/, accessed May 7, 2021.

3. James Lal Penick Jr., *The New Madrid Earthquakes*, rev ed. (1976; Columbia: University of Missouri Press, 1981).

4. Steven Biel, ed., *American Disasters* (New York: New York University Press, 2001).

5. Ted Steinberg, *Acts of God: The Unnatural History of Natural Disaster in America* (Oxford: Oxford University Press, 2000).

6. Rob Nixon, *Slow Violence and the Environmentalism of the Poor* (Cambridge, MA: Harvard University Press, 2011), 6–10.

7. Ksenia Chmutina and Jason von Meding, "A Dilemma of Language: 'Natural Disasters' in Academic Literature," *International Journal of Disaster Risk Science* 10 (September 2019): 283–92; Gregory Squires and Chester Hartman, eds., *There Is No Such Thing as a Natural Disaster: Race, Class, and Hurricane Katrina* (New York: Routledge, 2006).

8. Bas van Bavel et al., *Disasters and History: The Vulnerability and Resilience of Past Societies* (Cambridge: Cambridge University Press, 2020), 159–87; Theodore Steinberg, "What Is a Natural Disaster?," *Literature and Medicine* 15 (Spring 1996): 33–47.

9. Jacob A. C. Remes and Andy Horowitz, eds., *Critical Disaster Studies* (Philadelphia: University of Pennsylvania Press, 2021), 1; Andy Horowitz, *Katrina: A History, 1915–2015* (Cambridge, MA: Harvard University Press, 2020), 15.

10. Note that according to the United States Federal Emergency Management Agency (FEMA), an additional category of natural hazards also included in this list are *extraterrestrial hazards* such as those caused from meteorites and asteroids (Centre for Research on the Epidemiology of Disasters [CRED]—Emergency Events Database [EM/DAT], a catalog of 22,000 mass disasters from 1900 to the present day, compiled using data from "United Nations agencies, non-governmental organizations, insurance companies, research institutes, and press agencies," available at https://www.emdat.be; FEMA, Hazard and Disaster Classification Training Manual, https://www.training.fema.gov/ushazards101/surveyofhazardsanddisasters-session01-powerpoint-hazardanddisasterclassification.ppt).

11. FEMA, Disaster Information Hazard Page, Index of Hazards, https://www.fema.gov/disasters.

12. Gísli Pálsson, *The Human Age: How We Created the Anthropocene Epoch and Caused the Climate Crisis* (London: Welbeck, 2020); Susan Cutter, "The Changing Nature of Hazard and

Disaster Risk in the Anthropocene," *Annals of the American Association of Geographers* 111, no. 3 (2021): 819–27.

13. Michelle Landis, "'Let Me Next Time Be Tried by Fire': Disaster Relief and the Origins of the American Welfare State," *Northwestern University Law Review* 92 (1998): 967–1034; Gareth Davies, "The Emergence of a National Politics of Disaster, 1865–1900," *Journal of Policy History* 26 (2014): 305–26; Robert T. Stafford Disaster Relief and Emergency Assistance Act, PL 100–707, signed into law November 23, 1988, 42 U.S.C. § 5121 et seq.

14. Burnham, "A Neglected Field," 24.

A NEW WORLD OF DISASTER

HAZARDS, ENVIRONMENTS, AND EXPERIENCE IN COLONIAL BRITISH AMERICA

MATTHEW MULCAHY

In a classic essay published in 1982, Karen Kupperman highlighted what she called the "puzzle of the early American climate," namely that places like Virginia and New England were hotter and/or colder than places at the same latitude in Europe, contrary to colonists' expectations. Kupperman's essay focused mostly on climate as temperature, but other parts of the physical environment also differed between the Old World and the New, including the experience of various natural hazards. Indeed, in many ways, English migrants encountered a new world of disasters in North America and the Caribbean as they set about establishing permanent colonies. In some cases, they encountered entirely new phenomena, such as hurricanes, whose power exceeded anything that Europeans had known, or snowstorms that generated far deeper snows than most English men and women had experienced. In other cases, colonists encountered familiar natural hazards such as earthquakes, floods, and drought but did so in new contexts.[1]

Whether new or familiar, disasters played an important role in shaping the mental and physical worlds of colonists throughout British America across the seventeenth and eighteenth centuries. Just as colonists slowly learned to "unpuzzle" aspects of America's hot and cold climates, so too they had to understand and adapt to the natural hazards they encountered. In doing so, colonists everywhere drew on established, and evolving, European religious and intellectual frameworks to make sense of great storms, earthquakes, floods, drought, and the like, but they also modified such perspectives based in part on their contact with Native peoples and their lived experiences in the different physical environments of the New World.[2] Put simply, while colonists everywhere conceived of disasters in broadly similar ways, the relative frequency or infrequency of specific hazards in various regions influenced understanding of those events across the seventeenth and eighteenth centuries.

Perhaps no disaster better symbolized the novelty and dangers of the New World environment than hurricanes. As one commentator noted, "an European can form no just idea of a West Indian hurricane, far less the dire effects which accompany it." Europeans quickly appropriated the Native American word for the great storms and Native knowledge about their seasonality and the natural signs that seemed to indicate their onset. Such information soon became a Caribbean proverb: "June too soon, July stand by, August you must, September remember, October all over."[3]

Hurricanes came to shape all aspects of life in the Greater Caribbean, a region encompassing the major British islands in the Caribbean (Barbados, Jamaica, and the Leeward Islands of Nevis, St. Christopher, Antigua, and Montserrat) and including the mainland southeastern lowcountry of Carolina and Georgia. Contemporaries often recognized the Carolina lowcountry as the outer edge of the hurricane zone. The power of hurricanes, the eighteenth-century naturalist Mark Catesby wrote, was "much mitigated" by the time they reached Carolina, with "Virginia not having often much of it." Within the Greater Caribbean, hurricanes routinely disrupted the region's plantation economy, laying waste to sugar and rice plantations. The storms damaged or destroyed ships, docks, houses, and churches to such an extent that, according to one governor, a full accounting of the damage would "swell into a volume and puzzle belief." Colonists learned to adapt traditional English architectural styles to the threat, building lower-profile buildings with hipped rather than gabled roofs to lessen their vulnerability to winds, and stone buildings replaced wooden ones wherever possible.[4]

Countless storms pummeled the islands and lowcountry across the seventeenth and eighteenth centuries, but among the largest and most destructive were the twin hurricanes in September 1752 that caused extensive damage in Charleston and the surrounding lowcountry; the major storm that swept across the Leeward Islands in late August 1772, a newspaper account of which written by Alexander Hamilton helped secure him a placement at King's College in New York City; and the Great Hurricane, which struck the entire chain of the Lesser Antilles on October 10, 1780. That storm still ranks as the deadliest Atlantic hurricane, claiming the lives of at least twenty thousand individuals, including thousands of enslaved people.[5]

Notwithstanding Catesby's comments, hurricanes did occasionally strike Virginia and points farther north. A powerful hurricane swept along the Virginia coast in August 1667 and "overturned many Houses, burying in the Ruines much Goods and many people . . . whereby unknown numbers have perished." Most of the colony's corn and tobacco was destroyed. Another "most dreadful" hurricane struck the Chesapeake and mid-Atlantic Seaboard in 1769, again resulting in damage to tobacco and corn crops. New England, too, experienced several significant hurricanes. Governor William Bradford reported on August 15, 1635, that Plymouth suffered "a mighty storm of wind and rain as none living in these parts, either English or Indian, ever saw." Bradford wrote that the storm resembled "those hurricanes and typhoons that writers make mention of in the Indies." As Bradford's comment suggests, while hurricanes did strike New England, colonists there viewed them as exceptional events.[6]

Unlike hurricanes, earthquakes were not a new phenomenon for Europeans, and they had long inspired a particular dread. "In what Condition can a Man be safe," asked one seventeenth-century English commentator, "when the World itself is shaken?" All of Europe experienced occasional shocks, including England in 1580, 1692, and 1750, but with the exception of the Great Lisbon Earthquake in 1755, most tremors in northwestern Europe generated great fear but little damage. As a result, few colonists who migrated to British America had experience with earthquakes.[7]

All the colonies felt the ground shake at various points across the seventeenth and eighteenth centuries, but earthquakes struck most frequently and most violently in several of the Caribbean islands, particularly Jamaica and the Leeward Islands. Indeed, contemporary commentators noted that "Jamaica is remarkable for earthquakes" and that residents expected them yearly. The worst was the 1692 tremor that damaged plantations across the island and destroyed its principal urban center, Port Royal. In a matter of minutes, roughly half of Port Royal, the wealthiest city in British America, collapsed into the harbor, and some 1,500–2,000 residents, including roughly 600 enslaved Africans, perished in one of the great disasters of the early modern Atlantic world. News of the disaster circulated widely in other colonies and across the Atlantic. Two years earlier, a major earthquake struck the Leeward Islands, causing extensive damage on Nevis and St. Christopher (an island split between English and French sectors at the time). Frequent tremors occurred in all the islands across the eighteenth century, although none of the magnitude of the 1690 and 1692 events. Still, the frequency with which the earth shook meant the specter of another event like Port Royal hung over the heads of residents throughout the islands. As one visitor to Antigua observed, "We live here on shaking ground."[8]

Earthquakes struck the mainland colonies as well, although less frequently and with less intensity. Indeed, the experience of earthquakes in various colonies in North America more closely resembled that of England, where occasional tremors generated panic and fear but caused little damage, rather than the more frequent and occasionally devastating tremors that shaped life in the islands. New England experienced noteworthy earthquakes in 1638, 1663, 1727, 1744, and 1755, along with several other smaller tremors. The Massachusetts clergyman Cotton Mather reported that during the night of October 29, 1727, the earth began to "heave and shake so as to Rocque the Houses and cause here and there the falling of some smaller Things, both within Doors and without." Overall, however, damage was minimal, in part because most houses and other buildings were made of relatively flexible wood, which withstood shaking better than more rigid stone or brick, and no deaths occurred. Terrified residents nevertheless flooded into churches across New England in what several scholars have termed "earthquake revivals." The November 18, 1755, earthquake was perhaps that region's largest and most destructive during this period. Its effects were felt along large parts of the Eastern Seaboard and as deep into the interior as Lake Champlain in upstate New York. Houses shook, dishes fell from shelves, and hundreds of brick chimneys in and around Boston collapsed or were damaged, but no deaths occurred. The event took on added significance as reports of the great earthquake that devastated Lisbon on November 1 arrived in British America several weeks later, prompting both moral and scientific reassessments of the local tremor.[9]

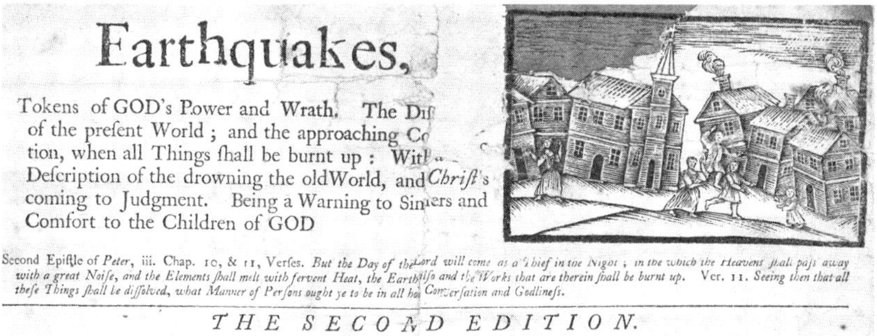

Earthquakes,

Tokens of GOD's Power and Wrath. The Di
of the preſent World ; and the approaching Co
tion, when all Things ſhall be burnt up : Wit
Deſcription of the drowning the old World, and *Chriſt*'s
coming to Judgment. Being a Warning to Sinners and
Comfort to the Children of GOD

Second Epiſtle of *Peter*, iii. Chap. 10, & 11, Verſes. *But the Day of the Lord will come as a Thief in the Night ; in the which the Heavens ſhall paſs away with a great Noiſe, and the Elements ſhall melt with fervent Heat, the Earth alſo and the Works that are therein ſhall be burnt up.* Ver. 11. *Seeing then that all theſe Things ſhall be diſſolved, what Manner of Perſons ought ye to be in all holy Converſation and Godlineſs.*

THE SECOND EDITION.

A woodcut depicting damage from the 1744 earthquake in New England, from a broadside printed in Boston. New York Public Library.

Earthquakes struck farther south as well. When the Virginia planter Landon Carter reported a tremor in March 1758 that awakened him from bed, he wrote, "It was very terrible to one not used to earthquakes and I never had any idea of such a thing before only from description to which this answered." Likewise, a short tremor in 1754 lasting only a few seconds "create[ed] no small Surprize and Astonishment" in Charleston, South Carolina, "being unusual in this Country."[10]

A far more frequent, and far more damaging, disaster that plagued all of the colonies at various times was drought. Unlike hurricanes and earthquakes, drought events unfold slowly over time and can linger for months and even years. Even short-term relief in the form of rain may not signal the end of a drought. In addition, drought does not affect physical infrastructure: houses, churches, and mills remain standing, and roads remain open. As with earthquakes, drought was not unknown to English migrants, although recent scholarship suggests that too much rain rather than too little posed the greater challenge to English agriculture in the medieval and early modern periods. This was not the case in the colonies, however, most of which relied on agricultural exports that were vulnerable to drought.[11]

Drought threatened the production of staple crops like sugar, tobacco, indigo, and, to a certain extent, rice, and that in turn threatened colonists' income. Diaries and newspapers routinely highlighted parched fields, "burned up" crops, and lost revenue. The governor of Antigua, for example, reported that a "great drought" in 1670 "has rendered the crops backward and bad, and brought the planters into debt." An extended drought plagued parts of New England across several months in 1748–49. George Washington wrote that an extended drought in the spring of 1755 "almost destroyd this part of the Country" and caused immense agricultural losses in Pennsylvania and Virginia. Tobacco exports from Virginia, which had averaged almost fifty-one thousand pounds per year between 1751 and 1755, plunged to roughly twenty-eight thousand pounds in the year following the drought.[12]

The impact of tobacco crops lost from drought was severe enough to generate a political conflict in Virginia. As output dropped, prices rose threefold, and local officials sought to regulate the price of tobacco used to pay the salaries of Anglican clergy in 1755. They did so again in 1758 when the "unseasonableness of the weather" ruined the crop. These "two-penny acts," so named for the regulated price of tobacco, generated protests from local churchmen, who organized to have the king veto the laws. They were successful in doing so in 1758, prompting a backlash among colonists and providing future revolutionaries like Patrick Henry a stage to criticize excessive Crown interference in local affairs.[13]

The loss of crops for export markets hurt planters' bottom lines, but the loss of provision crops like wheat and corn alongside them often produced periods of privation and, at times, famine conditions. This was especially true for enslaved individuals, who were often ill-fed in the best of times, and was especially true in the island colonies, which relied (to a greater or lesser extent) on food imported from the mainland to supplement local resources. An ongoing drought in the Leeward Islands during the 1730s exacted a heavy toll in human life. One plantation overseer wrote in December 1736, "Our famine still continues, or rather Increases . . . [and] swept off a great many people." Henry Laurens reported that dry weather destroyed much of South Carolina's corn and other provision crops in the summer of 1756 and that "Negro provision" in particular remained "scarce & dear" in early 1757. Local officials at times halted the export of corn or other provision crops to stave off famine conditions for all residents. In addition to food shortages, colonists (or their servants and enslaved laborers) often had to walk miles to secure fresh water for drinking, as happened in New England in the late summer of 1773. Animals, too, suffered from a want of adequate fodder and water, which had ripple effects for colonists who relied on livestock for dairy, meat, and as exports to other colonies.[14]

Perhaps the worst subsistence crisis developed during the 1770s and 1780s, when the combination of drought and the American Revolution resulted in a catastrophe for enslaved people throughout large sections of the Caribbean. As severe dry weather withered provisions on the islands, the ongoing war between Britain and the mainland colonies left the islands cut off from their closest and best supplier of food. Thousands of enslaved people died over the course of the war years. In Antigua alone, reports suggested that between 10 and 20 percent of the island's enslaved population perished from drought, famine, and disease linked to such shortages in the late 1770s.[15]

Too little rain often had tragic consequences for colonists, but so too did too much rain. Flooding, like drought, occurred periodically in all the colonies (or parts of colonies) during the seventeenth and eighteenth centuries. Melting snowpack in the northern colonies along with intense periods of rain and routine clearing of trees in all the colonies contributed to floods, or "freshes," as colonists frequently termed them. These freshes were seasonal occurrences in the mainland colonies, often occurring in the spring or following summer storms. In the islands they often occurred during the rainy season between May through November. The level of damage could be immense. William Byrd reported on a "deluge" that overflowed his Virginia plantation in late April 1685. The water "swept away all our fences, destroyed all that was on the ground," and "carryed away the Hills (that were made for Tobacco)." Almost all of his tobacco crop and most of his neighbors' were destroyed. Likewise, "A Dismal flood of rain" in the eastern part of Jamaica in April 1765 flooded plantations, swept away bridges, and drowned countless animals. "It is inconceivable what devastations it has made," wrote one experienced planter.[16]

As with drought, European colonists had experience with flooding, but the violence of rains and floods in parts of British America at times exceeded European precedents. Edward Long in Jamaica observed that "rain precipitates in this island with a violence rarely seen in England." In New England sudden spring thaws after snowy winters often unleashed what Samuel Sewall called "extraordinary excessive Floods." John Winthrop reported the combination of a deep snowpack, a "sudden thaw in the spring" of 1646, and "much rain" washed away bridges and overflowed roads in Hartford and New Haven. Several "great freshes" along Connecticut rivers in February 1767 swept up "boats, timber, parts of houses," and deposited them on the north shore of Long Island.

Winter conditions contributed to spring floods farther south as well. Parts of Philadelphia flooded when thick ice dams in the Schuylkill River gave way during rainy spring thaws in 1733 and 1737. Melting snows in the piedmont of Virginia and Maryland at times contributed to violent flooding. So too did increased settlement, as deforestation in western parts of the colonies allowed for greater runoff.[17]

The most destructive Chesapeake fresh occurred in the spring of 1771. A rainy spring characterized much of the Southeast that year. In Virginia, ten to twelve days of heavy rains in May filled the James, Rappahannock, and Roanoke Rivers as they headed east. In late May, floodwaters (perhaps exacerbated by a passing tropical storm) broke over the central and eastern parts of the colony, with the James River cresting at forty feet above normal levels at Richmond. Dozens of colonists and enslaved people perished (some accounts suggest more than one hundred deaths), hundreds of cattle drowned, and thousands of hogsheads of tobacco were swept away. One resident wrote it appeared as if the devil had "bored a Hole through the Mountains, and let in the South Sea upon them." The legislature allocated some thirty thousand pounds to reimburse revenues lost when public tobacco inspection warehouses were swept away. The effect on poorer colonists, although less documented, likely lingered for some time, as the flood washed away corn crops, "which numbers of poor families entirely depended upon for subsistence."[18]

The snowpack that at times contributed to flooding highlights another hazard colonists encountered in parts of British America: "deep snows." English colonists had limited experience with significant (and constant) snow as English winters were comparatively mild. Snow itself was not unfamiliar, of course, but few migrants had experience with the "deep snow" that periodically blanketed New England and the Middle Colonies. Indeed, severe winter storms, what we now call nor'easters, resulted in levels of snow that formed a distinct kind of disaster for colonists. Deep snowpack of several feet prevented or limited travel and trade, isolating both individual colonists and towns from one another, and often resulted in the death of large numbers of domesticated animals central to the economies of many northern colonies. The most intense event in New England was the Great Snow of 1717, a series of four major snowstorms in eleven days between February 18 and 28. The combined snowfall across large swaths of the region ranged from three to five feet, with snowdrifts in places between ten and sixteen feet.[19]

While New England and parts of New York experienced more frequent, and more frequently intense, snowstorms, "deep snow" occasionally blanketed parts of the Middle Colonies as well, causing similar disruptions and hardships. The hard winter of 1741 saw deep snowpack from New England throughout central Pennsylvania, where parts of Lancaster County were covered by three feet of snow. Newspapers reported "Great Numbers of the Back[country] inhabitants suffer'd much for want of bread" and were reduced to eating deer carcasses found near their houses. At least one woman froze to death. As in other blizzards, the storm killed countless horses and cattle. Likewise, a "long snow" across several months in the winter of 1764–65 killed an "abundance of Sheep" in New Jersey. The last major storm of that winter, in March 1765, dumped several feet of snow and disrupted the work of Charles Mason and Jeremiah Dixon measuring the Pennsylvania-Maryland border for days. In short, the New World's snowy winters periodically created a distinct form of disaster in many colonies across the seventeenth and eighteenth centuries.[20]

As colonists assessed the damage, calculated their losses, and worked to recover from various disasters, they also sought to make sense of these events. In doing so they built from intellectual foundations they had carried with them, especially regarding hazards with which they were familiar, but they also learned from Native Americans and from their own experiences. The balance between intellectual inheritance and lived experience varied across time, by region, and by the particular hazards colonists encountered.[21]

By far, the most important inherited framework for understanding disasters was providentialism. As was the case in Europe, for the overwhelmingly Protestant colonists, hurricanes, earthquakes, floods, and blizzards were not random occurrences. They were providential events, acts of God, sent to punish sinful humans or warn of a worse fate if they did not reform. There was no need to look for natural forces at work in such events, ministers routinely preached to their congregations. The cause of all such events was simple: human sin. The 1667 hurricane in Virginia resulted from colonists' "evil way[s]," while their "frequent and Crying sinns" and their "obstinate persisting in the same" were the cause of sickness, drought, and famine in the spring of 1688.

"Tis Sin, and that *only*, that enkindles the Anger of Almighty God and causes Him to march thro' a Land in Indignation," observed one commentator in the *Boston Gazette* following the 1755 earthquake. Pennsylvania's governor reminded colonists of the connection between "National Calamity and National Vice" during the drought of 1755. Colonists often recognized providential connections in such events even when they did not directly experience them. Thus, residents of New Haven feared the appearance of a blazing star and an earthquake in a neighboring town in March 1681 were "forrunners or . . . warnings of som great changes or Judgment neare."[22]

As sin was the ultimate cause of disasters, the proper response was prayer, remorse, and reform. Officials throughout British America responded to major disasters by calling for a day of fasting and prayer. Fast days required colonists to abstain from food, work, and other activities. Residents gathered in churches and ministers offered special prayers for the day. Not surprisingly, their sermons called upon listeners to recognize their responsibility for the disaster, to seek God's forgiveness, and to reform their sinful practices. At times, when a major disaster was avoided, such as when rains fell before a drought became calamitous, colonists organized a day of thanksgiving to recognize God's protection and their deliverance from harm.[23]

Fast days occurred in response to the full range of disasters across the seventeenth and eighteenth centuries. These rituals were organized most frequently in New England, reflecting the prominence of Puritanism and colonists' heightened attention to the providential meaning of various events in the region, including but not limited to disasters. In most cases fast days were called in response to specific events, although in the Caribbean, the frequency and seasonality of hurricanes led to fixed days of fasting and thanksgiving at the start and end of hurricane season. No systematic study exists of fast days in British America, but limited evidence in both diaries and official records from the Caribbean and New England suggests that drought events (on their own or in combination with other environmental challenges such as insect infestations or disease outbreaks) occasioned specific fasts more often than any other disaster. Why this was the case is not entirely clear. One factor may have been time: because droughts were prolonged events, colonists had time to organize such rituals, which was not the case during a storm or earthquake. Moreover, colonists recognized that prayer provided some possibility of immediate providential relief in the form of rains. As one account from Jamaica noted during a 1754 dry period, colonists "made frequent requests for rain." While colonists could and did reflect on their sins during rituals *in the wake of* hurricanes and earthquakes, they could enact such rituals *during* a drought, which may have resulted in more frequent fasts. Certainly, colonists everywhere routinely offered special prayers for divine relief in the form of rain, and often got results. John Hull's diary, for example, recorded fasts in response to extended droughts in 1662 and 1672 in Massachusetts, and in both instances, "The Lord heard prayer, and sent sufficient rain." So, too, a fast called during a severe drought in Massachusetts in the summer of 1749 resulted in "plentiful & seasonable Rains, as quite altered ye face of ye Earth."[24]

Providentialism served as the dominant interpretative framework for understanding disasters, but it was not the only one. As in Europe, some colonists looked to the movement of the stars for explanation. Astrology had many followers in colonial America, and astrologers often claimed to be able to predict disasters. The word "disaster" itself, meaning "ill-star," suggested such a connection. Although ministers often railed against such judicial astrologers, the idea that heavenly movements affected events on earth made sense to many. As late as 1769, one official in North Carolina posited a link between a "blazing planet or star . . . rising in the east for several nights" in late August and a hurricane that struck in early September.[25]

Such beliefs sometimes overlapped with knowledge gained from Native Americans in different parts of British America. Colonists in the Caribbean, for example, learned from Carib Indians various signs that presaged hurricanes, including that the number of rings around the moon in certain months could indicate the number of days before a storm struck. They remained dependent on Indigenous informants for decades. One account reported that having driven the Caribs out of St. Christopher, English colonies sent emissaries to them at Dominica and St. Vincent to "know whether there would be any Hurricanes that Year" and that their predictions "rarely or seldom failed." Likewise, some colonists in New England learned about the history of earthquakes in the region from Native Americans. Rhode Island's leader Roger Williams reported that after the 1638 earthquake the local Narragansett leader told him that this was the fifth earthquake (what they called *Naunaumemoauke*) during the previous eighty years and that "either plague or pox or some other epidemicall disease" always followed a few years later. The village of Moodus in Connecticut (now part of East Haddam) derived its name from the Algonquian word *Machetmadosset* or *Machitmoodus*, which translated as "place of noises" or "place of bad noises." As colonists soon learned, the sounds were powerful enough, according to one eighteenth-century minister, to occasionally shake the earth and "the houses and all that is in them."[26]

Belief in God as the ultimate cause of disasters did not foreclose efforts to understand the possible natural forces at work in various events. Natural philosophy, what we would now call science, flourished in all parts of British America as learned colonists sought to make sense of their New World environments. Regarding disasters, natural philosophers sought to understand the "secondary causes" (God remained the primary cause) that gave rise to storms, earthquakes, and the like. This was especially true during the latter decades of the seventeenth century and across the eighteenth. Such investigations did not deny that God could and did sometimes directly cause the winds to swirl or the earth to shake (such events were termed special providences), but they suggested that more often than not, God worked through established natural processes that were observable and understandable to humans, which contemporaries labeled God's general providence. In the case of earthquakes, colonists built from intellectual foundations that dated to Aristotle as they debated the role of underground vapors or exhalations in shaking the earth. By contrast, the encounter with hurricanes called for new data and new ideas as the ancients had no knowledge of such hazards. Instead, commentators called for information and observations "fetch'd fro[m] both Indies" to provide a foundation for investigations into what forces might give rise to these new and terrifying storms. Shifting intellectual frameworks on both sides of the Atlantic meant that by the eighteenth century, many learned elites increasingly viewed disasters as part of God's general ordering of the natural world rather than as special divine interventions into it. As terrifying as earthquakes were, Harvard professor John Winthrop observed following the 1755 tremor in Massachusetts, they formed one of God's "laws for the government of the world" and thus "promote the good of the whole."[27]

Finally, even as ministers preached about God's judgment and natural philosophers debated natural processes, colonists also recognized that their own actions at times contributed to or exacerbated the damage caused by disasters. Island colonists, for example, recognized by the eighteenth century that clear-cutting forests rendered them more vulnerable to the effects of drought. To forestall that, they passed laws limiting tree removal near ponds to limit evaporation or in some cases preserving what forested areas remained to help retain moisture and "to prevent the drought which in these climates is the usual consequence of a total removal of the woods." Likewise, in both Jamaica in 1692 and Massachusetts in 1755, residents recognized that some of the damage from earthquakes resulted from their building practices. Brick houses built on "low, loose Ground, made by encroachments on the Harbor" suffered the greatest damage in both Boston and Port Royal.[28]

In short, colonists drew upon diverse intellectual frameworks to make sense of the disasters they experienced, and they recognized that divine power, natural forces and processes, and human actions could all play a role in such events. The relative emphasis on these interpretations, however, varied. They varied over time, as ideas about special providences waned everywhere and were replaced by increasing emphasis on God's general providence over the course of the eighteenth century (although the idea of direct divine intervention did not disappear). They also varied by disaster and by region, reflecting colonists' increased experience with and knowledge about specific hazards in different parts of British America.

In most of the mainland colonies, the relative infrequency of large-scale events like hurricanes and earthquakes ensured that they retained more of their providential meaning well into the eighteenth century. As short, isolated, and often seemingly random events, such disasters continued to bring forth calls for repentance and reformation. The 1727 earthquake, which did relatively little damage in New England, resulted in major religious revival in the region, as colonists flocked into churches. Likewise, the Reverend Samuel Davies in Virginia used the 1755 earthquake to remind listeners that while "natural causes concur towards the production of earthquakes," they were "still directed by the divine hand." Earthquakes were one of the "extraordinary ministers of his vengeance." Even as some learned colonists increasingly joined transatlantic scientific conversations about the natural forces at work in earthquakes, the terror of the shaking earth meant that many viewed human sin and divine judgment as the cause. Following the 1755 earthquake, for example, John Adams complained that the tremors provoked "a very general if not universal apprehension" among colonists in Massachusetts and that most residents, including "some Persons of the highest Rank," viewed earthquakes "only as Judgements, Punishments, Warnings etc." One likely reason was that earthquakes were, as Adams noted in a different context, "rare" in New England and elsewhere on the mainland.[29]

Hazards that occurred more frequently and/or seasonally, by contrast, lost some of their providential associations. For example, as colonists in New England gained more experience with harsh winter conditions, major snowstorms appeared less as special providences and more as part of the natural order. Singular events like the Great Snow of 1717 remained "a Rebuke from Heaven" in the eyes of many and still brought forth calls for a day of fasting, but other wintry events passed with less moral commentary by the eighteenth century. Cotton Mather and others even began to see blessings as well as warnings in New England's snowy winters. Terrifying and treacherous at times, the great snows increasingly reflected God's general ordering of the natural world.[30]

A similar process played out in parts of the Greater Caribbean in response to repeated hurricanes and earthquakes. As colonists gained more experience with such events, the providential context of both shifted. In Jamaica and some of the Leeward Islands, minor earthquakes occurred so frequently (and often with little damage) that colonists early on came to view them as ordinary rather than as unusual and wondrous. One observer noted that the frequent earthquakes on Antigua frightened him when he first arrived, but after a few months, "I begin to be used to them, and they now hardly alarm me." Likewise, as colonists gained more understanding of the seasonality of hurricanes and the signs that preceded them, the storms became an "expected calamity," in the words of one observer, and thus lost some of the providential associations. The storms made more sense as part of God's general ordering of the natural world, and less as special markers of divine displeasure at specific human sins in specific places. This lack of religious response to various hazards in the region at times puzzled outside observers. One visitor to Jamaica in the

1710s expressed surprise that "a people to whome God speaks so frequently in Thunder, Lightning, fire and Earthquakes sho'd be so unmindfull of his power and Judgments."[31]

Unusual or particularly violent and destructive hurricanes and earthquakes in the Caribbean still resulted in fast days and calls for moral reform, as happened following the great earthquake in 1692 and the 1772 hurricane. More often, however, colonists increasingly viewed most such events as part of God's general providence rather than as particular judgments or warnings. Indeed, as with great snows in New England, some came to argue that despite the losses that accompanied them, both hurricanes and earthquakes had beneficial consequences and thus a role in the divine ordering of the natural world. They answered to some "wise, and perhaps salutary purpose in the economy of nature," wrote one observer in Jamaica, and colonists came to regard them as "necessary and propitious."[32]

These shifting attitudes were one part of a larger process of adapting to the New World across the seventeenth and eighteenth centuries. Adjusting to the New World involved not only shifts in colonists' understanding about climate in terms of heat and cold but also coming to terms with the various hazards they encountered, both new and familiar. While the relative impact of such disasters differed across the broad geography of British America, hurricanes, earthquakes, drought, snowstorms, and floods routinely terrified and amazed, claimed the lives of many, damaged property, destroyed settlements, instigated political conflict, challenged intellectual and religious ideas, and, in short, created distinct challenges for colonists.

NOTES

1. Karen Kupperman, "The Puzzle of the Early American Climate in the Early Colonial Period," *American Historical Review* 87 (December 1982): 1262–89.

2. Sam White, "Unpuzzling American Climate: New World Experience and the Foundations of a New Science," *Isis* 106 (September 2015): 544–66.

3. Hector M'Neill, *Observations on the Treatment of the Negroes, in the Island of Jamaica* (London: 1788), 39; John Taylor, *Newes and Strange Newes from St. Christophers of a tempestuous Spirit, which is called by the Indians a Hurry-Cano* (London, 1638).

4. Mark Catesby, *The Natural History of Carolina, Florida, and the Bahama Islands* (London,

1771), 1:ii; Jonathan Atkins to Joseph Williamson, October 13, 1675, *Calendar of State Papers, Colonial Series* (hereafter *CSPC*) (London: Her Majesty's Stationery Office, 1860s–), 294. For a survey of the impact of these and other storms, see Matthew Mulcahy, *Hurricanes and Society in the British Greater Caribbean, 1624–1783* (Baltimore: Johns Hopkins University Press, 2006).

5. Mulcahy, *Hurricanes and Society in the British Greater Caribbean*, 25, 60, 165–66.

6. *Strange Newes from Virginia, being a true Relation of the Great Tempest in Virginia* (London, 1667). For the 1769 storm, see David Ludlum, *Early American Hurricanes* (Boston: American Meteorological Society, 1963), 24–25; *Pennsylvania Gazette*, September 28, 1769; R. Nicholas to John Norton, September 16, 1769, in *John Norton & Sons: Merchants of London and Virginia, Being the Papers of their Counting House for the Years 1750–1795*, ed. Frances Mason (New York: A. M. Kelley, 1968); 106; and William Bradford, quoted in Ludlum, *Early American Hurricanes*, 11.

7. John Shower, *Practical Reflections on Earthquakes in Jamaica, England, Sicily, &c* (London, 1692), 54.

8. *Pennsylvania Gazette*, December 22, 1737; [Rev. E. Heath], *A Full Account of the Late Dreadful Earthquake at Port Royal in Jamaica* (London, 1692); *An Account of the Late Dreadful Earth-Quake in the Island of Mevis* [sic], *St. Christophers, &c* (London, 1690); John Luffman, *A Brief Account of the Island of Antigua* (London, 1789), 144.

9. Anne Stevens, "Eastern North American Earthquakes Prior to 1660," *Bulletin of the Seismological Society of America* 85 (October 1995): 1398–1415; Cotton Mather, *The Terror of the Lord: Some Account of the Earthquake that Shook New England* (Boston, 1727), 1. Accounts of 1755 include *Boston Gazette*, November 24, 1755; John Winthrop, *A Treatise on Earthquakes* (Boston, 1755); and Whitney Ann Robles, "Atlantic Disaster: Boston Responds to the Cape Ann Earthquake of 1755," *New England Quarterly* 90 (March 2017): 7–35.

10. *Diary of Colonial Landon Carter of Sabin Hall, 1752–1778*, ed. Jack P. Greene (Richmond: Virginia Historical Society, 1987), 1:208; *Pennsylvania Gazette*, July 4, 1754; Kathleen Murphy, "Prodigies and Portents: Providentialism in the Eighteenth-Century Chesapeake," *Maryland Historical Magazine* 97 (Winter 2002): 397–421.

11. On drought in England, see Kathleen Pribyl, "A Survey of the Impact of Summer Droughts in Southern and Eastern England, 1200–1700," *Climate of the Past* 16 (2020): 1027–41.

12. William Byam to William Lord Willoughby, n.d. 1670, *CSPC*, 205–6; George Washington to Robert Orme, May 22, 1755, https://founders.archives.gov/documents/Washington/02-01-02-0143; "Tobacco Export from Virginia, by Port, 1745–1773," in *Historical Statistics of the United States, Millennial Edition*, by Susan Carter et al. (New York: Cambridge University Press, 2006). See also Lorena Walsh, *Motives of Honor, Pleasure, and Profit: Plantation Management in the Colonial Chesapeake 1607–1763* (Chapel Hill: University of North Carolina Press, 2010), 509.

13. A good summary of the crisis is Jon Kukla's "Two Penny Acts (1755, 1758)," in *Encyclopedia Virginia* (2016), www.EncyclopediaVirginia.org, accessed January 5, 2021.

14. David Stalker to William Stapleton, December 15, 1736, 4/10, Stapleton Manuscripts, John Rylands Library, University of Manchester; Laurens to Meyler & Hall, January 20, 1757, in *The Papers of Henry Laurens*, 16 vols. (Columbia: University of South Carolina Press, 1968–2003), 2:423; *Pennsylvania Gazette*, October 13, 1773.

15. Richard Sheridan, "The Crisis of Slave Subsistence in the British West Indies during and after the American Revolution," *William and Mary Quarterly* 33 (October 1976): 615–41; Alexander Berland and Georgina Endfield, "Drought and Disaster in a Revolutionary Age: Colonial Antigua during the American Independence War," *Environment and History* 24 (May 2018): 209–35.

16. "Capt. Byrd's Letters Continued," *Virginia Historical Register and Literary Advertiser* 1–2 (1848): 81–83; Simon Taylor to Chaloner Arcedekne, April 23, 1765, in "The Letters of Simon Taylor of Jamaica," in *Travel, Trade, and Power in the Atlantic, 1765–1884*, ed. Betty Wood and Martin Lynn (Cambridge: Cambridge University Press, 2002): 12–13. See also William Cronon, *Changes in the Land: Indians, Colonists, and the Ecology of New England* (New York: Hill and Wang, 1983), 122–26.

17. On flooding in England, see John Emrys Morgan, "Understanding Flooding in Early Modern England," *Journal of Historical Geography* 50 (October 2015): 37–50; Edward Long, *The History of Jamaica* (London: T. Lowndes, 1774), 3:649–50; Sewall quoted in Thomas Wickman, *Snowshoe Country: An Environmental and Cultural History of Winter in the Early American Northeast* (New York: Cambridge University Press, 2018), 134; John Winthrop, *The History of New England, 1630–1649*, ed. James Kendell Hosmer (New York: Scribner's, 1908), 2:264; *Pennsylvania Gazette*, February 19, 1767, February 22, 1733, and February 3, 1737; and Arthur Pierce Middleton, *Tobacco Coast: A Maritime History of the Chesapeake Bay* (1953; repr., Baltimore: Johns Hopkins University Press, 1984), 57–59.

18. Kathleen Murphy, "Virginia's Great Fresh of 1771 and the Politics of Disaster Relief," *Virginia Magazine of History and Biography* 123 (2015): 298–323; Dennis Blanton, Michael Chenoweth, and Cary Mock, "The Great Flood of 1771: An Explanation of Natural Causes and Social Effects," in *Historical Climate Variability and Impacts in North America*, ed. Lesley-Ann Dupigny-Giroux and Cary Mock, 3–22 (Dordrecht, Germany: Springer, 2009).

19. Wickman, *Snowshoe Country*, 3; Thomas Wickman, "The Great Snow of 1717: Settler Landscapes, Deep Snow Cover, and Winter's Environmental History," *Northeastern Naturalist* 24 (2017): 81–115.

20. *Pennsylvania Gazette*, April 9, 1741; James Parker to Benjamin Franklin, March 22, 1765, https://founders.archives.gov/documents/Franklin/01-12-02-0040; David Ludlum, *Early American Winters, 1604–1820* (Boston: American Meteorological Society, 1966), 62.

21. On the importance of inherited frameworks shaping responses to natural events, see Sara Gronim, *Everyday Nature: Knowledge of the Natural World in Colonial New York* (New Brunswick, NJ: Rutgers University Press, 2007), 76–77.

22. *Strange Newes from Virginia, being a true Relation of the Great Tempest*; "Proclamation for a Day of Humiliation," May 1688, in *The Papers of Francis Howard, Baron Howard of Effingham, 1643–1695*, ed. Warren Billings (Richmond: Virginia State Library and Archives, 1989), 374–75; *Boston Gazette or Country Journal*, November 24, 1755; *Minutes of the Provincial Council of Pennsylvania* (Harrisburg, PA: Theo Fenn, 1851), 6:422; Franklin Dexter, ed., *New Haven Town Records, 1662–1684* (New Haven, CT: New Haven Colony Historical Society, 1919), 2:412.

23. Richard Gildrie, "The Ceremonial Puritan: Days of Humiliation and Thanksgiving," *New England Historical and Genealogical Register* 136 (1982): 3–16.

24. On the frequency of fasts called in response to drought in New England, see W. DeLoss Love, *The Fast and Thanksgiving Days of New England* (Boston: Houghton, Mifflin, 1895), 319; for Antigua, see Vere Langford Oliver, ed., *The History of Antigua* (London: Mitchell and Hughes, 1894–96), 2 vols.; *Pennsylvania Gazette,* June 20, 1754; *Diaries of John Hull* (Boston: John Wilson and Son, 1857), 206, 233; and *Annals of Dorchester,* quoted in Love, *Fast and Thanksgiving,* 320. See also Thomas Prince, *The Natural and Moral Government and Agency of God in Causing Droughts and Rains* (Boston, 1750).

25. For condemnation of the "Prophanity" of astrology following the 1727 earthquake, see John Barnard, *Sin Testify'd Against by Heaven and Earth* (Boston, 1727); and Governor Tyron to Lord Hillsborough, September 15, 1769, in Ludlum, *Early American Hurricanes,* 48–49.

26. Taylor, *Newes and Strange Newes from St. Christophers;* Mulcahy, *Hurricanes and Society,* 51; Roger Williams to John Winthrop, June 1638, https://www.masshist.org/publications/winthrop/index.php/view/PWF04d033#sn=; John Ebel, *New England Earthquakes: The Surprising History of Seismic Activity in the Northeast* (Lanham, MD: Globe Pequot, 2019), 132–34.

27. Ralph Bohne, *A Discourse Concerning the Origine and Properties of Wind* (London, 1671), 4; John Winthrop, *A Lecture on Earthquakes* (Boston: Edes and Gill, 1755), 1–31, quote on 27; Lauri Bauer Coleman, "Rain Down Righteousness: Interpretations of Natural Events in Mid-Eighteenth-Century Boston," in *Remaking Boston: An Environmental History of the City and Its Surroundings,* ed. Anthony Penna and Conrad Wright, 233–58 (Pittsburgh: University of Pittsburgh Press, 2009).

28. Oliver, *The History of Antigua,* 1:xcv; Matthew Mulcahy, "Miserably Scorched: Drought in the Plantation Colonies of the British Greater Caribbean," in *Atlantic Environments and the American South,* ed. Thomas Earle and D. Andrew Johnson (Athens: University of Georgia Press, 2020), 81; "Letter from Hans Sloane . . . with Several Accounts of the Earthquakes," *Philosophical Transactions of the Royal Society* 18 (1694): 90–99; *Boston Gazette,* November 24, 1755, quoted in Robles, "Atlantic Disaster," 27.

29. On earthquake revivals in 1727, see Eric Seeman, *Pious Persuasions: Laity and Clergy in Eighteenth-Century New England* (Baltimore: Johns Hopkins University Press, 1999), 149–58; Samuel Davies, "The Religious Improvement of the Late Earthquake" (1755), in *Sermons on Important Subjects* (New York: Robert Carter, 1854), 3:177, 179–80; *Diary of John Adams* [December 1758?], https://founders.archives.gov/documents/Adams/01-01-02-0003-0003-0002; Adams, "A Dissertation on the Canon and the Feudal Law," No. 3, https://founders.archives.gov/documents/Adams/06-01-02-0052-0006; and *Boston Gazette,* September 30, 1765.

30. Wickman, "Great Snow," 84; Cotton Mather, *Winter Meditations; Directions on How to Employ the Leisure of Winter for the Glory of God* (Boston, 1693); Wickman, *Snowshoe Country,* 245–52.

31. Luffman, *A Brief Account of the Island of Antigua,* 123; William Bedford, *Descriptive Account of the Island of Jamaica* (London, 1790), 1:393; Mulcahy, *Hurricanes and Society,* 33–64; Hugh Totterdell letter, May 27, 1712, Mss 2050, National Library of Jamaica, Kingston.

32. Long, *History of Jamaica,* 3:619, iv.

AN INCENDIARY WAR

CONSPIRACIES, DISASTERS, AND THE AMERICAN REVOLUTION, 1775–1790

BENJAMIN L. CARP

In the summer of 1778, two calamities struck the British garrison at New York City in rapid succession. First, on August 3, a fire that began in a ship chandler's house near Cruger's Wharf laid waste to about sixty-four houses, several other structures, and a couple of small ships. The next day, lightning struck a naval sloop lying in the East River that held almost 250 tons of gunpowder—the explosion killed the few men on board, unroofed houses, stove in window frames, and shattered dishes and windowpanes all over the city. As the German chaplain Philipp Waldeck wrote, "The rebels will certainly consider these [disasters] quickly following, one after the other, . . . to be comforting signs that heaven and all the elements are opposed to the King's Army." The second calamity was clearly an act of nature, but the first was more ambiguous: not all the disasters befalling the British army descended from the heavens. The king's supporters suspected that the rebels were trying to destroy the town, just as they had two years before. Shortly after the British army occupied New York in September 1776, an even more extensive fire had burned through about a fifth of the city, destroying two churches and hundreds of houses.[1]

The Revolutionary War's politics were fiery—sometimes quite literally. Dramatic wartime fires allow historians to explore people's fears about their enemies' actions and motivations. Although these fears were often groundless, sometimes wartime actors did set fires purposefully. Historians have considered evidence of covert action, mutinous behavior among soldiers, or radical action by discontented groups, including the enslaved. While the origins of some fires were mysterious and may never be uncovered, these fires are still worth further investigation. The calamities of the Revolutionary War—its flickering flames—accentuate the conflict's dynamism and volatility. Furthermore, these fires may reveal acts of irregular warfare that arose from radical politics and therefore became unsuited to national mythologies.

Colonial America had experienced many disasters, but no catastrophe was as dramatic and concentrated as the Revolutionary War. The war disrupted trade, mustered armies into camps, and forced people to migrate, all of which bred food scarcity and disease. The social order buckled: enslaved people made bids for freedom, rebels tore down old systems of government, and women rioted over food prices. Armies set fires, dispossessed neighbors, took prisoners, and slew enemies. Meanwhile, the new states set about displacing native peoples, perpetuating southern slavery, and exiling Loyalists. These upheavals exacerbated a series of major wartime calamities. Epidemics, forest fires, and hurricanes unleashed death and destruction during the years between 1775 and 1783. Whereas historians once heralded the American Revolution as the first revolution of the Enlightenment, they now regularly characterize it as a disastrous civil war. The Revolution, then, was as much ill-starred (the root meaning of "disaster") as star-spangled.[2]

How did people make sense of these events? Although laypeople and their religious leaders often attributed calamities to Divine Providence, philosophers had also introduced a more modern vocabulary to assess disasters rationally and recognize humans' responsibility to prevent or ameliorate them. Enlightenment thinkers tried to "control rebellious nature," urging societies to undertake the daunting task of curbing famine, limiting fire, and reducing disease, among other afflictions. Early modern thinkers also hoped to mitigate the effects of war on civilians and ordinary soldiers. As they tried to instill an ethos of humanity, reason, discipline, and honor in the face of various forms of calamity, their high-flown ideals led to important efforts in the realms of urban planning, immunization, and battlefield restraint. Yet these efforts also imperfectly held back the tide of disease, savagery, retaliation, and horror. Even as calamity inhered in warfare, Enlightenment philosophers struggled to contain wartime as well as peacetime disasters.[3]

Disasters and atrocities are, of course, particularly attendant upon wartime; it is hard to imagine otherwise amid the deployment of people—particularly young men—in unsanitary military camps, the mobilization of munitions, and countless other acts of aggression and disruption. The Reverend Jonas Clark tried to offer his Lexington congregation comfort: "When God designs the reproof and Correction of his people," he might visit them with natural disasters; or he might "give the enemy a commission, in war, with fire and sword, to distress and destroy." As fearful rumors abounded, it was natural to blame the enemy for the harsh effects of war. The Reverend Charles Inglis, a Crown supporter, charged Congress "before God and the world, with all the calamities that are suffered by America," while the revolutionary Thomas Paine, surveying the annals of Britain's atrocities, concluded that the mother country was "the greatest and most ungrateful offender against God on the face of the whole earth." Many other secular and religious leaders invited their faithful hearers to ponder how God would judge each side. If wars inherently invited disaster, then identifying which side had caused the war in the first place also focused the blame for any calamities, even accidents, that ensued.[4]

The catastrophic political upheaval of the American Revolution also revealed the limits of leaders' ability to control events. Refugees, suffering captives, and other victims of war indicted the enemy as well as their own government's claims to provide protection. Politicians needed networks of communication to mobilize the population, but these networks soon became choked with rumors about calamities and their origins. The frightful possibility of unrestrained warfare lurked beneath strategic and diplomatic decisions.

Wartime disasters thus offer particular insights into people's experiences of the Revolution and their broader responses to calamities. Human factors shape the impact of all disasters—they influence the damage to people's homes, what kind of public and private relief is available, and what preventive steps are undertaken. Moreover, rumors and misinformation prey on people's vulnerabilities and fears in the wake of war and calamity; the climate of fear and the difficulties of gathering clear intelligence helped conspiracy scares to flourish. This was especially true during fires and disease epidemics, which often led frightened people to wonder whether their origins (or spread) were deliberate. Americans, both native and white, traded fears of their enemies intentionally spreading smallpox, something the British actually did at Fort Pitt in 1763. During the siege of Boston in 1775, George Washington was initially skeptical of reports that "the enemy intended Spreading the Small pox amongst us" by sending inoculated refugees out of the city, but when outbreaks began, he was ready to believe.[5]

Fires, meanwhile, could arise from a spectrum of causes, ranging from the purely natural (lightning) and the tragically accidental to avoidable negligence and outright destructive intent (arson and incendiarism). People might well attribute fires and plagues to God's judgment, civic neglect, or errant individuals, but they also sometimes interpreted these events as signs of intentional action that reflected their nightmares: sabotage by Catholics, slave revolts, borderlands warfare, and civil unrest. Stated another way, the chaos that arose from war, political upheaval, and disease epidemics often compounded people's fears. One might argue that accusations of deliberate wartime sabotage were the products of overactive imaginations. Were such accusations merely a reflection of people's preexisting fears, or was there more to them?[6]

Fire had always threatened colonial towns, and as American cities' population density increased during the eighteenth century, fires held even greater potential for devastation. Occasionally incendiaries set deliberate fires, such as in the 1712 slave uprising in New York City or the acts of arson by Marie-Joseph Angélique, an enslaved woman in Montréal, who set two fires in 1734, either to cover her tracks as she escaped or as vengeance against a mistress she hated and the slave system in general.[7] North Americans had also witnessed large fires in Charleston (1740), Boston (1760), and Montreal (1765). When Charleston suffered its Great Fire of November 18, 1740, a rumor traveled to Newport and Boston that "in the Time of the Fire, the Negroes rose upon the Whites, which made it believed that those Rebels set the Town on Fire, to favour their Designs against the People." The rumor was later dispelled; and although all three of these fires were attributed to accidents, the extent of the damage reinforced colonists' anxieties about deliberate fires, particularly because they took place during wars, epidemics, or heightened political tensions.[8]

Throughout the long eighteenth century, war particularly gave rise to conspiracy fears, including fears of fiery disaster. Religious rivalries, racial paranoia, and geopolitics seemed to manifest as sabotage, civil unrest, and slave revolt when flames engulfed colonial towns. Conspiracy scares emerged during King William's War (which also manifested as civil disorder in the American colonies), Queen Anne's War, the War of Jenkins' Ear, the Seven Years' War, and the War of 1812.[9] Even smaller fires led to fearful murmurs and conspiracy theories: people were eager to blame society for its negligence or individual suspects for their malign intent.[10] In the North American colonies, the interest in fiery plots reached its deadliest peak in response to the supposed "Negro Conspiracy" of 1741. In the midst of the War of Jenkins' Ear, New Yorkers arrested 152 Black people and several whites after a series of ten fires terrified the city; in the end, the authorities executed thirty-four people (most of them enslaved) and forcibly deported seventy more.[11]

The devastating fires of the Revolutionary War are worthy of particular attention because the political upheaval that preceded the outbreak of fighting had already predisposed many to see the rebellious colonists as "incendiaries" who had instigated a civil war. Fire was a powerful signifier, but whether participants perceived it as the torch of liberty or the flames of discord was in the eye of the beholder. Crown supporters were quick to point out the anarchic tendencies that the American Revolution had introduced; for instance, Ambrose Serle, who became secretary to Admiral Richard, Lord Howe, criticized the "Factious and Republican Incendiaries" who wrote "inflammatory Publications" in Britain and America.[12]

As the war began in 1775, the leaders of the American rebellion were conscious of how the wider world might perceive a rebellious movement. They were eager to prove themselves by keeping things orderly, and so they tried to suppress any evidence of anarchy in their midst.[13] When fires destroyed homes, rebel leaders had to ensure that their allies weren't blamed for committing wanton devastation. They could claim that the British had driven them to acts of revenge, but they wanted to avoid the accusation that their rebellion had unleashed chaos beyond their control. In spite of the best efforts of more conciliatory leaders on both sides, soldiers and civilians pursued "flaming measures." British soldiers destroyed about four hundred buildings in Charlestown, Massachusetts, during the Battle of Bunker Hill (June 17, 1775); the opposing armies combined to burn 1,331 buildings in Norfolk, Virginia, in early 1776; southern militia forces burned dozens of Cherokee towns later that year.

On September 21, 1776, six days after the British occupied New York City, a fire raged across Broadway and burned perhaps eight hundred buildings, leveling more than a fifth of the city. The rebels had previously threatened to burn the city on their way out; as soon as they left, residents began finding caches of combustible materials and putting out mysterious fires. In the early-morning hours of September 21, a fire ignited and burned for many hours. Witnesses later said that the fire began in several places at once, and the British troops caught a number of perpetrators in the act of tampering with fire equipment, carrying combustibles, or even lighting buildings on fire. They summarily executed a few alleged saboteurs—including, supposedly, at least one woman and a mixed-race man—by piercing them with bayonets and throwing them into the flames. The British also believed that some of these incendiaries were rebel officers—William Tryon, New York's last royal governor, was not alone in his belief that "Mr. Washington was privy to this villainous act," while other observers blamed New Englanders, who deliberately targeted New York City as an Anglican-leaning, Loyalist-leaning trade rival. In the weeks before the fire, Washington was forced to disabuse the New York Provincial Convention of the "Report Prevailing amongst the Army, 'that if the fortune of War should oblige our Troops to abandon that City, it should be immediately burnt by the retreating Soldiery, and that any Man is authorized to set it on fire.'" Was the fire authorized from the top down, or had it begun from the bottom up? Leaders on both sides perceived Washington's army of 1776 (particularly the militia) as plagued with illness, regional rivalries, poor discipline, desertion, and insubordination, perhaps suggesting a climate where soldiers, in conjunction with civilian saboteurs, might take it upon themselves to burn the city. Aside from the summary executions, the British examined prisoners in an inquiry in the fall of 1776, but the records of the inquiry have been lost. The British never formally charged anyone else with incendiarism, so they never resolved the question of fault.[14]

British and Hessian officers also raised concerns about incendiarism after the Cruger's Wharf fire of August 3, 1778. Captain John Peebles of the Forty-Second Regiment heard it had "been done by design, as Matches & combustibles were found in several places," and so several people (some of them French) were "taken up on suspicion." A Hessian lieutenant also said, "Some disgruntled rebels were arrested." Waldeck, the chaplain, noted that "someone

This map, by a New Yorker who lived in the city during the Revolutionary War, shows the damage the urban landscape suffered from two large fires. David Grim, "This plan of the City of New York . . . shewing the progress and extent of the great fire which happened in the year 1776 . . . and also the fire of 1778" [1804–26], Black ink and pencil and color wash on paper. NS9 M25.1.6. New-York Historical Society, 84161d.

sympathetic to the rebels" had set the fire on August 3 and "will not rest until all New York lies in rubble." Major General Valentine Jones, the British commandant of New York, proclaimed on August 14 that "many inhabitants of this city, suspect that the late fire was not the effect of accident, but design"; he offered a hundred guineas and a pardon to informants. As a clue, he shared that one suspect had been "wounded in the back with a bayonet." Weeks later, royal officials were still looking for the fire's "perpetrators." Officials and inhabitants believed that the rebels were responsible, but once again, there is no evidence that the British successfully pursued justice.[15]

In the months after New York City experienced its dual disasters of August 1778, the Anglo-Iroquois borderlands suffered raids that left hundreds of houses in flames and dozens killed, including noncombatants. Continental forces then burned at least forty Iroquois towns during the Sullivan-Clinton expedition of 1779. British troops launched a number of notable raids; one of the last, under Benedict Arnold, burned 143 buildings in New London, Connecticut (September 6, 1781). All in all, the war—not just battlefield actions but hundreds of other destructive raids—left thousands of people homeless or economically devastated, in addition to the lives lost and the lasting physical and mental injuries. Such destruction disrupted communities, displaced refugees, and threatened Americans' sense of safety in a fundamental way.

Crown supporters and American rebels selectively politicized these events by fitting their opponents into atrocity narratives. In a letter from New York City in 1777, a British officer wrote, "We begin now severely to want part of the city which those unhappy destroyers of their country have consumed; as several good families, whom their army have ruined, come daily shivering in for our protection." In particular he noted, "Many of the poor ladies have scarce a petticoat to cover them." Henry Laurens, president of the Continental Congress in May 1778, wrote that the British were "endeavouring to distress them [the United States] by such extravagant Acts in predatory War as will Stain the annals of history with marks of Infamy & disgrace upon that once Magnanimous people." In their efforts to burn houses and goods, they had "improved upon the lessons learned from their Indian Consorts." Senior commanders on both sides professed to disavow acts of destruction (at least when committed upon white settlements), even as they perennially lamented the inherent impossibility of making every soldier and ally conform to an aristocrat's idea of strict military discipline.[16]

A 1780 fire in Charleston, South Carolina, offers another example of ambiguous circumstances surrounding a Revolutionary War disaster. Continental forces surrendered Charleston to the British on May 12. Three days later, the city suffered a horrific explosion. British artillery officers were storing the prisoners' muskets in an arsenal around 1:00 p.m., when one of the muskets discharged and ignited some stored gunpowder, blowing up the arsenal, six nearby buildings (including a brothel and poorhouse), a jail (filled with "the Lunaticks and negroes who were chained in Goal [gaol] for trifling Misdemeanours"), and a barracks, while destroying thousands of captured muskets and swords. Dozens of people died; one victim was thrown against the steeple of

Although there is no known illustration of the Charleston explosion of May 15, 1780, this image shows the drama of such a disaster. During the siege of British Pensacola, on May 8, 1781, the Spanish fired a shell that blew up the garrison's powder magazine. H. G. Berteaux and Nicolas Ponce, *The Taking of Pensacola,* in *Recueil d'estampes representant les différents événemens de la Guerre [. . .]* (Paris, 1784), Library of Congress, Rare Book and Special Collections Division.

the town's Independent (Congregational) meetinghouse. As the arsenal exploded, some of the weapons discharged, killing and wounding people who ran to put out the fire. Eventually a group of soldiers, militiamen, residents, and enslaved Blacks managed to extinguish the flames, but a witness estimated that more than two hundred people were killed, including English and Hessian officers and soldiers, civilian inhabitants, and some rebel soldiers. If this number was correct, it was twice the number of men the British had lost while besieging the city. Looking over the charred and mutilated corpses and injured survivors, Captain Johann Ewald wrote, "During the years that I have been a soldier I have witnessed many a sad spectacle of war, but never such a horrible one as this. . . . A battlefield could not look sadder."[17]

Observers wondered how this catastrophe had come about. Most appeared to agree that an artillery officer had hastily tossed an undischarged musket into the magazine, where it went off and ignited the gunpowder. Lieutenant Christian Friedrich von Bartholomai of the Ansbach Jaegers wondered, "What reasonable person would thoughtlessly throw loaded weapons into a powder magazine when a struck flint, resulting from a fall against another weapon, could cause the weapon to fire?" Captain Peebles, who was also present at this disaster, found this to be "Very Strange Management."[18]

The second possibility, however, was that a rebel had ignited the powder maliciously, which Ewald said was "more probable." Rebel leaders were sensitive to this charge. General William Moultrie recalled a Hessian officer confronting him: "you, General Moultrie, you rebel's have done this on purpose, as they did at New-York," while General Lachlan McIntosh replied that the charge of sabotage arose from "Some un[thin]king men of the enemy"; in other words, the accusation was without merit.[19]

Still, von Bartholomai wondered, "why wasn't such a dangerous place better guarded, and why was everyone allowed to enter?" Most Hessian officers held the British responsible for their carelessness, but some clearly saw the rebels' hands at work, too. Some remarked that the disaster could have laid a quarter of the city in ashes if a powder magazine only two hundred yards away (containing four or five hundred barrels of powder) had caught fire. Ewald had noticed before the incident that the British army was lax in its precautions when it came to open powder magazines.[20]

There is certainly not enough evidence to prove a deliberate action. Still, the broader context of the rebels' actions around Charleston is suggestive. In late April 1780, as rebel military leaders determined the necessity of surrendering Charleston, a French officer reported that this "had occasioned great discontent as well among the regulars as militia, who wish to defend the place to the last extremity."[21] By early May, members of the rebel garrison finally admitted that defeat was at hand. Desperate soldiers, running out of provisions, had resorted to plunder and desertion. In a Council of War on May 8, South Carolinians such as Colonel Charles Cotesworth Pinckney and Lieutenant Colonel John Laurens still wished to fight, whereas most officers were ready to capitulate. Major General Benjamin Lincoln tried without success to wring concessions from the British for civilians and the militia. After a "drunken Frensy" of British cannonading (including incendiary ammunition) on May 9 and 10, even Christopher Gadsden and the militia were willing to give up. The opposing generals agreed to terms on May 11, and the garrison surrendered the next day.[22]

The British had already learned at New York City in 1776 that the capture of an American city filled with disgruntled inhabitants was a risky proposition. In South Carolina, the rebels continued to threaten British-occupied Charleston, just as they did at New York City. A few days after the deadly explosion of May 15, the regimental quartermaster Carl Bauer reported that "the rebel officers' side-arms were taken from them because they had begun disorders in the city."[23] Months later, on August 16, Crown supporters spread a classic conspiracy rumor, based on documents allegedly found in the Continental officers' papers after the Battle of Camden. Loyalist newspapers reported a nefarious plot among prominent Charleston rebels and General Horatio Gates "to set the city on fire, open the prisons, and attack the busy garrison." In response, Lord Cornwallis sent twenty-nine prominent "conspirators and incendiaries" (including Gadsden, David Ramsay, Edward Rutledge, and Peter Timothy) to St. Augustine. Captain Peebles wrote, "this & many other cases plainly shews that they are villains in grain, & never to be trusted."[24]

Justice Thomas Jones, a New York Loyalist, wrote a manuscript history of the war in the 1780s with harsh characterizations of people on both sides of the conflict. Jones noted: "The Americans" and their sympathizers in Britain "made great complaints during the war against the royal army for burning houses, mills, and towns. It was called inhumanity, and contrary to the usage of civilized nations." Jones didn't approve of these British acts of destruction: "to rob, plunder, and burn, defenceless unfortified towns could answer to no purpose. . . . It occasioned rancor and inveteracy, and instead of conciliating, it widened the breach." Yet he insisted on putting these acts in context; he noted that the rebels, too, committed atrocities (including burning New York City twice, on September 21, 1776, and August 3, 1778) and still "had the impudence to charge Great Britain with carrying on an inhuman war." He concluded, "the burning of towns in times of war, in all civilized nations, is a usual practice." His voice found no audience in the immediate aftermath of the Revolution:

his nephew inherited the manuscript in 1835 but declined to publish it "from a feeling of delicacy," since "the children of a few parties mentioned in it were living." Jones's history wasn't published until 1879, and many historians have dismissed it as prejudicial.[25]

By contrast, two of the war's most influential early historians discussed fires and devastation in their published work. David Ramsay and Mercy Otis Warren were well connected to leading revolutionaries and wrote histories that were designed to be accepted by the American public. They chose to shroud the disasters of the Revolution in ambiguity. In some cases, Ramsay was quick to turn accusations around on the British. In 1785, he argued that the Charleston explosion of 1780 took place not because of rebel sabotage but "By the imprudence of the [British] guard, in snapping the guns and pistols." Four years later, he argued in his *History of the American Revolution* that the New York fire of 1776 was not set by rebels but "most probably occasioned by the disorderly conduct of some British sailors, who had been permitted to regale themselves on shore," and he made no mention the New York fire of 1778 or the Charleston explosion. Like Jones, Ramsay pointed out that both sides committed atrocities; unlike Jones, he argued that the United States did not need to take responsibility for them. Enumerating the "depredations" around New York, he wrote, would "fill a volume" but "answer little purpose but to excite compassion and horror." Indeed, he hastened to describe how "The calamities of war were followed by another class of evils," the popular movements of the 1780s such as Shays' Rebellion: the true calamity for Ramsay was the democratic impulses Americans unleashed along the way.[26]

Mercy Otis Warren mentioned none of these three fire disasters in her *History of the Rise, Progress, and Termination of the American Revolution.* Interestingly, however, she did hint at the kinds of resentment that might have led to war crimes. The rebels' evacuation from New York occasioned "the pains of anxiety, disappointment, and want, through a rapid flight from post to post, before a victorious army, who despised their weakness, and ridiculed their want of discipline." She also mentioned the persistent "animosities . . . between the southern and eastern troops," contrasting the "aristocratic spirit" of the former with the relative "equality of condition" among the latter. The rebels overcame these challenges, however, and looked forward to a bright future as an exemplar for humankind. Warren repeatedly enjoined her readers to "draw a veil" over the war's barbarities. Ramsay, too, wanted to move on, arguing that South Carolinians, "instead of repining at their losses, generally set themselves to repair them by diligence and economy." These contemporary historians must have suspected that it would be impossible for their audiences to coolly assess the disasters of the past.[27]

Recent historians have made clear that conspiracy discourse, groundless rumors, and reactionary violence (including racial violence) influenced early American political culture.[28] This climate of disinformation influenced perceptions of the Revolutionary War. When disasters took place—whether they resulted from accident, negligence, or sabotage—wartime purveyors of public opinion often found ways to project blame onto the other side or drown these events in misinformation and ambiguity. Conversely, when women, the enslaved, the propertyless, Native Americans, and other groups had asked for greater freedom, the leaders of the rebellion called it catastrophe. By failing to look disasters squarely in the face, chroniclers obscured real disasters and misnamed struggles for freedom as calamities of another kind.

After the war, political leaders continued to spread conspiracy theories when they were useful to suppress dissent, but they were often grimly fatalistic in the face of calamities. The new nation was awash in actual disasters, but federal and state governments made it clear that they would offer scant relief. Instead, these new governments offered infrequent aid beyond encouraging voluntary benevolence. Some disasters became rhetorically useful to journalists and politicians who wanted to stoke fear, rage, and vengefulness, but victims were still on their own.[29]

Revolutionary-era Americans experienced a series of calamities whose outcomes were impossible to deny, even if their origins were occasionally obscure. It may not be possible for historians to determine whether some of these calamities arose from insurgency, sabotage, and resistance, or whether they were mere accidents, but it may be worthwhile for historians to consider them as unheeded warnings. The Revolution was an agent of change as well as an agent of disaster. And the disasters continue: as one historian has argued, "the United States . . . has been fighting almost without pause since independence."[30] Rather than repeatedly tell the story of the Revolution as a birth of freedom, historians might also accentuate the catastrophic nature of insurgency. Such a retelling allows us to better appreciate the tragedies that unfolded while also allowing more room to explore the languages of popular rebellion.[31]

Arson and incendiarism were notoriously difficult to prove, which was one reason why American reformers later sought to remove arson from the list of capital crimes.[32] Historians, too, have been reluctant to attribute fires to incendiarism, seeing sparse or conflicting evidence as little more suitable than the spectral evidence used to condemn witches. White colonists' paranoia and the confessions they coerced under torture make historians skeptical of the archival evidence. Should historians, therefore, dismiss accusations of incendiarism in cases where the evidence is suspect or ambiguous? Were all suggestions of deliberate incendiarism the products of delusion, rhetoric, racial fear, and conspiracy theory? Or can historians define some of these clandestine deeds as acts of sabotage by opposing armies? Furthermore, why assume that all irregular acts of warfare had authorization from the leadership? Unauthorized deeds were not necessarily inchoate acts of mischief, and historians might potentially identify collective action on the part of dissenters and oppressed groups (including women or the enslaved) using the "weapons of the weak." Given the epistemological difficulties of working with shadowy evidence, it is understandable that many historians have backed away from looking for hard evidence of causation for mysterious events like fires. Scholars have focused instead on the fearful mind-set that pervaded American discourse and the inherent violence of slavery and settler colonialism. Still, perhaps historians should not abandon the job of trying to uncover intent at the heart of mysterious disasters. The American Revolution may well have been an incendiary movement in more ways than one.[33]

NOTES

1. *Eighteenth Century America: A Hessian Report on the People, the Land, the War, as Noted in the Diary of Chaplain Philipp Waldeck (1776–1780)*, trans. Bruce E. Burgoyne (Bowie, MD: Heritage, 1995), 79 ("signs"); Journals of Christopher French, Library of Congress; see also Louisa Susannah Wells, *The Journal of a Voyage from Charlestown, S.C., to London, Undertaken during the*

American Revolution by a Daughter of an Eminent American Loyalist in the Year 1778 and Written from Memory Only in 1779 (New York: New-York Historical Society 1906), 34–35, 38–40; *Royal Gazette* (New York), August 5, 1778.

2. Cindy Ermus, "Revolution as Disaster," paper presented at the 50th Annual Conference of the Consortium on the Revolutionary Era, 1750–1850, February 28, 2020; Sylvia R. Frey, *Water from the Rock: Black Resistance in a Revolutionary Age* (Princeton, NJ: Princeton University Press, 1991); Barbara Clark Smith, "Food Rioters and the American Revolution," *William and Mary Quarterly* 51, no. 1 (January 1994): 3–38; Elizabeth Fenn, *Pox Americana: The Great Smallpox Epidemic of 1775–82* (New York: Hill and Wang, 2002); Matthew Mulcahy, *Hurricanes and Society in the British Greater Caribbean, 1624–1783* (Baltimore: Johns Hopkins University Press, 2006); Matthew Mulcahy, "Miserably Scorched: Drought in the Plantation Colonies of the British Greater Caribbean," in *Atlantic Environments and the American South*, ed. Thomas Earle and D. Andrew Johnson (Athens: University of Georgia Press, 2020), 65–89, esp. 75–78; Thomas J. Campanella, "'Mark Well the Gloom': Shedding Light on the Great Dark Day of 1780," *Environmental History* 12, no. 1 (January 2007): 35–58; John Robert McNeill, *Mosquito Empires: Ecology and War in the Greater Caribbean, 1620–1914* (New York: Cambridge University Press, 2010), chap. 6; Maya Jasanoff, *Liberty's Exiles: American Loyalists in the Revolutionary World* (New York: Knopf, 2011); Holger Hoock, *Scars of Independence: America's Violent Birth* (New York: Crown, 2017).

3. Nicholas Guyatt, *Providence and the Invention of the United States, 1607–1876* (Cambridge: Cambridge University Press, 2007), chap. 3; Anson Rabinbach, *In the Shadow of Catastrophe: German Intellectuals between Apocalypse and Enlightenment* (Berkeley: University of California Press, 1997), 17, cited in Marie-Hélène Huet, *The Culture of Disaster* (Chicago: University of Chicago Press, 2012), 6–7; for a recent summary on wartime conduct, see T. Cole Jones, *Captives of Liberty: Prisoners of War and the Politics of Vengeance in the American Revolution* (Philadelphia: University of Pennsylvania Press, 2020), chap. 1.

4. Jonas Clark, *The Fate of Blood-Thirsty Oppressors, and God's Tender Care of his Distressed People: A Sermon, Preached at Lexington, April 19, 1776* (Boston, 1777), 9; [Charles Inglis], *The Letters of Papinian. in which the Conduct, Present State and Prospects, of the American Congress, are Examined* (New York, 1779), 64; [Thomas Paine], *American Crisis*, no. 2 (Philadelphia, 1777), 18; Glenn A. Moots and Phillip Hamilton, eds., *Justifying Revolution: Law, Virtue, and Violence in the American War of Independence* (Norman: University of Oklahoma Press, 2018).

5. George Washington to John Hancock, December 4, 11, 1775, *The Papers of George Washington: Revolutionary War Series*, ed. Philander D. Chase (Charlottesville: University Press of Virginia, 1986): 2:486, 533 ("Spreading"); Fenn, *Pox Americana*, 88–92, 131–33, 257–58; Gregory Evans Dowd, *Groundless: Rumors, Legends, and Hoaxes on the Early American Frontier* (Baltimore: Johns Hopkins University Press, 2015), 3–7, chaps. 2, 11.

6. Paul A. Gilje, *The Road to Mobocracy: Popular Disorder in New York City, 1763–1834* (Chapel Hill: University of North Carolina Press, 1987); Peter Silver, *Our Savage Neighbors: How Indian War Transformed Early America* (New York: Norton, 2008); Robert M. Owens, *Red Dreams, White Nightmares: Pan-Indian Alliances in the Anglo-American Mind, 1763–1815* (Norman: University of Oklahoma Press, 2015); Lauric Henneton, "Introduction: Adjusting to Fear in Early America,"

in *Fear and the Shaping of Early American Societies*, ed. Henneton and L. H. Roper (Leiden: Brill, 2016), 1–37; Peter H. Wood, *Black Majority: Negroes in Colonial South Carolina from 1670 through the Stono Rebellion* (New York: Knopf, 1975), 309–14; David Barry Gaspar, *Bondmen and Rebels: a Study of Master-Slave Relations in Antigua, with Implications for Colonial British America* (Baltimore: Johns Hopkins University Press, 1985), 141–44, 224–26.

7. Anne-Claire Faucquez, "'A Bloody Conspiracy': Race, Power and Religion in New York's 1712 Slave Insurrection," in *Fear and the Shaping of Early American Societies*, ed. Henneton and Roper, 204–25; Afua Cooper, *The Hanging of Angélique: The Untold Story of Canadian Slavery and the Burning of Old Montréal* (Athens: University of Georgia Press, 2007).

8. *Boston Evening-Post*, January 12, 1741 ("rose"); Matthew Mulcahy, "'Melancholy and Fatal Calamities': Disaster and Society in Eighteenth-Century South Carolina," in *Money, Trade, and Power: The Evolution of Colonial South Carolina's Plantation Society*, ed. Jack P. Greene, Rosemary Brana-Shute, and Randy J. Sparks (Columbia: University of South Carolina Press, 2001), 278–98; Cynthia A. Kierner, *Inventing Disaster: The Culture of Calamity from the Jamestown Colony to the Johnstown Flood* (Chapel Hill: University of North Carolina Press, 2019), 99–120.

9. Owen Stanwood, *The Empire Reformed: English America in the Age of Glorious Revolution* (Philadelphia: University of Pennsylvania Press, 2011); Jason T. Sharples, *The World That Fear Made: Slave Revolts and Conspiracy Scares in Early America* (Philadelphia: University of Pennsylvania Press, 2020), 46–57, 70, 86–96, chaps. 5–6; Eleonora Rohland, *Changes in the Air: Hurricanes in New Orleans from 1718 to the Present* (New York: Berghahn, 2019), chap. 4.

10. *Virginia Gazette* (Williamsburg) (Purdie and Dixon), July 30, 1767; *New-York Journal*, April 7, July 25, 1768.

11. Peter Charles Hoffer, *The Great New York Conspiracy of 1741: Slavery, Crime, and Colonial Law* (Lawrence: University Press of Kansas, 2003); Jill Lepore, *New York Burning: Liberty, Slavery, and Conspiracy in Eighteenth-Century Manhattan* (New York: Knopf, 2005); Sharples, *World That Fear Made*, 94–95, 98, 100–101, chaps. 3–4.

12. [Ambrose Serle], *Americans against Liberty: Or An Essay on the Nature and Principles of True Freedom* (London, 1775), 29 ("Factious," "inflammatory"); Janice Potter, *The Liberty We Seek: Loyalist Ideology in Colonial New York and Massachusetts* (Cambridge, MA: Harvard University Press, 1983), chaps. 2–3.

13. Peter S. Onuf, epilogue to *Between Sovereignty and Anarchy: The Politics of Violence in the American Revolutionary Era*, ed. Patrick Griffin, Robert G. Ingram, Onuf, and Brian Schoen (Charlottesville: University of Virginia Press, 2015), 287.

14. The British army did accuse some of their military prisoners of involvement, and they held another investigation of the fire in 1783, as they were evacuating New York; though most witnesses believed the fire was deliberate, the British government didn't disrupt the peace treaty by acting on these findings. William Tryon to Lord George Germain, September 24, 1776, *Documents Relative to the Colonial History of the State of New York [. . .]*, ed. E. B. O'Callaghan and Berthold Fernow (Albany, NY, 1853–87), 8:686 ("privy"); Abraham Yates Jr. to George Washington, August 22, 1776, *The Papers of George Washington, Revolutionary War Series*, ed. Philander D. Chase and Frank E. Grizzard Jr. (Charlottesville: University Press of Virginia, 1994), 6:108 ("prevail-

ing"); Benjamin L. Carp, "The Night the Yankees Burned Broadway: The New York City Fire of 1776," *Early American Studies* 4, no. 2 (Fall 2006): 471–511; Benjamin L. Carp, *The Great New York Fire of 1776: A Lost Story of the American Revolution* (New Haven, CT: Yale University Press, 2023).

15. *John Peebles' American War: The Diary of a Scottish Grenadier, 1776–1782*, ed. Ira D. Gruber (Mechanicsburg, PA: Stackpole, 1998), 206 ("combustibles," "suspicion"); Bruce E. Burgoyne, ed., *Enemy Views: The American Revolutionary War as Recorded by the Hessian Participants* (Bowie, MD: Heritage, 1996), 272 ("disgruntled"); *Diary of Waldeck*, 78 ("sympathetic," "rubble"); *Royal Gazette* (New York), August 19, 1778 ("inhabitants," "bayonet"); William Tryon to Lord George Germain, September 5, 1778, in *Documents Relative to the Colonial History of the State of New York [. . .]*, ed. E. B. O'Callaghan, vol. 8 (Albany, NY, 1857), 750 ("perpetrators"); Journals of Christopher French, Library of Congress.

16. *Letter from an Officer* (London, 1777), 2 ("severely," "petticoat"); Henry Laurens to David Espy and others, May 17, 1778, *Letters of Delegates to Congress, 1774–1789*, ed. Paul H. Smith (Washington, DC: Library of Congress, 1982), 9:693 ("predatory," "Consorts"); Benjamin L. Carp, "'The Unpleasing Part of the Drama': Fear, Devastation, and the Civilian Experience of the Revolutionary War," in *Fear and the Shaping of Early American Societies*, ed. Henneton and Roper, 284–303; Benjamin L. Carp, "'Disreputable among Civilized Nations': Destroying Homes during the Revolutionary War," in *Justifying Revolution*, ed. Moots and Hamilton, 168–89.

17. Lachlan McIntosh, "Journal of the Siege of Charlestown, 1780," *Lachlan McIntosh Papers in the University of Georgia Libraries*, ed. Lilla Mills Hawes, University of Georgia Libraries Miscellanea Publications, No. 7 (Athens: University of Georgia Press, 1968), 121 ("Lunaticks"), 122; Johann Ewald, "Short Description of the Expedition to Charleston and the Siege of the City, March 28 to June 19, 1780 [. . .]," in *The Siege of Charleston [. . .]*, ed. and trans. Bernhard A. Uhlendorf (Ann Arbor: University of Michigan Press, 1938), 89 ("sad spectacle"), 91; David Ramsay, *The History of the Revolution in South-Carolina [. . .]* (Trenton, NJ, 1785), 2:62–63; Carl P. Borick, *A Gallant Defense: The Siege of Charleston, 1780* (Columbia: University of South Carolina Press, 2003), 222; Joshua Shepherd, "A Melancholy Accident: The Disastrous Explosion at Charleston," *Journal of the American Revolution* (August 5, 2015), https://allthingsliberty.com/2015/08/a-melancholy-accident-the-disastrous-explosion-at-charleston/.

18. Bruce E. Burgoyne, trans. and ed., "The Bartholomai Diary, Extracts," *Diaries of Two Ansbach Jaegers* (Bowie, MD: Heritage, 1997), 150, 151 ("reasonable person"); *Peebles' American War*, 374 ("Strange Management"); Ewald, "Expedition to Charleston," in *Siege of Charleston*, ed. and trans. Uhlendorf, 89. For other German officers who did not suspect American sabotage, see "Diary of Captain Johann Hinrichs," in *Siege of Charleston*, ed. and trans. Uhlendorf, 297–99; and *Journal of a Hessian Grenadier Battalion*, trans. Bruce E. Burgoyne, ed. Marie Burgoyne (Westminster, MD: Heritage, 2005), 134. [Carl Bauer], "The 1780 Siege of Charleston as Experienced by a Hessian Officer," ed. George Fenwick Jones, pt. 2, *South Carolina Historical Magazine* 88, no. 2 (April 1987): 69, was uncertain but cited "lack of caution."

19. Ewald, "Expedition to Charleston," in *Siege of Charleston*, ed. and trans. Uhlendorf, 89 ("more probable") (curiously, this passage is omitted in Johann Ewald, *Diary of the American War: A Hessian Journal*, trans. and ed. Joseph P. Tustin [New Haven, CT: Yale University Press, 1979],

239–40); William Moultrie, *Memoirs of the American Revolution [. . .]* (New York, 1802), 2:109–12, 111 ("on purpose"); *McIntosh Papers*, 121 ("men of the enemy").

20. Burgoyne, "Bartholomai Diary," 151 ("dangerous place"); Ewald, "Expedition to Charleston," in *Siege of Charleston*, ed. and trans. Uhlendorf, 91.

21. John Lewis Gervais to Henry Laurens, April 28, 1780, in *Papers of Henry Laurens*, ed. David R. Chesnutt and C. James Taylor (2000), 15:284.

22. Harry Miller Lydenberg, ed., *Archibald Robertson, Lieutenant-General Royal Engineers: His Diaries and Sketches in America, 1762–1780* (New York: New York Public Library, 1930), 228 ("drunken Frensy"); Ewald, "Expedition to Charleston," in *Siege of Charleston*, ed. and trans. Uhlendorf, 85; Moultrie, *Memoirs of the American Revolution*, 2:79–108; Ramsay, *History of the Revolution in South-Carolina*, 2:54–62; Borick, *Gallant Defense*, 174–82, 194–228.

23. Bauer, "1780 Siege of Charleston," 69; see also Ewald, "Expedition to Charleston," in *Siege of Charleston*, ed. and trans. Uhlendorf, 87.

24. Bernard A. Uhlendorf, trans., *Revolution in America: Confidential Letters and Journals 1776–1784 of Adjutant General Major Baurmeister of the Hessian Forces* (New Brunswick, NJ: Rutgers University Press, 1957), 383 ("busy garrison"); *Royal Gazette* (New York), September 20, 1780, 3; *Peebles' American War*, 407 ("villains"); Anna Wharton Morris, contributor, "Journal of Samuel Rowland Fisher, of Philadelphia, 1779–1781," *PMHB* 41, no. 3 (1917): 309; George Smith McCowen Jr., *The British Occupation of Charleston, 1780–82* (Columbia: University of South Carolina Press, 1972), 58–61, 151–52; Charles, earl of Cornwallis, to Lord George Germain, September 19, 1780, in *The Campaign in Virginia, 1781: An Exact Reprint of Six Rare Pamphlets on the Clinton-Cornwallis Controversy [. . .]*, ed. Benjamin Franklin Stevens (London, 1888), 1:267; Sir Henry Clinton to George Washington, October 9, 1780, Cornwallis Papers, PRO 30/11/3, p. 201.

25. Thomas Jones, *The History of New York during the Revolutionary War [. . .]*, ed. Edward Floyd De Lancey (New York, 1879), 1:xi–xiii, xii ("delicacy," "children"), 314–15 ("plunder"); 2:307 ("great complaints"), 308 ("impudence," "usual practice"), 309–14; Joseph S. Tiedemann, "Thomas Jones: Embittered Long Island Loyalist," *Long Island History Journal* 21, no. 1 (Fall 2009), https://lihj.cc.stonybrook.edu/2009/articles/thomas-jones-embittered-long-island-loyalist/.

26. Ramsay, *History of the Revolution in South-Carolina*, 2:62 ("imprudence"); David Ramsay, *The History of the American Revolution*, foreword by Lester H. Cohen (1789; Indianapolis: Liberty Fund, 1990), 1:308 ("regale"), 2:281–88, 288 ("depredations," "volume," "compassion"), 2:340 ("calamities").

27. Mercy Otis Warren, *History of the Rise, Progress, and Termination of the American Revolution [. . .]*, foreword by Lester H. Cohen (1805; Indianapolis: Liberty Fund 1994), 1:325 ("anxiety"), 330 ("animosities," "aristocratic"), 331 ("equality"), for "veil" see 1:146, 2:33, 2:300; Ramsay, *History of the Revolution in South-Carolina*, 2:386 ("repining").

28. In a previous generation, historians of ideology identified conspiracy-mindedness as a way of structuring eighteenth-century epistemology (see Bernard Bailyn, *The Ideological Origins of the American Revolution* [Cambridge, MA: Belknap Press of Harvard University Press, 1967], 144–59; Gordon S. Wood, "Conspiracy and the Paranoid Style: Causality and Deceit in the Eighteenth Century," *William and Mary Quarterly* 39, no. 3 [July 1982]: 401–41; and Potter, *Liberty We Seek*, 5–7, 16–25, 34–38, 136–39, 150–52).

29. Rachel Hope Cleves, *The Reign of Terror in America: Visions of Violence from Anti-Jacobinism to Antislavery* (Cambridge: Cambridge University Press, 2009); Gareth Davies, "Dealing with Disaster: The Politics of Catastrophe in the United States, 1789–1861," *American Nineteenth Century History*, 14, no. 1 (2013): 53–72; Kierner, *Inventing Disasters*, chap. 5.

30. David Vine, *The United States of War: A Global History of America's Endless Conflicts, from Columbus to the Islamic State* (Oakland: University of California Press, 2020), 1.

31. Michael A. McDonnell, "War and Nationhood: Founding Myths and Historical Realities," in *Remembering the Revolution: Memory, History, and Nation Making from Independence to the Civil War*, ed. McDonnell, Clare Corbould, Frances M. Clarke, and W. Fitzhugh Brundage, 19–40 (Amherst: University of Massachusetts Press, 2013).

32. William Bradford, *An enquiry how far the punishment of death is necessary in Pennsylvania* (Philadelphia, [1793]), ETSC #W031893, pp. 31–32.

33. Historians of radicalism have argued that elite fears revealed moments of genuine agitation (see James C. Scott, *Weapons of the Weak: Everyday Forms of Peasant Resistance* [New Haven, CT: Yale University Press, 1985]; and Peter Linebaugh and Marcus Rediker, *The Many-Headed Hydra: Sailors, Slaves, Commoners, and the Hidden History of the Revolutionary Atlantic* [Boston: Beacon, 2000], chaps. 6–7).

AN AMERICAN PLAGUE

YELLOW FEVER IN THE UNITED STATES, 1793–1820

SARAH E. NARAMORE

At the turn of the nineteenth century, yellow fever brought sickness, death, and distress to thousands of Americans. After a particularly devastating outbreak in the nation's capital of Philadelphia in 1793, almost no summer went by without the illness striking the Atlantic coast. The ailment became the most feared disease of the era before its retreat from northern cities and emergence as an exclusively southern disease in the 1820s. Prior to that, newspapers and medical journals reported on yellow fever outbreaks from Boston to Charleston. Formal responses to the ailment included the creation of boards of health, quarantine of people and goods, and expanded public sanitary infrastructure including street cleaning and centralized water supplies. Together these actions against a specific ailment created a blueprint for nineteenth-century epidemic responses, most notably cholera, which reached the United States a generation after the peak of yellow fever.

Historians of the early United States have approached the yellow fever epidemics from multiple perspectives.[1] The fact that the disease ties into histories of race, politics, and economics as easily as it does the history of medicine attests to the immense scope of the ailment's consequences. This essay addresses that scope while framing the history of yellow fever in the Early American Republic as a series of disasters—and threat of disaster—that shaped American lives for a generation. For most towns, yellow fever season lasted from the height of summer in July until the hard frosts of late October and early November put an end to their worry. The disastrous toll of the fever came from these repeated visits before 1820 rather than a singular outbreak. And then, unexpectedly, the disease disappeared in the North and became a seemingly southern concern.

Yellow fever behaved differently than previous American epidemics like smallpox, measles, malaria, and diphtheria, which made it especially disastrous and frightening. Aside from a few sporadic epidemics in the eighteenth century, most British North American colonies were free of the illness for long stretches of time. Charleston, South Carolina, reported the most probable cases of yellow fever before 1793. Parts of Virginia experienced a severe but temporally isolated outbreak in 1741. In the early to mid-eighteenth century, yellow fever simply did not have the familiarity of measles or malaria. Moreover, unlike smallpox or diphtheria, which were considered common in cold climates, yellow fever was associated with warm and wet weather.[2]

When it struck, yellow fever disrupted daily activities, economies, and ended lives in the fragile young republic. It was variously referred to as "bilious remitting fever," "yellow jack," or simply the "black vomit," and physicians, journalists, and intellectuals like Noah Webster compared the social devastation from yellow fever to the plague.[3] Like plague, yellow fever became part of a disastrous and recurring pattern that killed quickly and marked sufferers with obvious physical signs of illness. Like plague, yellow fever led Americans to question themselves and their society. Was an angry God condemning them for some unspecified sin? Or were more mundane political, social, or medical failings to blame? Such questions became more common as yellow fever occurred more regularly beginning in the 1790s. For more than twenty years, newspapers, medical journals, and novels featured the disease and dissected its literal and metaphorical meaning for the nation.

Yellow fever—as it is known today—is a hemorrhagic fever caused by a flavivirus carried by the specific species of *Aedes aegypti* mosquitos. Historic and genetic evidence suggest that the pathogen entered human populations in Africa about 1,500 years ago and can infect both humans and nonhuman primates. The virus probably arrived in the Americas through the Atlantic slave trade, which significantly increased the movement of humans and mosquitos between West Africa, South America, and the Caribbean by the late seventeenth century.[4] To transmit yellow fever in the United States the insects need to be transported north and establish themselves in a seasonal population during the summer before dying with the first hard frosts.[5] The mosquito's bite can both deposit virus and pick it up from human or animal blood, transporting it to another body.

Once in a human population the virus spreads easily. Mosquitos lay their eggs and complete the larval state of their development in standing pools of water. Upon reaching adulthood, females fly off in search of a nearby blood meal to start the process over again. The higher the density of humans and standing water meant a greater the chance for an epidemic to take hold, which is why urban areas experienced the most frequent and deadly outbreaks. Three to six days after infection a human patient may develop flu-like symptoms. After a few days most people feel better. This generic beginning is one reason current physicians note that early diagnosis of yellow fever is difficult. It also makes yellow fever an especially tricky historical diagnosis.[6] Fifteen to 20 percent of patients develop more severe (and deadly) symptoms. These include high fever, jaundice, and hemorrhages. Even in modern cases, fatality rates at this point may be as high as 60 percent.[7]

In the eighteenth and nineteenth centuries, however, fevers were identified based on a shared collection of symptoms and local conditions; thus, yellow fever was defined by what it did to communities and individuals and where it appeared rather than the presence or absence of a specific microbe. People had yellow fever if they turned yellow, vomited black vomit, had raging fevers, and died in alarming numbers. Communities were at risk if they either had connections to sickly places (according to doctors who thought the illness was imported from other climates) or harbored dangerous local environments (according to those who thought unhealthy local conditions were to blame). This created public debates regarding both the appropriate treatment and prevention of the disorder. Doctors and politicians focused on contagious spread emphasized quarantine and fever hospitals, whereas those focused on local conditions called for long-term sanitation reform.[8] These realities also encouraged widespread reporting of the fever as the years went on. Making yellow fever a possibility gave communities permission to use it as a label for their dangerous summer fevers if they included yellowed skin and black vomit. Without modern testing, it is impossible to know exactly how much "yellow fever" was yellow fever.

The debates and discussion of yellow fever and its prevention began in earnest after the 1793 outbreak in Philadelphia. When an unprecedented four to five thousand Americans died in a single city, in a single summer, the nation took notice. As far away as Scotland, American medical student Edward Fisher wrote that he "longed" for more detailed information about what had taken place in his home country.[9] Meanwhile, London publisher Charles Dilly reported to Philadelphia physician Benjamin Rush in 1795 that the American's book on yellow fever—first released in 1794—had already sold one hundred copies of a second edition.[10] The country and world were taking notice of American yellow fever and American fever knowledge.[11] As large outbreaks continued in the following years, many Americans worried that a substantial change had occurred in their society, commerce, or environment. In his book on the fever, Rush reminded people that "yellow fever like all other diseases is influenced by climate and season."[12] This meant that the illness was shaped by its surroundings and even created by them. The events in Philadelphia, even from the beginning, were not interpreted in isolation. Observers understood that what happened there could happen elsewhere.

The 1793 Philadelphia outbreak has been recounted many times.[13] To summarize, roughly halfway through the city's notoriously humid and oppressive summer, residents around Arch Street started coming down with a fever accompanied by jaundice and producing a black vomit that looked like coffee grounds. The jaundice identified it as a bilious disease (affecting the liver), and the black vomit indicated bleeding into the upper gastrointestinal tract (hemorrhage).[14] According to his account of the fever, Rush first became aware of the illness in four related cases near the Delaware River and initially blamed rotting coffee left on a dock for the illness.[15] By late August rumors of its unusual malignancy and fatality encouraged Governor Thomas Mifflin to order a formal report on the ailment's cause, cure, and extent.[16] Port physician Dr. James Hutchinson published his conclusions on August 28 before dying of the fever himself. As part-time inspector of ship and crew health for the city, Hutchinson was in and out of areas hardest hit by the outbreak. Meanwhile, the College of Physicians of Philadelphia (a professional organization of mostly local doctors including Hutchinson and Rush) printed their own recommendations for fever prevention and cure on August 26.

Taken together, these recommendations formed an early public health response to the disease that blended individual and collective action. The documents included advice for individual self-preservation—like avoiding "all unnecessary intercourse" and dressing for the weather—as well as those related to public health, such as cleaning the city streets, marking the homes of infected people, establishing a fever hospital, and stopping the ringing of church bells to avoid a constant reminder of the increased number of funerals. Such steps became common following outbreaks of yellow fever in places like Wilmington, Delaware, and Baltimore, Maryland.[17] To eighteenth-century ears these suggestions would have been familiar from other epidemics, especially plague. Meanwhile, isolating the sick in hospitals, cleaning the streets, and marking the homes of the infected was thought to limit the disease's spread by either eliminating infectious people from the general population or removing the filth and effluvia that caused illness.[18]

Panic ensued, nonetheless. Thousands left the city as the epidemic grew, a pattern followed in other outbreaks. For example, many residents fled Baltimore during the summer of 1800, when yellow fever claimed roughly 1,200 lives.[19] Of course, many remained in the diseased cities throughout the epidemics. Those without means could not simply leave their businesses and hope to return and reopen after the fever ran its course.[20] This was especially true for Philadelphia's Black community in 1793. Economically disadvantaged and thought (mistakenly) to be immune from the disease, a theory that began in the plantation colonies of the Caribbean and was largely unchallenged by North American doctors, most free African Americans in the city had little choice but to try and find work throughout the epidemic. As a result, African Americans experienced high death rates that summer.[21] In their account of the epidemic, leaders of the Free African Society Richard Allen and Absalom Jones highlighted the role of the African American community as citizen responders to a crisis, focusing on their work as nurses, gravediggers, and caretakers at extreme personal risk and sacrifice. Allen and Jones noted that they coordinated with the mayor to procure nurses and concluded that "two thirds of the persons, who rendered these essential services, were people of colour."[22]

In the years following Philadelphia's epidemic, other East Coast cities experienced yellow fever epidemics. The remainder of the 1790s saw yellow fever hit numerous cities on the coast. It appeared in Baltimore, Philadelphia, Charleston, and New Haven, Connecticut, in 1794, Philadelphia again in 1797, and Wilmington, Delaware; Elizabeth, New Jersey; and New London, Connecticut, all in 1798.[23] One carefully documented outbreak in Boston in 1798 killed at least 186 people and led physician Samuel Brown to call for fundamental changes to urban infrastructure to avoid a repeat occurrence by cleaning the city.[24]

The outbreaks continued in the first decades of the nineteenth century. In 1805 the fever raged in Providence, Rhode Island, as well as Philadelphia and New York City.[25] Six years later the fever struck the Northeast again in the town of Perth Amboy, New Jersey.[26] New Yorkers watched in fear as the fever took off across the East River in Brooklyn in 1809, and physicians argued about whether or not it was locally produced or imported from Cuba on the ship *Concordia*.[27] In 1811 an anonymous "Observer" complained that many believed that "the golden age of our seaport towns is past, and that we have entered upon the age of clay" as a result of the continuous epidemics.[28] Physician John Crawford wrote in 1806, "the present century will be a type of the seventeenth when Epidemics raged," a century famous in the English-speaking world for plague.[29]

Farther south, others faced the threat as well, including residents of Waynesborough, Georgia, in 1802; St. Marys, Georgia, in 1808; and Charleston, South Carolina, in 1804. According to physician David Ramsay, the Charleston outbreak killed between two and three hundred people, nearly all recent arrivals to the region.[30] The horrific death tolls continued to disturb onlookers. One physician in Alexandria, Virginia, described the outcome of an 1803 epidemic, writing, "the traveler, as he passed in distant review of our city, must have been shocked at the heaps of monumental clay which potter's-field presented."[31] Like many cities, Alexandria organized a special council to deal with yellow fever, but such steps were not always productive. In Alexandria, special council meetings, "though intended to prevent unnecessary alarm, served but to encourage the fears of our citizens."[32]

Americans also continued to keep track of the fever beyond their borders, including outbreaks in tropical climates such as Grenada in the 1790s and more temperate regions in Europe such as those in Cartagena and Alicante, Spain, in 1811.[33] Nevertheless, many commentators focused on the disease and its appearance in the United States as a domestic concern. Just before the retreat of the fever from the mid-Atlantic, physician David Reese lamented from stricken Baltimore in 1819 that "the yellow fever appears to be the disease of our country" and "the scourge of America, the bane of our commercial intercourse."[34]

While large, urban outbreaks are best remembered, the fever also struck rural communities, inland communities, and small towns. Jaspar Cox and John Clairborne reported treating yellow fever in the rural, inland, and southern communities of Camden, South Carolina, and Brunswick County, Virginia, respectively in the first two decades of the nineteenth century.[35] Nor were southern practitioners alone in this rural and inland pattern of disease. Catskill, New York, a village in the mid–Hudson River Valley, suffered from an outbreak in 1803. As in urban outbreaks, the illness started in areas of questionable cleanliness and near the river, suggesting local causation.[36] Nevertheless, yellow fever maintained its reputation as an urban disease. Three years after the Catskill outbreak, Dr. William Baker from Bladensburg, Maryland (just outside of Washington, DC, on the Anacostia River), argued that the illness only existed in populated towns. He specifically claimed that the one common denominator in cases of yellow fever was the prevalence of human feces and their noxious fumes.[37]

The impact of yellow fever shocked Americans and clearly showed the limitations of pre-epidemic social safety nets. By the 1820s, cities knew to enact health boards and other forms of local support. Reese's account of the 1819 Baltimore epidemic emphasized poor relief as much as any medical procedures: "the first and most important duty which became requisite," he wrote, "was to provide for those who were unable to remove from the infected District, by reason of their poverty."[38] Officials had learned from earlier outbreaks to anticipate the needs of out-of-work, ill, and frightened citizens as well as the strain on infrastructure that dying and dead bodies placed on a community. At a time when social and physical health were understood as two sides of the same coin, Americans viewed the failure of individual and community health in urban areas as a threat to the social and political systems.

While individual outbreaks appear as isolated events in the historical records of various places, viewed as a group, important patterns emerge from these accounts that indicate the long-term nature of this disaster. Physicians responded to the new ailment by publishing and debating the causes, cures, and proper preventions of the fever. Medical journals from the period published some 1,700 articles and reviews between 1793 and 1815: roughly 10 percent were related to yellow fever, its appearance, nature, and prevention. Considering the scope of such journals—which covered everything from medical procedures to the weather to news of distant professional organizations—the concentration of yellow fever literature is remarkable and unlike the attention paid to any other specific disease.[39]

As yellow fever crashed into the young country again and again as both discrete and generalized disasters, Americans wondered what had changed in the United States to cause the fever to appear so frequently and in so many places, and what they could do to counter the danger. In terms of the disease's cause, medical authorities formed two camps. The first included physicians who believed the fever was imported from hot climates. These authors tended to focus on the connection between cases of illness on ships and connected them to diseases on shore. The other group (which included most American physicians by 1820, although the divide was more even in the 1790s) argued that the disease was not contagious and not passed from person to person.[40] These physicians emphasized how the fever tended to stay in port cities and not spread into the countryside despite the large numbers of urban dwellers who fled inland during outbreaks. For those who linked the fever to local conditions, weather was of particular concern. The Academy of Medicine of Philadelphia included weather observations and measurements of air quality as tasks assigned to their members. They believed that warm temperatures or putrefied air could trigger or worsen an epidemic.[41] According to contemporary sources, by 1820 most Americans saw local conditions as the culprit, as did some foreign visitors.[42] French observer C. F. Volney, for example, supported the idea of local production, writing, "I consider the doctrine of importation as dangerous and imprudent; both on account of the dogmatic and intolerant tone it has assumed . . . and because, in urging extravagant external measures it has rendered men indifferent to internal steps."[43] Those "internal steps" included early public health measures such as using clean water and washing streets.

Essays typically presented information and advice on dealing with the disease, as well as clues to how individual physicians understood its cause. Baker, the Maryland physician, explained that "in finding a cause for yellow fever we must not only resort to general principles . . . but to the particular situation in which it appears, the season, the weather; why the disease should appear in Baltimore, for instance, now it is populous, and was free from it while it was not populous, and the thousand other circumstances which . . . attend a proper inquiry."[44] He also recommended standard disinfecting techniques like the cleansing of streets and cleansing "necessaries" (outhouses) with lime. Another doctor, James Tounge, emphasized the sickly conditions near Fells Point in Baltimore, writing that in "many parts of it was almost insupportable from the smell produced by the putrefaction of filth. . . . [T]here are several acres of land which lay between the point and the Town which is overflowed by the tide when full; and is left naked . . . when the tide ebbs and leaves to the action of the sun a large quantity of grass which putrefies together with the roots." That putrefaction, in turn, was blamed for starting the disease, an idea shared by Rush and several of his Baltimore correspondents.[45]

In cases of large outbreaks, publications also included case studies or estimated fatality rates. Others included potential cures and tended to rely on their own experience. These "cures" ranged from bleeding and vomiting on the one hand to large doses of opium on the other. One Norfolk physician writing in 1804 claimed to help patients by emptying "the stomach with large draughts of warm water, or chamomile tea, and then administer[ing] an opiate; with aqua menthae, or a saline mixture. . . senna, and manna and cream of tartar . . . and immediately the antiseptics were thrown in. . . . During the fever a strong infusion of serpentaira with crocus . . . was given very freely."[46] Most of these treatments would have caused vomiting, voiding of the bowels, or some combination of both. Robust debates about treatment continued for some time.

Although many Americans abandoned cities when yellow fever appeared, physician Felix Pascalis Ouviere recommended a much more active and even invasive plan of medical action. He argued that the sick should be removed from their families (preventing a buildup of effluvia) and that all people should adapt to a vegetable-based diet to ensure healthy bile heading into fever season and exercise more regularly.[47]

Most medical professionals agreed that there was a need to purify American cities, quarantine trade vessels, and separate the ill from the healthy. Experience with fever encouraged cities to increase the power of some health authorities. Baltimore, for example, expanded its investment in fever prevention and physician power after their 1800 outbreak, taking steps that met or rivaled those of larger urban centers like New York and Philadelphia. Physician-led commissioners could enforce standards of cleanliness (even on private property) and block suspicious goods and people from entering the city in accordance with standard epidemic procedure. They were also paid well for their efforts, not always a guarantee during this period.[48] Cleanliness was not only a virtue for nineteenth-century cities; it was a necessity. Thus, port physicians or health officers (who were not necessarily doctors) inspected arriving ships for rotting or putrid cargo as well as sick passengers at Philadelphia and Baltimore's lazarettos (port quarantine stations and hospitals) and on ships by New York City's health boards.[49]

Altering urban landscapes likewise became an important way for mitigating potential disease. Writing in 1796, physician E. H. Smith claimed that he doubted "whether it would be possible to generate or import [yellow fever] . . . into well built & well ventilated Towns, whose inhabitants were temperate & cleanly."[50] Some of the assumptions about the fever's spread led to long-standing public health measures. The Philadelphia Lazaretto specifically targeted items associated with the fever for quarantine well into the new century including rags, coffee, and hides.[51] These "enumerated goods" placed the emphasis of contagion on cargo rather than people and borrowed from older assumptions about bubonic plague containment in European lazarettos.[52]

Cities also sought ways to secure reliable and clean water. By 1800 Philadelphia started receiving its new municipal water supply from Benjamin Latrobe's waterworks. The system included two steam pumps that moved water from the Schuylkill River into a system of wood pipes. Residents could obtain water for free at street corner pumps or pay to have it brought into homes (the fees were supposed to fund the project). This eliminated the need for rain-barrel water storage, which attracted mosquitos. The main purpose of these water systems, however, was not domestic use but to better clean the streets by washing detritus down the gutters and into the Delaware River.[53] Clean air was also deemed a medical necessity. Pascalis Ouviere praised the utility of public walks in European cities, which allowed residents to leave their homes and refresh their bodies with clean and "elastic" air. Walks outside the center of American cities could have the same healthy effects.[54]

Then, almost as suddenly as it began, yellow fever ceased to be a concern in the northern United States by the 1820s. By this point American physicians had finally (largely) agreed upon local production of the disease and developed a (mostly) uniform approach on prevention and treatment.[55] Major outbreaks north of the Chesapeake seemingly disappeared after 1821. Perhaps it was the result of successful public health and quarantine reform; perhaps it was due to a semantic shift in which doctors were less likely to report dangerous summer fevers as yellow fever. Whatever the reason, the medical crisis in the mid-Atlantic seemed to be over. While yellow fever faded as an immediate threat to Americans in places such as Philadelphia, New York, and Baltimore, its legacy lingered in the way those states, cities, and individuals responded to subsequent health disasters. The quarantines and public health measures that first coalesced during the yellow fever years in the Northeast came into sharper relief in the wake of the cholera pandemics of the mid-nineteenth century. In New York City the seasonal and occasional creation of a temporary board of health to prevent yellow fever turned into a year-round component of the municipal government in the wake of cholera by 1866.[56]

In the South yellow fever did not disappear and increasingly found itself included in lists of endemic "seasoning" disorders. As early as 1804 Virginia physician James Taylor referred to the illness as one peculiar to his region and relatively harmless for locals, noting that visitors "from Britain or northern climates have more symptoms of inflammation, and require power evacuations at the attack."[57] David Ramsay used similar language the next year, claiming, "as usual, the disease was confined to persons who were strangers to the air of Charleston," implying both local production and southerners' acclimation to the disease.[58]

In 1820, physician Matthew Irvine argued that it was an endemic disease in the South, most dangerous to foreigners and children but not long-term residents. As the southern medical profession focused more on the presumed distinctness of their region, yellow fever became wrapped into that new narrative, and by the 1840s many Americans viewed the disease as entirely regional.[59] The growth of port cities on the Gulf in the early 1800s and changes in trade patterns noted by historian K. David Patterson also explain the shift from yellow fever as an Atlantic disaster to southern disease. His statistics show the incidence of yellow fever reported in major cities moving from north to south over time, with a clear break after around 1819 to 1820.[60] This change is reflected in the historiography as well. Historians tend to either explore the northern outbreaks of the late eighteenth and early nineteenth centuries or the southern epidemics of the antebellum era but do not bridge the divide. Ideas about contagion (or lack thereof), seasonality, and association with urban spaces lingered, but the idea of the ailment as a national disaster waned, and its characterization as a distinctly southern calamity was ascendant.[61]

NOTES

1. The edited volume *A Melancholy Scene of Devastation* alone can attest to the diversity of approaches one can take with this disease (J. Worth Estes and Billy G. Smith, eds., *A Melancholy Scene of Devastation: The Public Response to the 1793 Yellow Fever Epidemic* (Sagamore, MA: Science History Publications/USA, 2013).

2. Benjamin Rush, *An Account of the Bilious Remitting Yellow Fever as It Appeared in the City of Philadelphia in the Year 1793* (Philadelphia: Thomas Dobson, 1794), 80; John Duffy, "Yellow Fever in Colonial Charleston," *South Carolina Historical and Genealogical Magazine* 52, no. 4 (1950): 189–97; Suman Seth, *Difference and Disease: Medicine, Race, and the Eighteenth-Century British Empire* (New York: Cambridge University Press, 2018), 74–79.

3. Noah Webster, *Noah Webster: Letters on Yellow Fever Addressed to Dr. William Currie* (Baltimore: Johns Hopkins University Press, 1947); Rush, *An Account of the Bilious Remitting Yellow Fever as It Appeared in the City of Philadelphia in the Year 1793*, 169–75; William Currie, "Facts and Arguments in Favour of the Foreign Origin and Contagious Nature of the Pestilential or Malignant Yellow Fever, Which Has Prevailed in Different Commercial Cities and Seaport Towns of the United States," *American Medical and Philosophical Register* 1 (1811): 181–96.

4. Juliet E. Bryant, Edward C. Holmes, and Alan D. T. Barrett, "Out of Africa: A Molecular Perspective on the Introduction of Yellow Fever Virus into the Americas," *PLOS Pathogens* 3, no. 4 (2007): 668–73; Billy G. Smith, *Ship of Death: A Voyage That Changed the Atlantic World* (New Haven, CT: Yale University Press, 2013).

5. Andrea Gloria-Soria et al., "Origin of a High-Latitude Population of *Aedes aegypti* in Washington, DC," *American Journal of Tropical Medicine and Hygiene* 98, no. 2 (2018): 445–52.

6. Catharine I. Paules and Anthony S. Fauci, "Yellow Fever—Once Again on the Radar Screen in the Americas," *New England Journal of Medicine* (2017): 1398–99; Lewis Markoff, "Yellow Fever Outbreak in Sudan," *New England Journal of Medicine* (2013): 689–91; "Yellow Fever—Symptoms, Diagnosis, & Treatment," Centers for Disease Control and Prevention, last modified

January 15, 2019, https://www.cdc.gov/yellowfever/symptoms/index.html; "Yellow Fever," World Health Organization, last modified May 7, 2019, https://www.who.int/news-room/fact-sheets/detail/yellow-fever.

7. Paules and Fauci, "Yellow Fever—Once Again on the Radar Screen in the Americas," 1397–98.

8. Thomas Apel, *Feverish Bodies, Enlightened Minds: Science and the Yellow Fever Controversy in the Early American Republic* (Stanford, CA: Stanford University Press, 2016); Suman Seth, *Difference and Disease: Medicine, Race, and the Eighteenth-Century British Empire* (Cambridge: Cambridge University Press, 2018); Mark Harrison, "Chapter 3: The Evils of Quarantine," *Contagion* 2013; Erwin H. Ackerknecht, "Anticontagionism between 1821 and 1867," *Bulletin of the History of Medicine* 22 (1948): 562–95; Christopher Hamlin, "Predisposing Causes and Public Health in Early Nineteenth Century Medical Thought," *Social History of Medicine* 5, no. 1992 (1992): 43–70.

9. Edward Fisher to Benjamin Rush (1794), Benjamin Rush Correspondence, vol. 5, Rush Family Papers, Library Company of Philadelphia.

10. Charles Dilly to Benjamin Rush (1795), Benjamin Rush Correspondence, vol. 31, Rush Family Papers, Library Company of Philadelphia.

11. For more on this pattern, see Katherine Arner, "Making Yellow Fever American: The Early American Republic, the British Empire and the Geopolitics of Disease in the Atlantic World," *Atlantic Studies* 7, no. 4 (2010): 447–71.

12. Rush, *An Account of the Bilious Remitting Yellow Fever as It Appeared in the City of Philadelphia in the Year 1793.*

13. Primary source accounts include Rush, *An Account of the Bilious Remitting Yellow Fever as It Appeared in the City of Philadelphia in the Year 1793*; William Currie, *An Impartial Review of That Part of Dr. Rush's Late Publication, Entitled "An Account of the Bilious Remitting Yellow Fever, as It Appeared in the City of Philadelphia, in the Year 1793 [. . .]," in Which His Opinion Is Shown to Be Erroneous; the Importation Of* (Philadelphia: Thomas Dobson, 1794); Charles Caldwell, *Medical & Physical Memoirs, Containing among Other Subjects a Partiuclar Enquiry into the Origin and Nature of the Late Pestilential Epidemics of the United States* (Philadelphia: Printed by Thomas and William Bradford, 1801); Abaslom Jones and Richard Allen, *A Narrative of the Proceedings of the Black People, during the Late Awful Calamity in Philadelphia, in the Year 1793: And a Refutation of Some Censures Thrown upon Them in Some Late Publications* (Philadelphia: Printed for the Authors, by William W. Woodward, At Franklin's Head, 1794).

14. B. Waterman, "Arthur Mervyn's Medical Repository and the Early Republic's Knowledge Industries," *American Literary History* 15, no. 2 (2003): 213–47; Sally F. Griffith, "'A Total Dissolution of the Bonds of Society': Community Death and Regeneration in Mathew Carey's *Short Account of the Malignant Fever*," in *A Melancholy Scene of Devastation: The Public Response to the 1793 Philadelphia Yellow Fever Epidemic*, ed. J. Worth Estes and Billy G. Smith (Science Publications/USA (1997).

15. Rush, *An Account of the Bilious Remitting Yellow Fever as It Appeared in the City of Philadelphia in the Year 1793*, 12.

16. Simon Finger, *Contagious City: The Politics of Public Health in Early Philadelphia* (Ithaca, NY: Cornell University Press, 2012), 126.

17. Rush, *An Account of the Bilious Remitting Yellow Fever as It Appeared in the City of Philadelphia in the Year 1793*, 18–23.

18. Rush, *An Account of the Bilious Remitting Yellow Fever as It Appeared in the City of Philadelphia in the Year 1793;* Mark A. Smith, "Andrew Brown's 'Earnest Endeavor': The Federal Gazette's Role in Philadelphia's Yellow Fever Epidemic of 1793," *Pennsylvania Magazine of History and Biography* 120, no. 4 (1996): 329.

19. Matthew A. Crenson, *Baltimore: A Political History* (Baltimore: Johns Hopkins University Press, 2017), 63–64.

20. Rush, *An Account of the Bilious Remitting Yellow Fever as It Appeared in the City of Philadelphia in the Year 1793*, 101–2.

21. Rana Asali Hogarth, "The Myth of Innate Racial Differences between White and Black People's Bodies: Lessons from the 1793 Yellow Fever Epidemic in Philadelphia, Pennsylvania," *American Journal of Public Health* 109, no. 10 (2019): 1339–41, https://doi.org/10.2105/AJPH.2019.305245; Mariola Espinosa, "The Question of Racial Immunity to Yellow Fever in History and Historiography," *Social Science History* 38, no. 3–4 (2012): 437–53.

22. Jones and Allen, *A Narrative of the Proceedings of the Black People, during the Late Awful Calamity in Philadelphia, in the Year 1793: And a Refutation of Some Censures Thrown upon Them in Some Late Publications*, 3–5.

23. John Vaughan, "An Account of the Origin and Cause of Yellow Fever as it appeared at Wilmington [. . .] in the Autumn of 1798," *Medical Repository and Review* 4 (1800); James Tilton, "Observations on the Yellow Fever as it appeared at Wilmington (Delaware) in the Summer and Autumn of 1798," *Medical Repository and Review* 2 (1800); George Lee, "A Short Account of an Epidemic Yellow Fever Which Prevailed in the Autumn of 1798 in the Village of Port-Elizabeth," *Medical Repository and Review* 3 (1800); Charles Holt, "A Short Account of the Yellow Fever, as it appeared in New-London, in August, September and October, 1798," *Medical Repository and Review* 3 (1800).

24. Samuel Brown, *A Treatise on The Nature, Origin and Progress of the Yellow Fever: With Observations on Its Treatment; Comprising an Account of the Disease, in Several of the Capitals of the United States; But More Particularly as It Has Prevailed in Boston* (Boston: Printed by Manning and Loring, 1800), 72–73, 109–12.

25. Parden Bowen, "Observations on the Nature of the Yellow Fever, Which Prevailed in Providence, R.I. in 1805," *American Medical and Philosophical Register* 4, no. 3 (1814); Charles Caldwell, "On the Yellow Fever at Philadelphia, 1805," *Medical Repository and Review* 5 (1808); Hardie "History of the Yellow Fever at New York, 1805," *Medical Repository and Review* 4 (1807).

26. "History of the Yellow Fever, Which Prevailed at Perth Amboy in 1811," *American Medical and Philosophical Register* 3 (1813).

27. John D. Gillespie, "Report on the Yellow Fever Which Prevailed at Brooklyn, in the Summer of 1809," *American Medical and Philosophical Register* 1 (1811); John R. B. Rodgers, "The Yellow Fever of Brooklyn in 1809," *American Medical and Philosophical Register* 1 (1811).

28. An Observer, "Conjectures, Respecting the Native Climate of Pestilence; in a Letter to the Editors of the Medical and Philosophical Register," *American Medical and Philosophical Register, or Annals of Medicine, Natural History, Agriculture and the Arts* (1811): 26.

29. John Carwford to Benjamin Rush, 1806, Benjamin Rush Correspondence, vol. 3, Rush Family Papers, Library Company of Philadelphia.

30. Joshua E. White, "Topographical Description of the Country around Waynesborough, in Georgia, with the State of the Thermometer and Weather for Part of the Year 1802," *Medical Repository and Review* 3, no. 1 (1806); James Seagrove, "Origin of Yellow Fever in the Contaminated Air of a Coasting Vessel, and of the Town of St. Mary's in Georgia," *Medical Repository and Review* 1, no. 2 (1810); James Seagrove, "Account of the Origin and Nature of the Yellow Fever Which Prevailed in 1808, at St. Mary's Georgia," *American Medical and Philosophical Register* 3, no. 4 (1813); David Ramsay, "Facts Concerning the Yellow Fever in Charleston, (South-Carolina), during the Hot Season of 1804," *Medical Repository and Review,* 2, no. 4 (1805): 365.

31. B. H. Hall "An Account of the Yellow Fever at Alexandria (Virginia) in 1803," *Medical Repository and Review* 2, no. 1 (1805): 19.

32. Hall, "An Account of the Yellow Fever at Alexandria (Virginia) in 1803," 19.

33. John Stewart, "Observations on the Nature and Treatment of the Malignant or Yellow Fever, Which Prevailed at Grenada in the Years, 1793, 4, and 5," *American Medical and Philosophical Register* 3, no. 2 (1813); R. Y. Vance, "Report on the Nature of the Yellow Fever Which Prevailed in the Cities of Carthegena and Alicant, in 1811," *American Medical and Philosophical Register* 2, no. 4 (1812). These patterns are also discussed in Arner, "Making Yellow Fever American," 450.

34. David M. Reese, *Observations on the Epidemic of 1819, as It Prevailed in a Part of the City of Baltimore* (Baltimore: John D. Toy, Printer, 1819), 14.

35. John Clairborne to Benjamin Rush, 1802, Benjamin Rush Correspondence, vol. 3, Rush Family Papers, Library Company of Philadelphia; Jaspar Cox to Benjamin Rush, 1810, Benjamin Rush Correspondence, vol. 3, Rush Family Papers, Library Company of Philadelphia.

36. Benjamin Dwight, "Some Remarks on the Origin and Progress of the Malignant Yellow Fever, as It Appeared in the Village of Catskill, State of New-York, during the Summer and Autumn of 1803, in a Letter from Dr. Benjamin W. Dwight to Eneas Monson, M.D. of New-Haven, Connecticut," *Medical Repository* 2 (1805): 105–21.

37. William Baker, "Remarks on the Origin and Cause of Yellow Fever, and on the Means of Prevention," *Medical Repository and Review* 9 (1806): 268–75.

38. Reese, *Observations on the Epidemic of 1819*, 55.

39. This includes articles and reviews published between 1793 and 1815 in the following periodicals: *American Medical and Philosophical Register, New-York Medical and Philosophical Journal, New England Journal of Medicine and Surgery, Philadelphia Medical Museum, Medical Repository and Review of American Publications, Eclectic Repository and Review,* and *Transactions of the American Philosophical Society.*

40. Apel, *Feverish Bodies, Enlightened Minds.*

41. William Baldwin, "To Dr. John Redman Coxe," *Philadelphia Medical Museum,* 1805, 67–69; Parden Bowen, "Observations on the Origin and Nature of the Yellow Fever, Which Prevailed in Providence, Rhode Island, in the Summer of 1805. In a Letter to James Hardie, Esq. Secretary to the Board of Health, N.Y.," *American Medical and Philosophical Register* 4 (1814): 331–40.

42. Apel, *Feverish Bodies, Enlightened Minds;* Nicholas Chervin, *De L'opinion des médecins*

Américains sur la contagion ou la non-contagion de la fievre jaune, our réponse aux allégations de MM. Les Docteurs Hosack et Townsend de New-York, publiées, l'an dernier, dans La Revue Médicale la Gazette de France et le New-York (Paris: Chez J.-B. Bailliere, Libraire, 1829); Manfred J. Waserman and Virginia Kay Mayfield, "Nicolas Chervin's Yellow Fever Survey, 1820–1822," *Journal of the History of Medicine and Allied Sciences* 26, no. 1 (1971): 40–51.

43. Constantin-François Volney, *View of the Climate and Soil of the United States of America: To Which Are Annexed Some Accounts of Florida, the French Colony on the Scioto, Certain Canadian Colonies, and the Savages or Natives* (London: Printed for J. Johnson, 1804), 318.

44. Baker, "Remarks on the Origin and Cause of Yellow Fever, and on the Means of Prevention," 270.

45. James Tongue to Benjamin Rush (1800), Benjamin Rush Correspondence, vol. 17, Rush Family Papers, Library Company of Philadelphia; Nathaniel Potter to Benjamin Rush (1799–1808), Benjamin Rush Correspondence, vol. 13, Rush Family Papers, Library Company of Philadelphia; James Smith to Benjamin Rush (1799–1812), Benjamin Rush Correspondence, vol. 23, Rush Family Papers, Library Company of Philadelphia.

46. James Taylor, "Notices of the Fevers of the City of Norfolk, in Virginia," *Philadelphia Medical and Physical Journal* 1 (1804): 6.

47. Felix Pascalis Ouviere, *An Account of the Contagious Epidemic Yellow Fever, Which Prevailed in Philadelphia in the Summer and Autumn of 1797* (Philadelphia: Snowden and McCorkle, 1798), 111–12.

48. Crenson, *Baltimore: A Political History*, 66–67.

49. David S. Barnes, "Cargo, 'Infection,' and the Logic of Quarantine in the Nineteenth Century," *Bulletin of the History of Medicine* 88, no. 1 (2014): 75–101.

50. E. H. Smith to Benjamin Rush (1796), Benjamin Rush Correspondence, vol. 16, Rush Family Papers, Library Company of Philadelphia.

51. Barnes, "Cargo, 'Infection,' and the Logic of Quarantine in the Nineteenth Century."

52. Alex Chase-Levenson, *The Yellow Flag: Quarantine and the British Mediterranean World, 1780–1860 (Cambridge:* Cambridge University Press, 2020).

53. Finger, *Contagious City: The Politics of Public Health in Early Philadelphia*, 154; Jan Golinski, "Debating the Atmospheric Constitution: Yellow Fever and the American Climate," *Eighteenth-Century Studies* 49, no. 2 (2016): 159.

54. Pascalis Ouviere, *An Account of the Contagious Epidemic Yellow Fever, Which Prevailed in Philadelphia in the Summer and Autumn of 1797*, 115.

55. Arner, "Making Yellow Fever American," 463; Waserman and Mayfield, "Nicolas Chervin's Yellow Fever Survey, 1820–1822."

56. Charles E. Rosenberg, *The Cholera Years: The United States in 1832, 1849, and 1866* (Chicago: University of Chicago Press, 1962); Barnes, "Cargo, 'Infection,' and the Logic of Quarantine in the Nineteenth Century."

57. James Taylor, "Notices of the Fevers of the City of Norfolk, in Virginia," *Philadelphia Medical and Physical Journal* 1 (1804): 7.

58. Ramsay, "Facts Concerning the Yellow Fever Which Prevailed in Charleston (South-Carolina), during the Hot Season of 1804," 366.

59. Lindsay Rae Privette, "'We Yet Survive': Physician Patient Relationships and the Yellow Fever Epidemic of 1853," *Social History of Medicine* 32, no. 1 (2019): 81–82.

60. K. David Patterson, "Yellow Fever Epidemics and Mortality in the United States, 1693–1905," *Social Science & Medicine* 34, no. 8 (1992): 856–58.

61. Margaret Humphreys, *Yellow Fever and the South* (New Brunswick, NJ: Rutgers University Press, 1992), 18–19.

MISINFORMATION AND THE POLITICS OF REPORTING ON DISASTERS IN THE EARLY REPUBLIC

JONATHAN TODD HANCOCK

According to eyewitness John Edwards, a volcano erupted outside Asheville, North Carolina, at the end of 1811. He reported the alarming details in a letter to the *Raleigh (NC) Star.* Likely related to hot springs in the area, a mountain "burn[ed] with great violence," and lava had cooled to form a dam across the French Broad River. Part of the crater had collapsed in on itself, issuing "a greater noise than the loudest artillery" that echoed across the Appalachian Mountains. An itinerate preacher told locals that, at night, the lava coursing through the mountains transformed into spirits and devils. The reported eruption of the Asheville volcano came several weeks after the newspaper reported a major and unprecedented earthquake that had shaken a huge swath of the continent, which Edwards also had described in a separate (and earlier) letter. Communities had cowered at the religious significance of the amazing destruction accompanying the earthquakes. Now with news of a volcanic disaster, many feared even more manifestations of divine wrath.[1]

The year 1811 had already given readers across the United States ample cause for concern. News of the volcano came at the end of a year that featured waves of stories about environmental and geopolitical instability, particularly on the nation's territorial periphery. In January, as many as five hundred enslaved people conspired to march on New Orleans from their German Coast plantations before Louisiana militias quickly and violently quelled the brewing insurgency. Spring flooding gave way to extreme summer heat and stagnant pools of water that spread a "pestilential vapour" along the Mississippi River. On the Ohio River, observers noted squirrels marching "by tens of thousands in a deep and sober phalanx to the South," many of whom drowned. A September hurricane pounded Charleston, and inland tornadoes wracked the South. Observers looked to the sky that fall, as a solar eclipse complemented the Great Comet of 1811, which had a two-pronged tail that was widely visible across the globe. Then December brought news of the earthquake, volcano, and a tragic theater fire in Richmond, Virginia, where seventy-two people, including the state's governor, died on the night after Christmas.[2]

By year's end, the United States also faced mounting geopolitical pressures from all sides. Republican war hawks sought military conflict with Great Britain as an alternative to the disastrous embargo levied against the empire for impressing US sailors into the Royal Navy, and in the Ohio Valley, they accused the British military of aiding a new wave of Native American militancy against encroaching US settlers. Led by the Shawnee brothers Tecumseh and Tenskwatawa, the Native American militants faced off against the US Army at the Battle of Tippecanoe in November. Though the Native Americans were defeated and dispersed after the battle, news of a renewed movement confronted US readers early the next year. So too did rumors of another slave revolt in New Orleans. Looming over the year were the pronouncements of Nimrod Hughes. In his pamphlet *A Solemn Warning to All the Dwellers upon the Earth*, the Virginia prophet foretold the "Certain DESTRUCTION of ONE THIRD OF MANKIND" on June 4, 1812. Although first published in 1810, the pamphlet garnered renewed attention after the earthquakes. Former US presidents John Adams and Thomas Jefferson regularly corresponded about it, and shortly after a major temblor, a New Jersey newspaper announced that new copies were available for purchase. "I hope these things are not ominous of national calamity," wrote a congressman to his wife. "The Natural World is in turmoil as well as the political," former First Lady Abigail Adams wrote to her son John Quincy.[3]

John Edwards's volcano account thus was a fitting conclusion to the year, but it had a major problem: it was a hoax. Newspapers across the country had published Edwards's vivid descriptions, no doubt eager to compete with one another to publish the latest and strangest news to grip readers that year. Other writers had been skeptical, though not entirely dismissive, of Edwards's story. A contributor to Richmond's *Virginia Argus* found the story plausible, as there was evidence of ancient volcanoes in Virginia, while the *Charleston Courier* warned readers to treat the account with "great caution." Then the Raleigh postmaster reported that a "John Edwards" did not exist in Asheville. The *Virginia Argus* retracted its previous reporting, and Washington City's *National Intelligencer* lamented, "It is to be regretted, that this personage, whoever he may be, has no better employment."[4]

Having previously reported on the genuine earthquake, the volcano hoaxer had sought more notoriety at a time when US newspaper editors could not dismiss even the most outlandish claims. The New Madrid earthquakes, as they came to be known, were the true culmination of what a North Carolina preacher called "a time of extraordinaries." Their magnitude and uncommonness alarmed people from the eastern Great Plains to the Atlantic coast and from the Great Lakes to the Gulf of Mexico. The strongest shaking in the North American interior in at least the past five centuries, they reversed the course of the Mississippi River near their epicenters in the Missouri Bootheel. Along with the oddities and instability preceding them in 1811, they led observers to speculate about all manner of environmental and spiritual causes and consequences, including divine judgment, volcanoes, and other underground and airborne mechanisms. Readers craved new information about them, which included the sensory assault that they leveled on observers, with strange sights, sounds, smells, and bodily sensations. With rumors of war and accounts of environmental instability swirling across information networks, the earthquakes fired the fears and imaginations of everyone within their reach.[5]

Adding to the fear and fascination around the tremors was the fact that Tenskwatawa had actually predicted them. In the winter 1807–8, he warned of powerful underground and airborne forces that would be unleashed on unbelievers in four years. Tenskwatawa's prediction helps to explain why intertribal militants regathered after their defeat at Tippecanoe. And just as Hughes's prophecy gained renewed attention in US print after the shaking, so too did newspapers link the earthquakes with the Shawnee prophet.[6]

As eastern North America continued to quiver through the early months of 1812, volcanoes in particular remained a steady topic of discussion, even after Edwards's account was debunked. Many earthquake observers in the United States supposed links between the shaking and volcanoes. In an influential

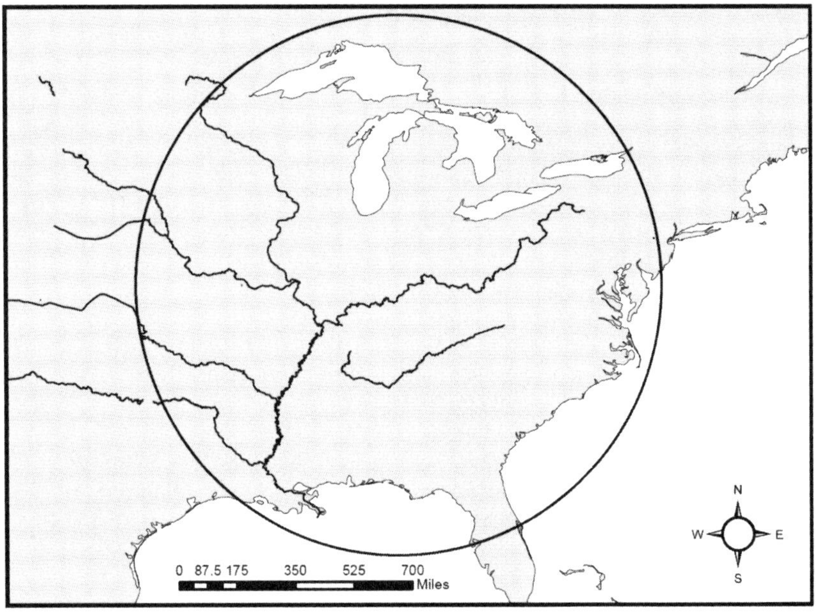

The approximate geographical scope of the New Madrid earthquakes of 1811–12. The earthquakes consisted of three major temblors between mid-December 1811 and early February 1812, as well as aftershocks that continued into the spring. Near the earthquakes' epicenters in the Missouri Bootheel, numerous eyewitness accounts reported that the Mississippi River flowed backward during the strongest shaking. Map by Jasmine Zandi.

1804 survey of US geology, French naturalist Constantin-François Volney theorized that underground combustion was responsible for both earthquakes and volcanoes, which explained the "confusion of all the strata of earth and stone" along the Atlantic coast. US naturalists cited Volney in their discussions of the earthquakes of 1811–12, though alongside Edwards, there was another curious source of misinformation about volcanoes in US newspaper discussions and private correspondence about the earthquakes: Native Americans. Whereas Edwards likely fabricated his volcano story for national print attention, the wave of Native misinformation about volcanoes constituted a geopolitical misinformation campaign intended to cast trans-Mississippi lands as dangerous and unpredictable. Long after discussion of Edwards's story subsided, Native American reports of distant volcanoes remained central to print discussions about the earthquakes' potential causes. Tenskwatawa's earthquake prediction may have lent them further credibility.[7]

For contemporary seismologists and disaster mitigation specialists, tall tales about volcanoes cloud assessments of the real seismological risks faced by communities in the New Madrid Seismic Zone today. But for historians, examining earthquake misinformation—how and why it flowed, as well as efforts to curtail it—reveals the promise and perils of the early republic's information landscape. The immediate context of mounting anomalies and geopolitical intrigue in 1811 certainly widened the range of possibilities that readers were willing to consider, but reporting on the earthquakes reflected sturdier features of scientific study, information brokering, and publishing in the early republic. Regardless of the momentousness of particular years, these means of reporting on early national disasters were sites of tension between elite and popular impulses. In early US print, the observations and concerns of commoners mingled with those of experts and elites, demonstrating the possibility for broad public input into matters of national interest. Print discussions of the earthquakes and related phenomena exhibited a nascent version of what today might be called "citizen science," a more democratic form of inquiry and debate in which people across social stations and education levels could contribute their observations and ideas about the natural environment. But astounding earthquake observations tested this broadened media landscape, as sifting fact from fiction about the earthquakes was no easy task. If multiple accounts corroborated the backward flow of the Mississippi River, why not entertain alarmingly precise apocalyptic predictions or the possibility of a volcano in the southern Appalachians? Established US political, religious, and scientific authorities ultimately closed rank and attacked propagators of misinformation (or true, but disturbing, earthquake details) as threats to national order and unity. In so doing, these authorities also undermined the collective nature of the new nation's study of these remarkable earthquakes. And despite their efforts, volcano accounts did not subside, as Native Americans propagated them to stoke US concerns about western lands.[8]

As they managed the flood of earthquake accounts, among other noteworthy topics in 1811 and early 1812, newspaper editors sought to balance objectives often in tension with one another: attracting readers' attention, competing among their peers, and printing trustworthy news. Competition for readers in Cincinnati spilled out into the pages of *Western Spy* and *Liberty Hall*, two of the city's newspapers. The editors of *Liberty Hall* accused their counterparts of exaggerating the number of shocks felt in the city. *Western Spy* responded by appealing to Cincinnati's citizens, "respectable for their number and intelligence, their diligence and accuracy of observations," to confirm that they had experienced three times as many shocks as had been previously reported. The editors argued that it was important to inform readers of the full risks they faced, because minimizing those risks could have deadly consequences. When officials in New York City and Philadelphia had understated a mid-Atlantic yellow fever outbreak in 1793 to protect their cities' reputations, the editors explained, they "wantonly sacrificed hundreds of lives, which might have been saved by a timely flight from the seat of pestilence—and thus narrow prejudice fortified by avarice and self-interest, warred against humanity." *Western Spy* granted that the earthquakes were less predictable than the steady spread of an epidemic, but the publication cautioned that it had a duty to report the full extent of the shaking. It also accused *Liberty Hall* of its own exaggerations by printing a letter claiming that "*Millions* of trees!" had floated to the top of the Mississippi River during the shaking. *Western Spy* editors claimed to have reviewed the same letter, and the word "millions" was not present.[9]

Former president John Adams was especially concerned about earthquake misinformation as a threat to national order. At the same time, he was also immersed in a range of apocalyptic literature. In correspondence with former president Thomas Jefferson, he took up prophecies that were swirling through the early republic in the unsteady months of early 1812. They discussed Tenskwatawa, foreteller of the earthquakes and instigator of the Battle of Tippecanoe; Nimrod Hughes, author of *A Solemn Warning to All the Dwellers upon the Earth;* and Christopher McPherson, a former congressional clerk and fellow prophet. McPherson sent his writings on the Book of Revelations, as well as Hughes's book, to a range of world leaders. Adams received these works and actually read them. He described Hughes and McPherson to Jefferson as "two such Mulattoes [who] might raise the Devils among the Negroes in that Vicinity," suggesting they might foment slave rebellions. McPherson was a free person of color in Virginia who had met Jefferson and James Madison while

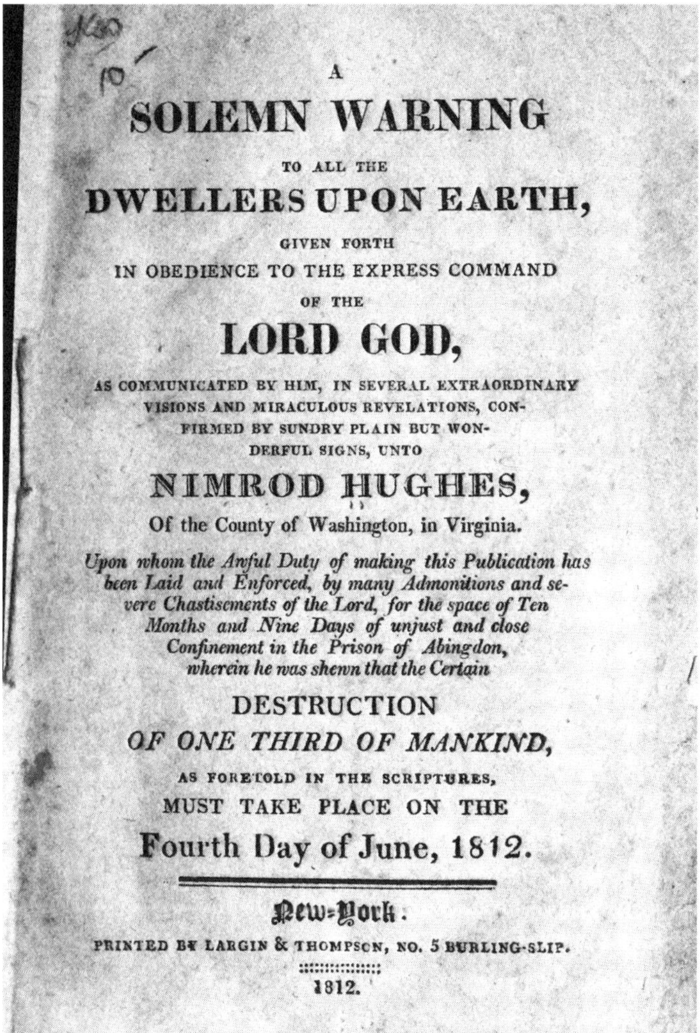

A
SOLEMN WARNING
TO ALL THE
DWELLERS UPON EARTH,
GIVEN FORTH
IN OBEDIENCE TO THE EXPRESS COMMAND
OF THE
LORD GOD,
AS COMMUNICATED BY HIM, IN SEVERAL EXTRAORDINARY VISIONS AND MIRACULOUS REVELATIONS, CONFIRMED BY SUNDRY PLAIN BUT WONDERFUL SIGNS, UNTO
NIMROD HUGHES,
Of the County of Washington, in Virginia.
Upon whom the Awful Duty of making this Publication has been Laid and Enforced, by many Admonitions and severe Chastisements of the Lord, for the space of Ten Months and Nine Days of unjust and close Confinement in the Prison of Abingdon, wherein he was shewn that the Certain
DESTRUCTION
OF ONE THIRD OF MANKIND,
AS FORETOLD IN THE SCRIPTURES,
MUST TAKE PLACE ON THE
Fourth Day of June, 1812.

New-York:
PRINTED BY LARGIN & THOMPSON, NO. 5 BURLING-SLIP.
1812.

The title page of an 1812 edition of Nimrod Hughes's pamphlet *A Solemn Warning to All the Dwellers upon Earth.* First published in 1810, Hughes's pronouncements gained notoriety amid the New Madrid earthquakes and other instances of environmental and geopolitical disorder in 1811 and 1812. Former US presidents Thomas Jefferson and John Adams corresponded about the pamphlet, and a minister in Maryland published a sermon decrying Hughes as a "false prophet" on the June 1812 day when Hughes predicted that one-third of humankind would perish. Library of Congress.

clerking for the US Congress and who had protested an 1810 law forbidding Black people from driving carriages and wagons if they were not transporting white people. In addition to his civic activity, he had experienced a series of visions in which Jesus slayed a dragon and cast it into a "dismal gulph of fire." By contrast, Hughes was not a free person of color, as Adams feared, but a white, likely college-educated prophet who had visions of widespread destruction on a June 1812 day that he had divined with creative calculations based on the Book of Daniel. His writing from southwest Virginia attracted McPherson's notice in Richmond, and McPherson joined their prophecies together.[10]

With news of comets, earthquakes, and volcanoes circulating through US newspapers, Adams and Jefferson took Tenskwatawa, Hughes, and McPherson seriously. The retired US Founders were less concerned about the prophets' vivid scenes of destruction coming to pass than the fear and instability that their writings had generated. Adams explained to Jefferson that the prophecies were "unphilosophical and inconsistent with the political Safety of States and Nations." Like many Americans, he was concerned about Tenskwatawa's influence on Native American communities in the Ohio Valley. And while Hughes and McPherson did not seek political clout, their writings had garnered attention across the United States. Adams cast his Massachusetts neighbors as "far from being remarkably Superstitious," but Hughes's pamphlet had nonetheless "Spread a great deal of terror and a Serious Apprehension." A writer noted similar alarm in his western Pennsylvania community, as did missionaries in Ohio, who complained that the "prognostications of a so called prophet among the whites in Virginia," along with the earthquakes, had led people to believe that the world's end was at hand. In a likely adaptation of Hughes's prognostication, an African American man in New Orleans decreed that two-thirds of humanity would be destroyed on a particular day. Whether contending with contrived volcano stories or biblically inspired forecasts of widespread destruction, Adams and Jefferson recognized how the strange and menacing reports of environmental and geopolitical disturbances could legitimate these prophetic claims. Popular print accelerated their circulation.[11]

Hughes tapped into two overlapping trends that framed inquiry into natural disasters in the early nineteenth-century United States: evangelicalism and empiricism. While religious enthusiasm and enlightenment rationalism seem at first to be oppositional frameworks for understanding disasters, both relied on the experience and authority of the individual, a principle also enshrined in the United States' founding documents. Earthquake observers often joined detailed descriptions of sounds, shaking, and weather alongside meditations on sin and divine judgment. Conversions to evangelical congregations spiked during the earthquakes, and just as readers evaluated the validity of earthquake observations, people questioned the authenticity of their conversion experiences during the earthquakes. Among preachers, "Earthquake Christians" became a popular term for those who joined churches during the shaking but abandoned their commitments when it subsided. Edwards's volcano story and Hughes's predictions tested the boundaries of the nation's republican media landscape, as they sought attention by offering detailed observations in popular print that incorporated input beyond experts and elites. Adams's concerns about the threats they posed to "political Safety" reflected the perils of misinformation and alarmism in a republic that ideally sought input beyond elite scholarly circles.[12]

Although Hughes surprisingly never updated editions of his work to incorporate the earthquakes, backlash against him demonstrated his pamphlet's wide circulation among readers in 1812. Critics assailed his character and fearmongering. Hughes claimed to have received his visions while falsely imprisoned in southwest Virginia; a personal acquaintance wrote about his reliability and his crime: stealing bacon and burning a barn. "There is no man who is acquainted with him who would believe a word he says; much less have confidence in his prophecy, and I was never more astonished to hear that his pamphlet excited a single enquiry," the writer explained in the New York City newspaper the *Columbian*. Another editorial writer characterized Hughes's visions as those "of a bigot, just let loose from prison." As the June 4 day of destruction approached, criticism intensified. On June 3, the *Georgia Journal* pilloried Hughes as a throwback to the seventeenth-century Salem Witch Trials and warned that harboring concerns about the following day would return to the nation to the "mists of superstition": "Away then with his nonsense, and let us hear no more of Hughes or his prophecy." Episcopal minister James Jones Wilmer gave a sermon in Maryland on the day that one-third of humanity was supposed to disappear. He acknowledged the "extraordinary changes and commotions," including many natural phenomena, that had befallen the nation and rebuked the "false prophet." A former chaplain of the US Senate, Wilmer published the sermon and mailed a copy to President Madison.[13]

While these authority figures ridiculed Hughes in print, he was not the marginal outcast that his critics assumed him to be, nor were his predictions entirely out of step with elite thinking about these seemingly apocalyptic times. A property owner and likely college graduate, he landed in his southwest Virginia county's middle tax bracket. His land-trading business resembled that of the more well-known and widely published itinerate evangelist Lorenzo Dow, and his prognostications were more precise, but no more foreboding, than those of Dow and Congregationalist theologian and Yale College president Timothy Dwight. Earthquakes were central to Dwight's warning that humanity was living through either the penultimate or final plague of Revelation. "At no time, since the deluge, has the situation of the human race been so extraordinary; *the world so shaken;* or its changes so numerous, sudden, extensive, and ominous," he wrote in a published sermon delivered on a national fast day in August 1812. As with Edwards's volcano story, what might first appear as a peculiar and isolated quirk in the documentary record was instead a more common feature in this age of revivalism and burgeoning popular print.[14]

Adams sought to combat speculation and exaggerations regarding the earthquakes by encouraging careful studies sponsored by elite scholarly societies. He urged physician and fellow US Founder Benjamin Rush to organize an American Philosophical Society inquiry into the "Truth of the terrible accounts of Earthquakes at the Southward and Westward." This distinguished body could examine the flood of newspaper accounts of volcanoes, backward river currents, strange atmospheric conditions, and other odd activity that accompanied the earthquakes. A comprehensive study by elite naturalists would not only correct the record for posterity; misinformation worried Adams about "something very wicked at the bottom of most of those stories that *falsis terroribus implet* [falsely alarm] our good Ladies and innocent Children." False reporting about the earthquakes registered among other complaints about US banks, distilleries, and expansionism as threats to national unity.[15]

Adams also served as an information broker between an eyewitness in Mississippi Territory and correspondents at another scholarly society. Over the course of the winter of 1811–12, Mississippi Territory governor Winthrop Sargent compiled accounts from his vantage point at the edge of the United States' growing southern plantation complex. He sent this information to his sister Judith Sargent Murray in Boston. Praising him for his "terrific" contribution, she wrote, "We have been alarmed and distressed by various reports of Earthquakes, and volcanic eruptions, but hitherto we have learned these things only by hearing of the ear." Murray forwarded her brother's study to Adams, who found it "made with the perspicuity and accuracy of an able Philosopher" and promised to send it to the nation's prominent naturalists. "The facts are so curious in the history of our Globe, so interesting and alarming to the inhabitants of America that all the societies for the promotion of science and history ought to use their best endeavours to ascertain the facts with precession," Adams wrote to Murray.[16]

The American Academy of Arts and Sciences in Boston eventually published Sargent's account, which included an array of Sargent's firsthand observations and instrument readings as well as those of local correspondents. When he did mention other contributors to his report, Sargent was careful to flag his trust in their information. Those correspondents included "an intelligent traveller," "a gentleman of respectability," and an enslaved person, whom Sargent characterized as "an old servant, who is very wakeful, and in whom I have some confidence." As with newspaper reporting on the earthquakes, Sargent's published study reflected early national commitments to empiricism, which rendered few solid conclusions about the temblors, and to the contributions of other earthquake observers, even those on the social margins. But as was befitting of his elitist Federalist political leanings, those outside contributions remained mediated through networks of correspondence among gentlemen scientists.[17]

Despite these efforts to limit misinformation, a theory linking faraway volcanoes to the earthquakes remained unchallenged. The eruptions in question were not in the southern Appalachians, as Edwards had suggested, but in the trans-Mississippi West, where US readers knew very little about the land and its people. Native Americans fueled reports of these volcanoes in a likely misinformation strategy to stem US interest in distant lands. In personal correspondence and newspaper stories alike, numerous reports cited Indigenous people as the source of information about volcanoes related to the earthquakes. The volume of these stories suggests a deliberate Native campaign to mislead settlers about the dangers that awaited them if they traveled farther west. From Philadelphia, American Philosophical Society member Benjamin Smith Barton received multiple letters about possible volcanoes from correspondents in Kentucky. In one, "reports derived from the Indians" claimed "immense Volcanic eruptions" accompanied earthquakes with epicenters somewhere between the Arkansas and Red Rivers. The correspondent also found "a substance somewhere similar to pumice Stone" floating down the Kentucky River. Based on its time of discovery and the speed of the river current, he estimated that the specimen came from a volcano three to four hundred miles north of Kentucky, and he promised to send it to Philadelphia for further investigation.[18]

Newspapers also began printing Native American–derived volcano accounts shortly after the shaking began. On December 21, the *Louisiana Gazette* mentioned a volcano near the "great Osage village," and in early January, the *New-York Evening Post* featured a letter suggesting that "the Burning Mountain, up the Washita River, had been rent to its base." The writer heard the report from a US settler "through the medium of some Indians," and just as Sargent attested to his correspondents' reliability, the writer described the settler's appearance as "such as to attach credit to his information." Indian stories about volcanoes soon appeared in newspapers in Tennessee, Georgia, Indiana, Ohio, and New York, and many other newspapers linked the volcanoes and earthquakes without explicitly mentioning Native informants. "No doubt volcanoes in the mountains of the west, which have been extinguished for ages, are now opened," explained the *Louisiana Gazette.* Volcano descriptions in Tennessee's *Carthage Gazette* and New York's *Columbian* were especially graphic. In the *Carthage Gazette,* Native Americans depicted mountains that "appeared to be tumbling to pieces" as "rocks as large as houses were thrown into the vallies from the tops of mountains; and in many places the earth appeared to be much heated, and in every direction there were seen to be evident signs of volcanic eruptions." According to a letter from Kentucky in the *Columbian,* "Some Indians who were in search of some other Indians that were lost, had returned, and stated that they had discovered a volcano at the head of the Arkansas, by the light of which they traveled three days and nights!" One reader in Ohio weighed these reports alongside Edwards's account and found the Native Americans more credible. Writing home to his family in North Carolina, he mentioned the Asheville volcano possibility, but the reports of the strength of shaking in New Madrid led him to believe Native Americans more than Edwards. Their report was that "a tremendous Volcano [had] opened in the great Northern or White mountains near the head of the Missouri."[19]

The New Madrid earthquakes posed a challenge to early US print culture. With the strong, unprecedented shaking in the North American interior, far from major hubs of printing, the nation relied on a wide range of observers. Information gathering about the earthquakes had the potential to be a collective enterprise that engaged people across social stations and education levels. Misinformation, the earthquakes' scale, and the environmental and geopolitical context in which they shook proved to be major obstacles to this undertaking. In an era of revivalism, war, and expanded popular print, and amid prophecies and accounts of comets, rivers running backward, and volcanoes, verifying authentic reporting became increasingly difficult in the winter of 1811–12. John Edwards's volcano story gained traction in a media landscape in which readers were eager for new information about the earthquakes, and newspapers were eager for readership. While his fabrication and Hughes's prophecy could be dismissed as attention-seeking alarmism or curious marginalia in the larger history of the New Madrid earthquakes, consternation among US Founders reveals the seriousness of the threat that misinformation posed to the new nation. Doubts about the truthfulness of earthquake accounts could contribute to the erosion of trust and the decline of civil society.

Despite authority figures' efforts to counter misinformation by denouncing its purveyors and encouraging elite institutions to sponsor official inquiries into the earthquakes, volcanoes remained a stubborn topic of print discussions well after Edwards's hoax. Native Americans planted these stories of menacing eruptions in a misinformation campaign to discourage further US interest in western territorial expansion. While the War of 1812 ended major Indigenous military resistance east of the Mississippi River, Native Americans could still exert geopolitical influence in subtler ways. In this case, they manipulated earthquake reporting to foment US newspaper readers' uncertainty and fear.

NOTES

1. *Raleigh Star*, January 10, 1812; *Chillicothe Fredonian*, February 19, 1812. Newspapers in at least Connecticut, Georgia, New Jersey, New York, Pennsylvania, South Carolina, and Virginia printed Edwards's account in the month after it appeared in North Carolina's *Raleigh Star* (see *New-York Herald*, January 25, 1812; *Connecticut Mirror*, February 2, 1812; *New-Jersey Journal*, February 4, 1812; *Georgia Journal*, February 5, 1812; and *Pennsylvania Gazette*, February 19, 1812).

2. Charles Joseph Latrobe, *The Rambler in North America, 1832–1833*, vol. 1 (London: R. B. Seeley and W. Burnside, 1835), 102–3; "Retrospect of the Year 1811," *Monthly Magazine and Literary Journal*, May 1812, 29–33. On the year's remarkable events, see Jonathan Todd Hancock, *Convulsed States: Earthquakes, Prophecy, and the Remaking of Early America* (Chapel Hill: University of North Carolina Press, 2021), 12–21. On the Richmond Theater Fire, see Meredith Henne Baker, *The Richmond Theater Fire: Early America's First Great Disaster* (Baton Rouge: Louisiana State University Press, 2012); and Cynthia A. Kierner, *Inventing Disaster: The Culture of Calamity from the Jamestown Colony to the Johnstown Flood* (Chapel Hill: University of North Carolina Press, 2019), 152–65.

3. Nimrod Hughes, *A Solemn Warning to All the Dwellers upon the Earth*, 2nd ed. (New Jersey: printed for the booksellers, n.d.); John Adams to Thomas Jefferson, February 10 and April 20, 1812, in *The Papers of Thomas Jefferson, Retirement Series, vol. 4*, ed. J. Jefferson Looney (Princeton, NJ: Princeton University Press, 2007), 483–85 and 642–43; John Adams to Thomas Jefferson, May 3, 1812, in *The Papers of Thomas Jefferson, Retirement Series, vol. 5*, ed. J. Jefferson Looney (Princeton, NJ: Princeton University Press, 2008), 11–14; *New-Jersey Journal*, January 21, 1812; Abijah Bigelow to Hannah Bigelow, January 1 and 5, 1812, in Brigham, "Letters of Abijah Bigelow," *American Antiquarian Society, Proceedings* 40 (1930): 323–24; Abigail Smith Adams to John Quincy Adams, March 12, 1812, reel 413, Adams Family Papers, Massachusetts Historical Society, Boston. On Nimrod Hughes, see Susan Juster, *Doomsayers: Anglo-American Prophecy in the Age of Revolution* (Philadelphia: University of Pennsylvania Press, 2003), 178–215; and Hancock, *Convulsed States*, 59–61, 100–101.

4. *Virginia Argus*, February 6 and February 13, 1812; *Charleston Courier*, February 15, 1812; *National Intelligencer* (Washington, DC), February 15, 1812.

5. Samuel L. Mitchill, "A Detailed Narrative of the Earthquakes Which Occurred on the 16th Day of December, 1811, and Agitated the Parts of North America That Lie between the Atlantic Ocean and Louisiana," *Transactions of the Literary and Philosophical Society of New York* 1 (1815): 299. For historical studies of the New Madrid earthquakes, see James Lal Penick Jr., *The New Madrid Earthquakes*, rev. ed. (Columbia: University of Missouri Press, 1981); Conevery Bolton Valencius, *The Lost History of the New Madrid Earthquakes* (Chicago: University of Chicago Press, 2013); Conevery Bolton Valencius, "Accounts of the New Madrid Earthquakes: Personal Narratives across Two Centuries of North American Seismology," *Science in Context* 25, no. 1 (2012): 17–48; and Hancock, *Convulsed States*.

6. On Tenskwatawa's earthquake prediction, see John Sergeant to Reverend Dr. Marsh, March 25, 1808, John Sergeant Letters, Society for Propagating the Gospel among the Indians

and Others in North America Records, MSS 48, Phillips Library, Peabody Essex Museum, Salem, MA; and Hancock, *Convulsed States*, 1–2, 82–84.

7. Constantin-François Volney, *View of the Climate and Soil of the United States of America* (London: J. Johnson, 1804), 117–21.

8. On the tensions between popular and elite impulses in early US civil society, education, and print culture, see Joyce Appleby, *Inheriting the Revolution: The First Generation of Americans* (Cambridge, MA: Harvard University Press, 2000), 129–60; Johan Neem, *Creating a Nation of Joiners: Democracy and Civil Society in Early National Massachusetts* (Cambridge, MA: Harvard University Press, 2008), 81–182; and Mark Boonshoft, *Aristocratic Education and the Making of the American Republic* (Chapel Hill: University of North Carolina Press, 2020), 75–181. On US print culture in era of the War of 1812, see Nicole Eustace, *1812: War and the Passions of Patriotism* (Philadelphia: University of Pennsylvania Press, 2012); and Nicole Eustace and Fredrika J. Teute, eds., *Warring for America: Cultural Contests in the Era of 1812* (Chapel Hill: University of North Carolina Press for the Omohundro Institute of Early American History and Culture). On scientific inquiry and writing about nature in the early US republic, which also reflected tensions between elite and popular impulses, see Conevery Bolton Valencius, David I. Spanagel, Emily Pawley, Sara Sidstone Gronim, and Paul Lucier, "Science in Early America: Print Culture and the Sciences of Territoriality," *Journal of the Early Republic* 36, no. 1 (2016): 73–123; Katherine Pandora, "Popular Science in National and Transnational Perspective: Suggestions from the American Context," *Isis* 100, no. 2 (2009): 346–58; and Andrew J. Lewis, *A Democracy of Facts: Natural History in the Early Republic* (Philadelphia: University of Pennsylvania Press, 2011). On early modern and modern earthquake inquiry in Europe and the United States, see Deborah Coen, *The Earthquake Observers: Disaster Science from Lisbon to Richter* (Chicago: University of Chicago Press, 2013).

9. *Western Spy*, February 8, 1812.

10. Adams to Jefferson, February 10, 1812, in *The Papers of Thomas Jefferson, vol. 4*, 483; Christopher McPherson, *A Short History of the Life of Christopher McPherson*, 2nd ed. (Lynchburg, VA.: Christopher McPherson Smith, 1855), 26.

11. Adams to Jefferson, February 10, 1812, in *The Papers of Thomas Jefferson, vol. 4*, 485; John Widney to Samuel Williams, November 13, 1811, Samuel Williams Manuscripts, Eli Lilly Library, Indiana University; Goshen Mission Diary, February 7, 1812, Moravian Archives, Northern Province, Bethlehem, PA; *Louisiana Gazette and Daily Advertiser* (New Orleans), November 27, 1811.

12. On the interplay of evangelicalism and empiricism in the early United States, see Juster, *Doomsayers*, viii; Christopher Grasso, "The Religious and the Secular in the Early American Republic," *Journal of the Early Republic* 36, no. 2 (2016): 359–88; and Hancock, *Convulsed States*, 44–45, 66–71. For an example of the fusion of empirical and evangelical considerations in US settler accounts of the earthquakes, see "Mrs. Lydia B. Bacon's Journal, 1811–1812," ed. Mary M. Crawford, *Indiana Magazine of History* 40, no. 10 (1944): 385. On the growth of trans-Appalachian evangelicalism during the earthquakes, see Hancock, *Convulsed States*, 62–66.

13. *Columbian*, January 3, 1812; *New-York Herald*, February 1, 1812; James Jones Wilmer, *An Address, Delivered in Havre-de-Grace, June 4, 1812: In Consequence of a Pamphlet Set Forth by a Certain Nimrod Hughes* (Baltimore: B. W. Sower, 1812), 1–15; Wilmer to James Madison, June

13, 1812, in *The Papers of James Madison, Presidential Series: vol. 4, November 5, 1811 to July 9, 1812*, ed. J. C. A. Stagg et al. (Charlottesville: University Press of Virginia, 1999), 481–82.

14. Washington County Deed Book, 1810–1812 Indentures, 373, Property Tax Census, 181–1816, and Unfiled Court Records of Washington County, 8:163–64, all in Historical Society of Washington County, Abindgon, VA; Timothy Dwight, *A Discourse in Two Parts, August 20, 1812, on the National Fast* (New York: J. Seymour, 1812), 6, 16–39.

15. John Adams to Benjamin Rush, March 19, 1812, in *Old Family Letters: Copied from the Originals for Alexander Biddle, Series A*, ed. Alexander Biddle (Philadelphia: J. B. Lippincott, 1892), 372; Benjamin Rush to John Adams, June 27, 1812, in *Letters of Benjamin Rush, vol. 2: 1793–1813*, ed. L. H. Butterfield (Princeton, NJ: Princeton University Press for the American Philosophical Society, 1951), 1145.

16. Judith Sargent Murray to Winthrop Sargent, March 26 and May 8, 1812, and John Adams to Judith Sargent Murray, September 11, 1812, all in Murray (Judith Sargent) Papers, Mississippi Department of Archives and History, Jackson.

17. Winthrop Sargent, "Account of Several Shocks of an Earthquake in the Southern and Western Parts of the United States," *Memoirs of the American Academy of Arts and Sciences* 3, no. 2 (1815): 350–59.

18. Alexander Montgomery to Benjamin Smith Barton, February 16, 1812, and M. Harvey to Benjamin Smith Barton, May 28, 1812, both in Benjamin Smith Barton Papers, American Philosophical Society, Philadelphia.

19. *Louisiana Gazette*, December 21, 1811; William Leigh Pierce, *An Account of the Great Earthquakes, in the Western States, Particularly on the Mississippi River; December 16–23* (Newburyport, MA: Herald Office, 1812), 13–14; *Louisiana Gazette*, February 29, 1812; *Carthage Gazette*, February 8, 1812; *Columbian*, April 1, 1812; Robert G. Wilson to William J. Wilson, February 27, 1812, L. C. Glenn Papers, Southern Historical Collection, University of North Carolina, Chapel Hill. For other newspaper stories that cited Indian reports of volcanoes, see *Western Sun*, February 22, 1812; *Western Spy*, March 14, 1812; and *Georgia Journal*, March 25, 1812. For newspaper stories that linked the earthquakes to volcanoes without mentioning Native informants, see *Western Spy*, December 28, 1811, and January 4, 1812; *Savannah Evening Journal*, February 8, 1812; *Georgia Journal*, February 12, 1812.

THE GREAT NEW YORK FIRE OF 1835 AND THE LEGAL ARCHITECTURE OF DISASTER

JANE MANNERS

Sometime between eight and ten o'clock on December 16, 1835, a fire broke out in the heart of New York's mercantile district. The night was windy and bitterly cold—one recollection put the temperature at ten below—and the fire, which had started in the chimney of a dry goods store, spread quickly. The new City Hall fire bell signaled the alarm, but although firefighters arrived at the blaze within ten minutes, the water in their engines and hoses froze almost immediately, and they were unable to contain the flames. Feeding on the silk and other flammable goods housed in the surrounding warehouses, the fire burned through the night and much of the next day. By the time it was over, it had leveled twenty-three blocks containing approximately six hundred buildings, including two thought to be fireproof. Estimates of the losses of real and personal property ranged as high as $20 million—well over half a billion dollars today.[1]

Mayor Cornelius W. Lawrence, himself a city merchant, arrived at the fire soon after it started. James Hamilton, the son of Alexander, was also there, having been summoned shortly before midnight to try to salvage a statue of his father that had recently been installed in the Merchants' Exchange, an ornate, three-story structure that had been completed only eight years earlier. Recalling that his first thought had been "powder must be used," Hamilton wrote in his memoirs years later of the hasty consultations among the mayor, several aldermen, and others. All agreed with Hamilton that the way to stop the fire was to deprive it of fuel by blowing up the buildings in its path. Mayor Lawrence and this ad hoc committee spent the next several hours gathering gunpowder from nearby stores, the Red Hook Arsenal, the Brooklyn Navy Yard, and the military fortifications on Governor's Island. At approximately six o'clock in the morning, Lawrence ordered the first explosion, at No. 48 Exchange Place.[2] It was a decision he might well have come to regret.

In New York City in 1835, fires were a near daily occurrence. The night before what came to be known as the "Great Fire" of December 16, a blaze had destroyed several buildings in the same neighborhood; the fact that fire-

Nicolino Calyo, *View of the Ruins after the Great Fire of New York, 16 and 17 December 1835, as Seen from Exchange Place, New York City*, 1836. Gouache on heavy paper, 16 9/16 × 24 in. Thomas Jefferson Bryan Fund, New-York Historical Society, 1980.54. This painting of the fire's aftermath is one of a series by Calyo, the son of a Neapolitan army officer who had immigrated to the United States in 1834. Exchange Place was the heart of the commercial district and the home of the newly built Merchants' Exchange, the burned-out building on the left, which had been thought to be fireproof. Newspaper accounts published in the days after the fire often commented on the expensive goods, such as those in the lower right, that merchants had piled in the middle of the street to save them from the flames.

men were still recovering from their earlier exertions was cited as a reason for the disastrous consequences of the fire the following night. "Fires are so frequent here," wrote one dismayed British architect in 1834, "that they excite no alarm . . . and the rule is, if the alarm is given during the night, to put the hand on the wall at the head of the bed, and, if it feels rather warm, to get up; but, if otherwise, to turn about and go to sleep again."[3] Ads for fire insurance dotted local newspapers.

While most fires were not as destructive as the Great Fire, the possibility of such a catastrophe was never out of mind for New York's leaders. What could officials do to stem such a blaze once it had started? The trouble was not that the city did not have solutions: blowing up or pulling down buildings to stop the progress of a fire was in 1835 a well-known firefighting technique. The trouble was liability. Under the common law—the mass of judicial precedents that judges use to guide their decisions in similar cases—an official who ordered a building's destruction to stop a fire could be sued by the building's owner. If a jury found that the destruction had not, in fact, been absolutely necessary to stop the fire, the official could end up personally liable for the damage.

From the vantage point of today, when public officials are generally immune from suits seeking to hold them accountable for discretionary acts taken under color of law, it is easy to forget the limited nature of officials' emergency powers in the early republic, when courts often held officials liable for their wrongful acts, even if they had been acting in good faith. Sometimes legislatures would reimburse officials ordered to pay damages. Through this practice, known as indemnification, there was a theoretical balance between ensuring that the victims of an official's unlawful acts were compensated, on the one hand, and enabling legislatures to reimburse officials whose acts did not warrant such punishment, on the other. But legislative indemnification often took months or years, and it was far from assured. To be an official in early America was thus to navigate a world in which performing one's duty carried a significant risk of legal liability, or even financial ruin.

The hazards of this regime of officer liability were nowhere more apparent than in moments of disaster. Floods, fires, plagues: in times of crisis, the effectiveness of a society's response often depends on the timeliness of officers' actions, their ability to induce certain behaviors, and their authority to alter preexisting legal rights and privileges. Containing a pandemic required quarantines and other limits on individual liberty and property, and containing a fire required depriving flames of the fuel in their path, regardless of who owned that fuel. Yet to lawfully take such action—to seize cargo suspected of being infected with cholera or to blow up a building to stop a fire—officers needed to be legally justified, by the common law or by legislation. Without such justification or if, in the exercise of their power, they went beyond what was justified, officials in the early republic would be liable for the losses caused by their actions.

Scholars who study disasters often highlight the human element behind what we colloquially refer to as "natural disasters," showing how people both generate destructive agents and create the conditions of vulnerability that enable these agents to have catastrophic effects.[4] Historians have revealed how government officials across space and time have contributed to disasters through their ineptitude, negligence, and corruption and then benefited politically and personally by providing relief to favored groups.[5] But when it comes to explaining the often tragic failure of leadership in the face of disaster, incompetence and self-dealing are only part of the story. The other part, a part to which disaster historians typically pay less attention, is what we might call the legal architecture of disaster: the backdrop of statutes and common law doctrines that set the parameters of official response. If a society's "pattern of vulnerability"—its physical infrastructure and location combined with its sociopolitical organization and ideology—is the key determinant of whether a destructive agent becomes a full-blown disaster, then the law that shapes the incentives and possibilities of the government's response to that destructive agent is a critical piece of the puzzle.[6]

To New Yorkers in the early decades of the nineteenth century, the conflict between officer liability and effective urban fire control was a deeply familiar problem. How, exactly, was an officer supposed to determine precisely which buildings needed to be destroyed to stop a fire? The obstacles to making an accurate, dispassionate decision in the midst of a massive conflagration were obvious, and yet under the common law, making the right call could well be the difference between being feted as a hero and being liable for damages. What if, for instance, the fire veered in another direction after city officials blew up a building that had seemed in imminent danger? This had happened in Charleston, South Carolina, in 1833; when the building's owner sued the town, witnesses at trial confirmed that the building's destruction had not, in fact, been necessary.[7] Treatise writers and other jurists often used an anecdote from the memoirs of the English statesman Edward Hyde, Earl of Clarendon, to illustrate the problem. Clarendon had written that on the first night of the Great London Fire of 1666, at a moment when the blaze might still have been halted, the lord mayor had blanched at the suggestion of pulling down buildings, making "no other answer, 'than that he durst not do it without the consent of the owners.'" His hesitation was "the less wondered at," Clarendon added, after "some gentlemen of the Inner Temple"—some of England's most influential lawyers—refused to remove goods from the houses of absent owners "because . . . it was against the law to break up any man's chamber."[8] The moral of the story was clear: the common law of necessity, which immunized officers only when a court determined after the fact that the destruction of the property in question had been necessary to stop the fire, was a porous shield against liability, pitting officials' self-interest against the public well-being.

But the common law was not the only possible protection against officer liability in such situations. There was another source of law—legislation—that could be used to plug the holes in the common law of necessity. In early nineteenth-century New York, this too was well known. Statutes authorizing officers to blow up buildings to stop fire had by then been on the books in other jurisdictions for over a hundred years. Sometimes, these laws promised compensation to the owners of the buildings thus destroyed; at other times, they simply declared the officers immune from suit for any damages.[9] They almost always required consultation among multiple decision-makers to determine which buildings needed to be pulled down or blown up. Their aim was to remove the common law's disincentive to action by replacing the court's determination of necessity with the officer's, thereby carving out a wider space for official discretion in the midst of disaster.[10]

When Mayor Lawrence gave the order to blow up several buildings on the night of December 16, he was acting under just such a statute. Thirty years earlier, on the heels of another singularly destructive fire in December 1804 and spurred by reports from the city inspector, the Street Commission, and the engineer of the Fire Department "that the means employed in the extinguishment of fire are susceptible of considerable improvement," the New York Common Council had drafted an act giving the mayor and aldermen the power to destroy buildings to fight fire and petitioned the state legislature to pass it.[11] A year later, the state legislature had enacted a statute granting city officials the power the Council sought and establishing a process for compensating anyone with an "estate or interest" in the destroyed buildings. The statute made it lawful for the mayor, or in his absence either a group of three aldermen or the city recorder and two aldermen, to order the destruction of any building then on fire or likely, in their judgment, to catch fire or spread the blaze to other buildings. As compensation, the statute provided that anyone "interested in any such building" could apply to assemble a jury to "enquire of and assess the damages which the owners of such buildings, and all persons having any estate or interest therein, have respectively sustained" through the building's destruction. The sums assessed would be deemed "in full satisfaction of all demands of such persons," to be paid by the city.[12] Interested parties, in other words, had a choice: they could sue the city by following the statutory process or they could sue the mayor at common law, but not both. It was this law that the mayor had in mind in December 1835, when he ordered the destruction of several city buildings to stop a raging fire.[13]

The mayor's use of gunpowder on the night of New York's Great Fire was the first test of the 1806 law, and the lawsuits his actions gave rise to soon revealed disagreement as to the law's scope. Everyone accepted that the statute had done two things: it had given specified officials, rather than a jury, the final word on whether the buildings' destruction had been necessary, and it had promised compensation to people with "an estate or interest" in the destroyed buildings. By requiring deliberation among multiple high-ranking city officers, the legislature had aimed to ensure the soundness of the decision. By establishing the lawfulness of decisions taken according to the statute's process, it had aimed to alleviate officers' fear of personal liability. And by promising compensation, the law rewarded those individuals whose property had been sacrificed for the good of others by leaving them in most cases better off than they would have been under the common law, where their damages would have been limited to the value of any property whose destruction a jury found had been unnecessary, and where the defendant officer's ability to pay was far from assured.

But how, exactly, was the jury to determine compensation under this new regime? Under the common law, damages would have been limited to property that (*a*) was destroyed unnecessarily and (*b*) would not have burned had it not been for the officials' actions, a no-harm, no-foul rule that often ended up reducing if not eliminating any damages. Thanks to the statute, the jury no longer needed to determine whether the destruction had been necessary. Necessity had been a defense to liability under the common law, one the statute had rendered superfluous by establishing that any decision to detonate that was reached through the statute's collaborative process was by definition lawful. But did the jury still need to decide whether the building would have burned anyway? And what about the property inside the buildings—did the statute mean that the city had to compensate interested parties for the value of their destroyed goods as well as their real estate? If so, did that mean that the statute's compensation scheme extended not only to the buildings' owners and tenants but also to the owners of goods stored on the premises? In an ordinary dwelling, such property might not make up a significant portion of the destroyed goods. But in the stores and warehouses and manufactories that constituted Manhattan's commercial district, much of the buildings' most valuable contents were not owned by the buildings' owners and renters. Instead, they were owned by firms like the Louisiana Sugar Refining Company, which had consigned merchandise valued at $12,423.68 to the lessee of a building blown up on Water Street,[14] and the American Print Works, a textile company owned mostly by wealthy New York and Boston shareholders, which claimed to have lost goods totaling $64,747.02 in the destruction of No. 52 Exchange Place.[15] Had the law intended to provide any compensation to these individuals, who under the common law would have been entitled to compensation for any goods unnecessarily destroyed? If not, did that mean that they were out of luck—or might it mean, despite the legislature's best efforts to avoid the perils of the common law of necessity, that the mayor could still be held personally liable? In the circumstances of the fire of 1835, which ravaged stores full of expensive goods owned by a range of different parties, the answers to these questions mattered a great deal.

Another factor that would further complicate the court's analysis was the 1821 addition of an eminent domain clause to the New York state constitution. Like the Fifth Amendment of the US Constitution, the clause forbade the taking of private property for public use without compensation. Even before it was added to the constitution, the principle that the state must compensate individuals whose property it took for public benefit was widely recognized, and many statutes authorizing the taking of private property for development included a provision spelling out how the amount of compensation should be assessed, just as the fire statute did. But unlike statutes authorizing the taking of land for a canal or a road, the fire statute did not actually take any property; it simply authorized the mayor to do so. And while it did provide for compensation to most of the individuals whose property might be taken by the mayor's act, it did leave some people out—those who lacked an interest in the actual physical buildings that were destroyed by conflagration. Perhaps these differences meant that the statute did not actually authorize a "taking" within the meaning of eminent domain, and so avoided this constitutional pitfall. But there was also a more problematic possibility: that the statute's failure to provide compensation to all potential sufferers conflicted with the eminent domain clause, rendering the law unconstitutional and greatly increasing the damages the city or the mayor would have to pay.

The courts' efforts to square the statute with the constitution's eminent domain clause dragged on for seventeen years. At stake were not only the fates of those individuals who suffered material losses as a result of the buildings' explosion. The mayor's and the city's fates hung in the balance as well. If either or both parties were to be found liable for all damages resulting from the mayor's actions, including those claimed by people who lost goods but lacked an interest in the destroyed buildings, the total bill would be astronomical: at least $700,000, a little less than half of the city's total receipts for the year 1836.[16] And the implications of such a broad reading of the clause's compensation requirement posed an even greater threat. Would officials no longer be able to quarantine vessels suspected of cholera or to seize cargo suspected of infection without paying the owners? By 1835, New York was the country's largest port, through which a vast quantity of valuable imports flowed every year. It could not possibly afford to compensate the owners of the vessels its officials detained or the goods they destroyed to protect the city, just as it would be hard-pressed to make good all the losses caused by the mayor's decision to save the city by blowing up buildings on the night of December 16, 1835. A holding that New York City owed compensation so widely would imperil the city's power to perform its most basic function: protecting its people.

The first trial in the fire cases, David N. Lord and Rufus Lord against the mayor and the Corporation of New York, took place over three days in February 1836, only two months after the fire itself. Rufus Lord had been the owner of No. 50 Exchange Place, which had caught fire from the explosion at No. 48, and his brother David, a dry goods importer, had been his tenant. Rufus sought compensation for the building, and David, a lessee, sought compensation for the goods inside. Judge John Treat Irving reminded the jury of prominent city merchants that it was the first case arising under the statute, which meant that no prior court had determined the law's scope. Judge Irving believed its coverage extended not only to the plaintiffs' interest in the building but to their contents as well.[17]

The Lords' attorney, Robert Sedgwick, opened with a thinly veiled threat: "If a doubt could be raised as to the right of the mayor and the two aldermen to order the destruction of property"—if, in other words, the court found that the statute did not authorize the officers' actions—"it would then follow that the mayor was a trespasser," rendering his destruction of the buildings unlawful and leaving him liable at common law. But Sedgwick trusted this would not be the case, as the mayor's actions were warranted "under the law and the constitution." He assured the jury that if necessary, he was prepared to show that most if not all of David Lord's goods could have been removed had the building not been blown up, thereby demonstrating that the cause of their destruction had been the mayor's act, not the fire itself. But this question really should not arise, he told the jurors. Their duty was simply "to inquire most particularly as to the fact that these goods were destroyed," determine their value, and calculate the damages.

Although Sedgwick evidently hoped that the jury would compensate his clients for their entire loss without considering questions of causality, most of the witness testimony he and his co-counsel elicited went to proving two points: that Mayor Lawrence had intervened too soon and that, but for this intervention, David Lord would have saved all or most of his goods before the fire reached his brother's building. Henry W. Rool and Nelson G. Elliot testified that one or two carmen were working constantly to cart Lord's goods from the hatchway at the back of the store. Rool added that he had spent half an hour removing goods from the fourth story of No. 50 and had managed to save between sixty and seventy packages during that time; Elliot guessed that "with forty or fifty persons there might have been saved four or five hundred packages of goods," and noted that at his store at No. 42, he had been able to save "from 30 to $40,000 worth, with eight or ten men, not laborers, in two hours, and without carts." Thomas Grocer produced the list of men hired to rescue Mr. Lord's goods; "there were from fifteen to twenty men employed all night." Asaph Stone, of No. 48's Stone, Swan & Mason, who thought he might also "have a claim, on the same grounds," was confident that "if Mr. Lord's store had not been blown down, he might have saved every thing." Benjamin Marsh, who had been working at Stone's store, stated that nearly an hour was wasted between the time the evacuation order was given and the explosion and that the flames did not reach the site where Lord's store had been until a full hour after that. The testimony of these witnesses all indicated that Mayor Lawrence had acted too early, causing David Lord to lose valuable goods that might otherwise have been saved.

Like the plaintiffs' lawyers, the city's attorneys focused on the size of the damages award, eliciting testimony to show that the explosion of No. 48 had not meaningfully reduced the amount of time Lord had had to save his goods. James Hamilton testified that No. 48 "would have burnt down in fifty minutes" had it not been blown up when it was, impliedly not a moment too soon. Uzziah Wenman testified that only half an hour had passed between the first shouts of powder and the explosion of No. 48. Nelson Elliot admitted on cross-examination that in addition to the "one hundred and fifty packages of goods at least" in Lord's storeroom, "there were three hundred packages of goods in Mr. Lord's third story," which was only one of four stories full of goods. The implication was that another half hour of carting, give or take, would not have made much of a dent in Lord's vast inventory.

In charging the jury, Judge Irving reminded them that the statute extended to goods as well as buildings and to lessees as well as owners, but not to property that would have been burnt anyway. "By common law," he explained, "any man has a right to pull down a house on fire to prevent the extension of the flames" and "could justify himself by the necessity of the case." The legislature could not have meant to alter this arrangement; rather, it had hoped "to prevent property being improperly destroyed, or neglected to be destroyed, from timidity as from either cause the consequence might be the destruction of great masses of property, which might otherwise be saved." It followed that the city was not responsible for the entire loss, just as the mayor would not have been under the common law: the jury was to give damages only for "the amount of whatever property would not otherwise have perished." In such a case, Irving emphasized, the jury's job was not simply to add and subtract, like human calculators. Their job was to reach an equitable outcome—to determine, "under all the circumstances of the case, whether the plaintiff or the city should suffer the whole or a part of the loss." The jury retired at ten o'clock at night and returned its verdict at one o'clock the following afternoon: $7,168.60 to Rufus for the building, and $156,274.80 to David, the value they assigned to the property he would not have lost but for the mayor's actions. It was less than the $250,239.39 the Lords were hoping for, but it was nevertheless an indication that the jury believed the city should bear a large part of the loss for both the building and its contents.[18]

On appeal, New York's higher courts twice affirmed the Court of Common Pleas' verdict. Chief Justice Samuel Nelson of the New York Supreme Court held that Irving's court had been right about both the property covered by the statute (it did extend to goods as well as buildings) and which losses it encompassed (only that property which would not have burned but for the mayor's decision).[19] Nelson's reading of the statute was animated by the state constitution's eminent domain provision, which Nelson called "the great fundamental principle." The common law necessity defense had developed not because the claims for compensation had not had merit, but because it seemed unjust to make such a heroic defendant liable. But here, the heroic defendant, the mayor, was *not* liable—the city was. And that was precisely where, under the principle of eminent domain, the burden should lie, Nelson explained, since it was for the city's benefit that the property was destroyed. The statute's instruction to assess damages "in full satisfaction of all demands of such persons respectively by reason of the pulling down or destroying the building" meant exactly that: to compensate for all consequences of the building's destruction, including the destruction of property therein. How else could the legislature have justified making the payment of damages conclusive upon the individual? The following year, New York's highest court, the Court of Errors, affirmed.[20]

Despite Nelson's eminent domain analysis, not everyone agreed that "the great fundamental principle" should control the outcome. Before the Supreme Court, the city's lawyers had argued that the statute could not possibly be governed by the constitution's eminent domain provision, for if it was, how could one account for the fact that the statute left some sufferers uncompensated—those who had lost goods yet lacked an interest or estate in the building?[21] The lawyers had asked the question to point out the absurdity of the eminent domain argument, since even the Lords' lawyers conceded that the statute left such claimants out of luck. Some justices had been persuaded—Justice Bronson, writing in dissent, argued that eminent domain had nothing to do with the statute's meaning, and if the legislature had failed in its moral duty to compensate individuals for property sacrificed for public use, there was nothing the court could do about it.[22] But others took the lawyers' *reductio ad absurdum* argument seriously: how could the statute's omission of these sufferers be squared with the principle of eminent domain? And if it could not, did that mean the law itself was unconstitutional?

In 1838, the New York Supreme Court faced this question head-on. Asaph Stone, the merchant from No. 48 Exchange Place who had testified in *Mayor v. Lord* that he thought he might "also have a claim, on the same grounds," had indeed sought relief under the statute, both for goods that he owned and those he was holding as an agent for others to sell on commission.[23] Other merchants had done the same. The Court of Common Pleas judge had instructed the jury that recovery was allowed, but on review Chief Justice Nelson disagreed. The statute promised compensation only to those individuals with an estate or interest in the building; the owners of goods merely stored there did not fit this description. Forced to address the question that had initially been posed to show the limits of interpreting the statute through the lens of eminent domain, Nelson retreated from his earlier embrace of the "great fundamental principle." Instead, he reasoned that at common law, a person who pulled down a building to stop a fire was not a trespasser, and the owner consequently had no right to recover. Glossing over the fact that at common law, this outcome hinged on whether a jury thought the destruction had been necessary, he reasoned that here, a claimant's only right to recovery stemmed from the statute, which clearly did not cover the plaintiffs in *Mayor v. Stone.*

On review, the Court of Errors again agreed. One of that court's members, Senator Alonzo C. Paige, concluded that the statute did not provide compensation for such claimants and the court could do nothing to change that; to ignore the statute's plain meaning would be to assume a "legislative authority" that the court did not possess.[24] Even if the constitution's eminent domain provision did apply, Paige explained, all that meant was that the plaintiffs could apply to the legislature for indemnification.[25] To Paige and his brethren, a court's interpretation of a statute could only stretch so far. Here, where the statute undeniably failed to provide recovery to the plaintiffs, the court's hands were tied.

And yet the lawsuits did not stop. Denied relief under the statute, wealthy, out-of-town merchants who had lost property in the blast yet lacked an interest in the destroyed buildings filed suit against the City of New York at common law. Reasoning that the statute had delegated the state's eminent domain power to the City of New York, they argued in *Russell v. Mayor of New York* that the mayor had been acting as the city's agent when he took the plaintiffs' private property for public use. It followed that city was constitutionally obligated to compensate all individuals injured through the exercise of that power, regardless of what the statute provided.[26]

In 1845, five years after the Court of Errors' decision in *Stone,* New York's highest court rejected this argument as well. Even if the mayor had been exercising the state's eminent domain power, Senator George C. Sherman reasoned, it did not follow that the *city* had to provide more compensation than the statute provided, because that duty, if it existed, had not been delegated. But in fact, Sherman went on, the power the mayor had exercised had *not* been the power of eminent domain. Instead, his right to act stemmed from the "law of overruling necessity," which Sherman defined as "a natural right belonging to every individual, not conferred by law." The statute, in designating the mayor as the decisionmaker, had merely specified how this natural right should be exercised, just as the state did in other matters of public health and safety. State law subjected mariners and their vessels to quarantine without compensating them for loss and delay, Sherman reminded his audience. In the cholera epidemic of 1832, the state had authorized agents of the Board of Health to destroy property to prevent the spread of disease, also without compensation. Why should fighting fire be any different?[27]

Russell ended the out-of-state merchants' efforts to win compensation in New York's courts. But a little over a year later, another group of out-of-state merchants arranged to have now-former mayor Cornelius Lawrence—by then

This image of Cornelius Lawrence, now part of the daguerreotype collection at the Library of Congress, was created by the photographer Mathew Brady in his studio in 1852, the year in which the fire lawsuits were finally resolved. Library of Congress, Prints & Photographs Division.

the US customs collector for New York—arrested in Newark, New Jersey.[28] Over the course of the next four and a half years, Lawrence defended himself against multiple common law trespass suits in New Jersey courts, brought on the grounds that the New York statute was indeed a delegation of the state's eminent domain power and thus unconstitutional and void with regard to the property owners it failed to compensate—those who, like the plaintiffs, lacked an interest in the destroyed buildings.

Remarkably, in 1848, New Jersey's highest court sided with the plaintiffs, rejecting the New York Court of Errors' interpretation of New York's own statute and constitution and obliging Lawrence to defend the necessity of his actions before a jury, just as he would have had to do had no statute existed.[29] In the trial that followed, the jury was not limited to determining mere causation, as in *Mayor v. Lord*. Instead, in addition to determining whether the mayor's actions had prevented the plaintiffs from saving their goods, the jury also had to decide whether the buildings' destruction—an event then seventeen years in the past—had in fact been necessary at the precise moment Lawrence gave the order, with Lawrence on the hook for any damages caused by a flawed judgment. At stake was $200,000, a little over $7 million in today's dollars.[30] This was precisely the scenario that the New York Common Council, in seeking the passage of a firefighting statute in the winter of 1806, had hoped to avoid.

After nine days of testimony and argument, the Newark jury found in favor of former mayor Lawrence: the buildings' destruction *had* been necessary, and Lawrence had not acted too early. He owed no damages. Yet despite this outcome, the case was a perfect example of the flimsiness of the common law necessity defense. Would the jury believe Charles Haswell, who testified that it was "a great mistake to blow up No. 48"?[31] Or would they believe John Cox, who asserted that had Lawrence not acted when he did, "the whole southern part of the city" would have burnt?[32] In their efforts to win compensation for their losses, the plaintiffs unwittingly demonstrated the inadequacy of the common law better than any judicial opinion or legislator's speech could hope to do. The muddled incentives of the common law necessity defense did not meet the needs of antebellum America's crowded city centers, where fire was an ever-present threat. To prevent such disastrous consequences, city leaders needed greater power and greater security than the common law provided.

* * *

To legal historians, the New York fire cases remain a marker of the outer bounds of the state's power to take private property for public use without compensation.[33] Yet curiously, the standard account of the cases attributes Lawrence's right to destroy private property to fight fire not to the actions of the state legislature but to the very common law whose inadequacy had created the need for a firefighting statute in the first place.[34] Outside legal circles, meanwhile, the fire is remembered mostly as a spur to the city's emerging penny presses and downtown development.[35] Both accounts overlook the critical role played by legislation in expanding the city's firefighting powers. By making the mayor and aldermen the judges of necessity, rather than a jury, the 1806 statute aimed both to free these officials from the fear of personal liability and to centralize discretion in the individuals best situated to make an informed, judicious decision. Its compensation scheme, meanwhile, spread the cost of the mayor's actions over the entire city, obliging those whose property was saved to compensate those whose property was sacrificed. The story of the 1835 fire and its legal aftermath reveals how that statute worked in practice, as the "great fundamental principle" of eminent domain threatened to upend the legislature's purpose. It is a vivid example of law's role in determining whether a destructive agent sparks a full-blown disaster or sputters out, deprived of fuel.

NOTES

1. Charles Haynes Haswell, *Reminiscences of New York by an Octogenarian (1816–1860)* (New York: Harper and Brothers, 1896), 305–7; Mary Louise Booth, *History of the City of New York, from Its Earliest Settlement to the Present Time* (New York: Clark and Meeker, 1859), 741–43; *American Print Works vs. Cornelius W. Lawrence: Proceedings at the Trial of above Entitled Cause, at Essex Circuit, October, 1852, Compiled from Notes of a Reporter at the Trial, and Revised by the Counsel for the Defendant* (hereafter *Trial Proceedings*) (New York: Collins, Bowne, 1852), 122–34; *Reminiscences of James Alexander Hamilton; or, Men and Events, at Home and Abroad, during Three Quarters of a Century* (hereafter *Hamilton Reminiscences*) (New York: Scribner, 1869), 284–88.

2. Joseph Alfred Scoville, *The Old Merchants of New York City* (New York: Carleton, 1863), 113–14; *Trial Proceedings*, 88–89, 91–92, 103, 115, 167–68; *Hamilton Reminiscences*, 285–86.

3. William Ross, "Street Houses of the City of New York," *Architectural Magazine*, November 1835.

4. Anthony Oliver-Smith and Susanna M. Hoffman, "Introduction: Why Anthropologists Should Study Disaster," in *Catastrophe & Culture: The Anthropology of Disaster*, ed. Oliver-Smith and Hoffman (Santa Fe: School of American Research Press, 2002), 3–4.

5. Skillful examples include Alan Taylor, "'The Hungry Year': 1789 on the Northern Border of Revolutionary America," in *Dreadful Visitations: Confronting Natural Catastrophe in the Age of Enlightenment*, ed. Alessa Johns (New York: Routledge, 1999); and Ted Steinberg, *Acts of God: The Unnatural History of Natural Disaster in America* (Oxford: Oxford University Press, 2000).

6. Oliver-Smith and Hoffman, "Introduction," 3.

7. *White v. City Council of Charleston*, 2 Hill (SC) 571 (1835).

8. Edward Hyde, *The Life of Edward Earl of Clarendon, Lord High Chancellor of England*, vol. 3 (1827): 100.

9. "An Act to Prevent and Suppress Fire in Charles Town" (November 4, 1704), in *The Statutes at Large of South Carolina*, ed. David McCord, vol. 7 (Columbia: A. S. Johnston, 1840), 41–42; "An Act for the Government of the City of Raleigh, and for Repealing All Former Acts for This Purpose" (Sec. XVIII [November 21, 1803]).

10. In *White v. City Council of Charleston*, for instance, Judge Harper reasoned that an ordinance authorizing city officials to destroy buildings "as may be judged necessary" should be read as "as [the officials] may judge necessary" (2 Hill [SC] 571, 576 [1835]).

11. *Minutes of the Common Council of the City of New York*, vol. 3 (New York: City of New York, 1917), 662, 689–90 (January 7, February 18, 1805).

12. "An Act for the Better Government of the City of New-York, and to Grant Certain Additional Powers and Rights to the Mayor, Aldermen and Commonalty Thereof, and to Explain, Continue and Amend the Respective Acts Therein Mentioned," Sections VIII & X, *Laws of the State of New York, Vol. IV, Containing All the Acts Passed at the 28th and 29th Sessions of the Legislature, 1801–5 and 1806* (Albany: Websters and Skinner, 1806). The act stated that the jury proceedings should mirror the proceedings spelled out in a 1787 law that provided damages to the owners of land taken for public roads.

13. Alderman Egbert Benson testified in 1852 that "[t]he Mayor [and aldermen] consulted as magistrates of the city. . . . We all had the statutes given to us when we went into office. I had informed myself a little of my duty" (*Trial Proceedings*, 96).

14. *Henry Shelton, Jacob Wilcox, & John Hiddleston, Plaintiffs in Error, vs. The Mayor, Aldermen, and Commonalty of the City of New York, Defendants in Error* (New York: Craighead and Allen, 1839), 8.

15. *Trial Proceedings*, 35.

16. Charles Bowles Fripp, "Statistics of the City of New York," *Journal of the Statistical Society of London* 2 (February 1839): 7.

17. "Court of Common Pleas: D.N. Lord and Rufus Lord vs. the Mayor and Corporation," *New York Spectator*, March 7, 1836.

18. "Court of Common Pleas," *New York Spectator*, March 7, 1836.

19. *Mayor of New York v. Lord*, 17 Wend. 285 (N.Y., 1837).

20. *Lord*, 126.

21. *Lord*, 303.

22. *Lord*, 300.

23. *Mayor of New-York v. Stone*, 20 Wend. 139 (1838).

24. The Court of Errors consisted of the justices of the New York Supreme Court, the president of the state senate, all state senators, and the state chancellor (New York Constitution, Article V, Section 1 [1821]).

25. *Mayor of New-York v. Stone*, 25 Wend. 157, 166 (1840).

26. *Russell v. Mayor of New York*, 2 Denio 461 (1845).

27. *Russell*, 473–74.

28. *Trial Proceedings*, 74–75.

29. *Hale v. Lawrence*, 1 Zab. 714 (1848).

30. *Trial Proceedings*, 7, 247.

31. *Trial Proceedings*, 159.

32. *Trial Proceedings*, 130.

33. *Penna. Coal Co. v. Mahon*, 260 U.S. 393, 415–16 (1922).

34. William J. Novak, *The People's Welfare: Law & Regulation in Nineteenth-Century America* (Chapel Hill: University of North Carolina Press, 1996), 71–79.

35. Edwin G. Burrows and Mike Wallace, *Gotham: A History of New York City to 1898* (New York: Oxford University Press, 1999), 596–601.

BRAVE MEN AND MANGLED LADIES

SPECTACLE, SENTIMENT, AND EXPLODING STEAMBOATS IN ANTEBELLUM AMERICA

CYNTHIA A. KIERNER

Unprecedented technological hazards threatened nineteenth-century Americans. The steam engines that powered innovative factory machinery and pumped water from mines often exploded, leaving workers dead or injured and their bosses largely immune from both civil and criminal action. In such cases, courts and middle-class observers alike tended to blame the workers, and, in part for that reason, there were few calls for government regulations to promote workers' safety in antebellum America. But the same technology that fueled early industries also drove steamboats that carried passengers from every class and region. Seemingly ubiquitous and horrifically deadly, steamboat explosions evoked public outcry and political action because, unlike other industrial hazards, these highly visible disasters endangered even the most privileged Americans.[1]

Between 1816 and 1848 alone, some 233 American steamboats exploded—an average of more than ten per year—leaving thousands dead, many thousands more injured, and, because steamboat operators were not required to keep complete passenger lists until 1852, thousands of other casualties unrecovered and uncounted. In all, roughly 30 percent of all steamboats built in the United States during these years were lost to explosions or other disasters, such as collisions with submerged tree trunks and other hazardous debris (known as "snags") or other vessels. As one contemporary observed, "we look as regularly, when we open a newspaper, for a steamboat disaster, as for the foreign news." Indeed, when antebellum Americans used the word "disaster," they were most likely referring to a deadly steamboat debacle.[2]

Occupying one extreme end of the continuum between so-called natural disasters and those caused wholly by human intervention, steamboat explosions raised the specter of human agency and culpability and consequently, unlike most other contemporary disasters, gave rise to protracted and highly publicized community meetings, coroners' inquests, scientific investigations, and even legislative hearings to assess blame and propose ameliorative reforms and regulations. The duration of these proceedings, along with the frequency of steamboat explosions and the often-grotesque spectacle of their human costs, meant that they were always in the news. Stoked by lurid press accounts of the mangled bodies of innocents—especially those of white women and children—public awareness and outrage eventually led to changes in public policy with the enactment of statutes, in 1838 and 1852, imposing nationwide safety standards in the steamboat industry. Although other industries remained unregulated for decades thereafter, this landmark legislation was an important first federal effort to promote public safety by overseeing the practices of private corporations.

In the decades following Robert Fulton's famous trip up the Hudson River on the *North River Steamboat* (later known as the *Clermont*) in 1807, steam revolutionized travel throughout the United States and facilitated the westward expansion of white settlement and agriculture. After their initial success in New York, Fulton and his partner, Robert R. Livingston, established a shipyard in Pittsburgh to bring waterborne steam transportation to the West. Their ship, the *New Orleans*, became the first steamboat on the western waters when it traveled the 1,100 miles from Pittsburgh to New Orleans—a journey that took as much as four months by land—in fourteen days in 1812; steamboats traveled that same route in less than a day by 1844. A demonstrably faster and less expensive way to transport both goods and people, steamboats crowded American waterways in the early nineteenth century. By 1838, there were more than seven hundred steamboats operating on the nation's rivers, lakes, and coastal waters. By 1850, there were twice that number.[3]

Steamboats fascinated Americans because of their enormous size and power. These vessels were likely the largest objects that most people ever encountered, and, though they were neither the first nor the only steam-powered mechanisms in antebellum America, they were more familiar to more people than new steam-driven machines that were increasing the speed and efficiency of processes as diverse as printing, shoemaking, and textile production. When Fulton's *Clermont* made its first trip from New York to Albany in 1807, people along the riverbanks watched in dread and amazement at its "huge black pipe vomiting fire and smoke" amidst sounds they likened to "hoarse breathing," conjuring "all the dark pictures of goblins that romancers have invented since the foundation of the world," according to one observer. Spectators panicked as the 142-foot craft noisily moved through the waters of the mighty Hudson River. While some imagined the *Clermont* as a "monster of the sea," others feared it was a "herald of the final conflagration at the day of doom."[4]

The sight of an exploding steamboat was even more terrifying. In June 1816, the *Washington* suffered the first reported steamboat explosion in North America. Shortly after its departure from Marietta, Ohio, the vessel's boiler exploded, drenching passengers in scalding water and launching them violently through the air, leaving eight dead and others injured. The explosion was a remarkable spectacle. Those ashore witnessed the "melancholy sight" and heard "the screams and groans of agonizing sufferers, rendering the scene horrible, beyond description." The deck of the *Washington* was reportedly "strewn with mangled and writhing human beings, uttering screams and groans of intense suffering." The Ohio River carried the scalded and mutilated corpse of the last of the victims fourteen miles downriver to Parkersburg, Virginia (now West Virginia), where townspeople found it three days later.[5]

Stirring descriptions of exploding steamboats and their "mangled and writhing" victims flooded the cultural landscape of early nineteenth-century America. The wreck of the ominously named *Aetna* became the first of many steamboat disasters to make national news when its boilers burst on Raritan Bay during a trip from Philadelphia to New York City in May 1824. The response to the *Aetna* explosion by both press and public set important and enduring precedents. In what became the standard format for the genre, newspaper reports described the horrors of the explosion and listed its victims, who, in this case as in so many subsequent steamboat disasters, represented a cross-section of the American population. Those who died aboard the *Aetna* included a middle-class family, a young Irish immigrant, the wife of an "amiable young gentleman," and three members of the ship's crew, two of whom were Black. Of the thirty-four people aboard the *Aetna*, six died in the explosion, two drowned, and five more died soon afterward of burns and other injuries in a New York City hospital.[6]

Accounts of the *Aetna* disaster were notably graphic. News reports, published first in New York newspapers and then reprinted or excerpted elsewhere, described the explosion as "so violent that almost everything in the cabins was demolished, the deck torn to pieces, and the vessel rendered a complete wreck." The impact was both ruinous and immediate, "spreading instant destruction among the passengers, machinery, &c." Another account noted that the "loud and awful crash" of the exploding boiler sent "hot water and steam expanding in every direction with the velocity of lightning," which "instantaneously scalded to death several of the passengers, demolished the cabins, ripped up the deck, broke the machinery in pieces, fired the vessel with the scattered brands from the furnace, rendered the whole midship a complete wreck, and filled the minds of the survivors with indescribable horror and dismay."[7]

News reports also emphasized that the *Aetna* disaster and its aftermath inflicted trauma on a wider community of people who felt sympathy for the victims and perhaps gained moral or spiritual insights from their sad and grisly fate. Observers noted that "this occurrence . . . cast gloom over the city" of New York, where burnt and dismembered bodies were brought ashore and a collective funeral for four of those who perished in the wreck attracted thousands of "sympathizing friends and spectators" who mourned the dead and pondered the fragility of human life. Clergy urged their flocks to look inward and repent lest they, too, die unprepared to meet their maker. As one minister put it, "I deem it a duty incumbent on me to assist you in learning a few important lessons from this scene of misery, which I hope may never be forgotten."[8]

Some commentators also scrutinized the conduct of the ship's captain and crew, debated the safety of high-pressure boilers—the powerful but volatile type of engine used on the *Aetna*, though at the time found mainly on western riverboats—and, in some cases, urged government intervention to prevent future tragedies. "Instead of speaking in terms of approbation of astonishing instances of despatch in stages and steamboats, especially in the races of opposition lines, which in all cases jeopardize the lives of the passengers," asked the editor of the *New York Commercial Advertiser*, "ought we not rather to censure them loudly and boldly, and point our pens steadily against every thing of the kind?" One contributor to Virginia's *Richmond Enquirer* supposed that the "universal attention" attracted by the *Aetna* disaster would end the use of high-pressure engines. "If public opinion do not effect that object," this Virginian mistakenly predicted, "we have no doubt legislation will."[9]

Public outcry was driven in large part by heartrending human stories that accompanied initial reports of the disaster and became more detailed in subsequent accounts. The earliest published account of the *Aetna* explosion almost cheerily informed readers that though four members of a single family, the Furman family of Brooklyn, had perished in the debacle, a "young lad about 13 years of age, belonging to the same family, [who] was, at the time of the explosion, sleeping on the covering of the boiler, was thrown into the air, and fell into the vacuum caused by the removal of the machinery, and received no injury!" Readers learned later that this unfortunate family was returning from a funeral in New Jersey for a young female relative whose infant child had also died during their visit "and was placed by the cold bosom of its mother, in the same coffin, and deposited in the same grave." Another account added that, after the wreck of the *Aetna*, Job Furman waited hopefully for the safe recovery of his wife, daughter, niece, and sister, only to have them arrive "not in health and activity, but fast bound in the fetters of death . . . their mangled persons exhibit[ing] a spectacle too appalling to recite!"[10]

In the years after the *Aetna* disaster, newspaper accounts of steamboat disasters became, if anything, more graphic and more detailed for at least two reasons. On the one hand, the burgeoning popularity of steamboat travel made such stories both newsworthy and relatable to many Americans. On the other hand, the steamboat's heyday coincided with a dramatic expansion of American print culture, which brought newspapers to every corner of a rapidly expanding nation. By one count, there were 2,270 newspapers in the United States in 1840, compared with 746 in 1820 (and only 71 in 1776). In larger population centers especially, many of these newspapers were dailies that attracted readers with human-interest stories that included explicit accounts of suffering and scandal. These were publications whose profits depended, in the candid words of one New York editor, "on the calamities of others."[11]

In reporting steamboat explosions, the nineteenth-century press perfected the genre of affecting personal narratives that even today circulate in the aftermath of disasters. Such stories typically reflected and reinforced readers' assumptions and biases—for instance, mostly portraying white men as heroic and women and children as passive victims—and therein lay their power. Lurid and tearful stories of the sad fates of so many respectable and otherwise ordinary people fueled readers' growing sense of the potential dangers that awaited them in such an exciting but challengingly changing world in which travel was becoming a commodity produced and marketed by remote capitalist entrepreneurs and corporations whose fierce competition and desire to garner public attention and maximize profits led them to build ever-bigger ships, overload their vessels, travel at excessive speeds and under unsafe conditions, and hire inexperienced engineers—all of which made American steamboats uniquely dangerous, with far more explosions and fatalities than their European counterparts. American steamboats were extremely profitable for owners and operators, despite the fact that they averaged only a few years of service because of their cheap, flimsy construction and lack of safety features, such as water and steam pressure gauges. Although some contemporaries lauded the safety of steamboat travel compared with other modes of conveyance, anyone who read the newspapers knew that explosions were common and had spectacularly fatal consequences.[12]

In the decades following the *Aetna* explosion, graphic accounts of steamboat disasters appeared in periodicals of every sort, as well as in lithographs and commercial entertainments, such as museum exhibits and theatrical presentations. Significantly, more than one-fourth of the two hundred lithographs of steamboats that the popular printmaker Nathaniel Currier published (first on his own and later in partnership with James Merritt Ives) depicted explosions or collisions. The popularity of steamboat disaster narratives and their visual representations were artifacts of what one historian has called the "pornography of violence" that complemented (and stimulated) the burgeoning humanitarian sensibilities of the antebellum era. Even words alone could convey such "dreadful pleasure," as was the case with a widely reprinted account of the explosion of the steamboat *Louisiana* in New Orleans in 1849. "The sight of the mangled bodies on every side, the groans of the dying, and the shrieks of the agonized sufferers, produced a general thrill of horror among the multitude," one eyewitness reported. "The body of a man was seen, with the head and one leg off, and the entrails torn out. A woman, whose long hair lay wet and matted by her side, had one leg off, and her body was shockingly mangled. A large man, having his skull mashed in, lay dead on the levee; his face looked as though it had been painted red, having been completely flayed by the scalding water. Others of both sexes, crushed, scalded, burned, mutilated and dismembered, lay about in every direction. Two bodies were found locked together, brought by death into a sudden and close embrace."[13]

Stories of exploding steamboats and their gruesome aftermaths were particularly shocking to prosperous white Americans, who typically experienced death with dignity and in private. While soldiers might die in battle and some unfortunates were murdered on city streets or mutilated by factory machinery, middle-class Americans—especially women and children—mostly died quietly at home, surrounded by family and friends. Having accepted their fate and prepared their souls, they experienced what contemporaries called a Good Death, expiring peacefully with loved ones then performing the intimate task of preparing the body for burial. Their mortal remains rested at home for several days before the casket was sealed and piously interred. The deaths of victims of steamboat explosions, by contrast, were sudden and brutal, leaving dismembered and sometimes naked bodies exposed to voyeuristic public view.[14]

As steamboat explosions became common and their death tolls mounted, personal stories of suffering and loss increasingly dominated newspaper coverage. When some 150 passengers died in the *Moselle* explosion near Cincinnati in 1838, newspaper reports predictably described the disaster and its aftermath as a spectacle experienced by people on shore—and vicariously by readers—as a ghastly cascade of "heads, limbs, and bodies . . . flying through the air in every direction, attended by the most horrible shrieks and groans from the wounded and the dying" with "twenty or thirty mangled and still bleeding corpses" scattered along the shore. But they also told tales of innocents who met their violent demise because an ambitious young captain's "most silly and culpable vanity" led him into a dangerous race with another boat. "Death," the press reported, "had torn asunder the most tender ties. . . . One man had saved a son, but lost a wife and five children. A father, partially demented by grief, lay with a wounded child on one side, his dead daughter on the other, and his expiring wife at his feet. . . . A little boy, about five years old whose head was much bruised, . . . cried continually for a lost father, while another lad a little older was weeping for his whole family. One venerable looking man wept for the loss of a wife and five children. Another was bereft of his whole family, consisting of nine persons."[15]

Such family dramas resonated among antebellum readers who sentimentalized domestic life and imagined home as a refuge from the harshly masculine world of commerce and politics, a construction of gender powerfully reflected in many narratives that featured real or imagined tableaux of strong and resourceful men saving women's and children's lives. Sometimes these accounts highlighted the heroics of ships' captains or of male passengers working together to save women and children by helping them to escape a burning vessel. Others told inspiring stories of individual men who rescued female family members or even total strangers. One of the more remarkable cases was that of young Robert Bullock, who reportedly went from cabin to cabin saving women and children aboard the burning *Shepherdess*, gave his coat to one freezing woman, and, after swimming ashore, brought two "young ladies" to a nearby town, where they "met with the attention which their half frozen condition required."[16]

Newspaper coverage of steamboat explosions tacitly acknowledged readers' interest in—and sensitivity to—the frequent and violent deaths of women and children. One key component of news reports was the roster of the dead, which listed most casualties by name, though sometimes women and children were identified only as wives or offspring of a named man. Some reports, however, supplemented these lists by specifically quantifying the deaths of women and children. Accounts of the explosion of the *Ben Sherrod* on the Mississippi River in 1837, which killed some two hundred people, informed readers that only two of nine or ten "ladies" aboard the ship survived the disaster and that "six dead bodies, those of two women and four children," were found near the burning vessel. When the *Erie* exploded on Lake Erie the following year, newspapers reported that "wives, mothers, helpless infants [were] all sunk . . . into the deep tomb of water." Only one female passenger, Mrs. Lynde, was saved.[17]

Such reports could be read either as acknowledgments of male chivalry and strength or, conversely, as subtle recognition of the limitations of those celebrated qualities. In the case of Mrs. Lynde, though her husband tried to save her and brought her the life preserver that ultimately allowed her to escape unscathed, newspapers reported that this "lady of superior intellect . . . conducted herself throughout the whole trying scene with exemplary fortitude," while Mr. Lynde "was much excited," despite his wife's urging him "to be more calm and self-possessed." The agitated Mr. Lynde failed to secure his life preserver properly and drowned as a result. The Lyndes' story must have left readers pondering whether he rescued his wife or whether she saved herself.[18]

The continuing appeal of these stories, which invited readers to be vicarious spectators at scenes of destruction and death, spurred the publication of anthologies that repurposed and sometimes expanded the original newspaper stories as sources of entertainment and moral instruction. Southworth Allen Howland's *Steamboat Disasters and Railroad Accidents in the United States*—which, despite its title, focused overwhelmingly on steamboat explosions and other shipwrecks—was a 408-page compilation that went through three editions in six years in the 1840s. Howland explained that the purpose of his book was not only to catalog "the many disasters that have occurred on our waters since the introduction of steam navigation, and, as far as practicable, [explain] the principal causes that led to such disasters," but also "to perpetuate the memory of those who have been the innocent sufferers thereby." Unlike most authors of earlier shipwreck stories, however, Howland did not view these "sufferers" as sinners justly punished by an angry God. Though he sought to inspire moral improvement in his readers, Howland also promoted a broader reform agenda aimed at reversing the fatal effects of capitalist malfeasance. "Although the laws of the land, with strange apathy, refuse to award the condign punishment such aggravated cases demand," he wrote, "yet the stern voice of an indignant public should denounce the reckless indifference, the gross carelessness, and the criminal neglect, through which so many of their fellow-beings are suddenly swept into eternity."[19]

This image appeared in Southworth Allen Howland's *Steamboat Disasters and Railroad Accidents in the United States,* as well as in a contemporary children's book called *Disasters by Steam, Fire, and Water: With Elegant Engravings.* The human drama of steamboat explosions appealed to readers of all ages in the antebellum era. Here survivors cling to floating furniture from a wrecked steamboat. An active man shields a passive woman as he waves in hopes of attracting potential rescuers. Courtesy of the American Antiquarian Society.

Steamboat disasters were so appallingly fascinating, and calls for government oversight so persistent, in part because of growing recognition that, in this new modern industrializing era, individual men could not always fulfill their socially prescribed protective role. Under the common-law doctrine of coverture, a wife's legal rights and obligations were subsumed by those of her husband; by law and custom, fathers also wielded near-absolute authority over their children. Because these patriarchal powers derived in part from the belief that women and children were inherently inferior and weak, they were also at least theoretically tied to men's corresponding responsibility to protect and provide for their domestic dependents. Steamboat architecture and etiquette gave physical expression to these legal strictures by enclosing respectable women in interior spaces to shield them from less refined passengers on deck, though these so-called "ladies' cabins" sometimes proved more deadly than protective in times of crisis. When the *New England* exploded on the Connecticut River in 1833, the ladies' cabin felt "the most destructive effects" of the blast. Eleven years later, aboard the *Lucy Walker,* the ladies' cabin "took fire and burned with great rapidity" immediately after the ship exploded. Cumbersome clothing and other cultural conventions—such as the belief that "ladies" should be frail and dependent—along with confinement in the interior ladies' cabin, contributed to the high numbers of female steamboat fatalities.[20]

The HMS *Birkenhead* (1854) and the more famous RMS *Titanic* (1912) are the only two known cases in which women numbered disproportionately among the survivors of a shipwreck, and circumstantial evidence overall suggests that women, who were the minority of travelers, were far more likely than men to die in steamboat disasters. The fact that both the *Birkenhead* and the *Titanic* were so amply and strenuously commemorated—in images, poetry, monuments, and even (in the case of the *Titanic*) movies—suggests that they were unusual and worth celebrating precisely because they validated gender conventions that vaunted white male strength, valor, and overall superiority. The case of the *Aetna,* for which a complete list of passengers and crew members is extant, was likely more typical. There were thirty-four people aboard the *Aetna* when it exploded in 1824, nine females (at least one of whom was a child) and twenty-five males. Thirteen people died. Eight of those thirteen were females, including a ten-year-old girl. Nineteen men and one thirteen-year-old boy, but only one woman, survived the disaster.[21]

More certain is the fact that those who reported (and read) stories about exploding steamboats fixated on the horrific and very public deaths of women passengers, as coverage of the *Lexington,* which exploded on the Long Island Sound in 1840, amply shows. All but one of the *Lexington*'s passengers died as a result of the disaster; because there were very few women aboard this ship, of the 140 known fatalities, all but 6 were men. Yet stories about the *Lexington* focused disproportionately on the suffering of women (especially mothers) and children: the little child "floating on the water" whose mother "cared only for her child when her own death was certain"; a mother pressing her child "to her breast amid the horrors" and using her veil to shield "the features of her boy from the advancing flames"; the doomed child "with his little hands clasped to his ears, as if to shut out the horrid noises that assailed him and filled his soul with terror"; the "deservedly beloved" eighteen-year-old Sophia

Wheeler, who tragically delayed her trip home to be married so that she might travel aboard the *Lexington* with her betrothed; the "body of a young lady . . . [in] a white flannel petticoat, fine muslin night gown and night cap, prunella shoes and black hose," which washed ashore in New Jersey six weeks later.[22]

These stories of suffering women and children and male heroics had well-heeled white protagonists, though fatalities among working-class deck passengers and crew members were, if anything, typically higher. Ships' crews got little sympathy in part because they included large numbers of immigrants and free and enslaved African Americans, a circumstance that likely made it easier for steamboat corporations—and the white middle-class general public—to attribute boiler explosions and other deadly equipment malfunctions primarily to the ignorance or negligence of the workers who oversaw them, just as they typically blamed workers for factory and mining fatalities. Moreover, on steamboats, as in the expanding antebellum economy more generally, women (and children) who toiled in dangerous, poorly paid jobs and routinely experienced workplace hazards were, in the eyes of many, unsexed by virtue of their employment as wage laborers. As a result, the same reports of the *Aetna* explosion that sentimentally recounted the loss of the Furman women only mentioned in passing that an African American ship's cook named Ann Thomas had also died. Similarly, when the chambermaid Mary Anderson was among the victims of the *Lioness* explosion in 1833, at least one account of that disaster nevertheless happily declared that "all of the women were saved."[23]

Even when they were passengers, people of color were not featured in the preferred narrative either as victims or heroes of steamboat disasters. Steamboats were employed in the removal of some eighteen thousand Creek Indians from Georgia and Alabama in the 1830s. When the *Monmouth* exploded after colliding with another boat on the Mississippi River in 1837, some four hundred Indians died, the highest death toll to date as a result of a single steamboat disaster. Yet, as some sympathetic observers noted, this tragedy "attracted but little attention, (comparatively speaking,) in any part of the country," and even when "journalists and news-collectors" reported the incident, they included "scarcely a word of commiseration for the sufferers." African Americans, who sometimes appeared (with their race specified) on published casualty lists, were also missing from most steamboat stories, even if their actions were truly praiseworthy. When the SS *Arctic* collided with a French steamer off

A. Pharazin, *Terrible Conflagration and Destruction of the Steam-Boat "New-Jersey."* This steamboat explosion on the Delaware River took the lives of sixty-one people in 1856. Of thirteen women known to have been aboard the ship, only three survived; forty-one of seventy-three known male passengers were saved. The first two columns of the print's caption list "The Dead" and "The Missing," with the names of "Colored" passengers enumerated separately at the bottom. Although the image shows an African American man swimming toward shore, no Black passengers were among "The Saved." Library of Congress, Prints & Photographs Division.

the coast of Newfoundland in 1854, Mrs. Anna Downer, a free Black passenger from Connecticut, labored "alone, working at the pumps" to expel water from the sinking vessel. Downer died aboard the *Arctic*, and though the ship's captain lauded her heroic efforts, the white press ignored her story. Noting the possible creation of a monument to honor a white man who had also acted bravely aboard the *Arctic*, a contributor to *Frederick Douglass's Paper* observed, "Mrs. Downer, beautiful and prepossessing, was brave; but she was a *woman*, and a *colored* woman. Who would think of erecting a monument to her?"[24]

The common admonition to save "women and children first," which originated during this period, is best understood as referring to white "ladies" and their offspring and, more importantly, as an ideal that defensively sustained a belief in the efficacy of male protection that had often little basis in reality.[25] While in some cases well-intentioned men were simply unable to shield women and children from raging flames and tempestuous waters, in others they clearly shirked these culturally prescribed responsibilities.

Among the era's many steamboat disasters, the explosion of the *Arctic* resonated more than most because, though eighty-six people survived, all of the women and children died in the explosion and its aftermath. The contrast with the 1852 wreck of the British steamboat *Birkenhead*—in which 458 men died, but all the women and children were saved—was especially chilling. One widely circulating report praised the "heroic band" of British men aboard the *Birkenhead*, who stoically accepted death, while condemning the "unmanly spectacle" of the American *Arctic*'s "robust cowards . . . treacherously deserting feeble and delicate women, and shutting their ears to cries from little children" as they fled the scene in the ship's lifeboats. According to one popular ballad:

> There were infants and fair maidens left shivering on the deck,
> And mothers with their cherished ones close clinging to the wreck;
> The aged, too, and sick were there—oh, tell us how it be,
> That all these helpless creatures were swallowed by the sea?
>
> And did you not stand by them—reached forth no hand to save,
> Those dear ones of the country from such a cruel grave?
> No! were all left to perish? and—ha, ye gallant few!
> The meanest other thing alive I'd be, than such as you![26]

Two years earlier, in 1852, public outrage had played a pivotal role in enacting a more effective steamboat safety law, which likely made the *Arctic* story even more shocking. Citizens and scientists had advocated such legislation for decades. Nationwide anger in the immediate aftermath of two particularly deadly explosions in 1838—the *Moselle* near Cincinnati and the *Pulaski* off the coast of North Carolina—helped persuade Congress to pass "An Act to provide for the better security of passengers on board vessels propelled in whole or in part by steam" in July of that year. A precedent-setting effort to prevent disasters by imposing safety regulations on private industry, the law was nonetheless weakened by loopholes and omissions—so much so that the number of people who died in steamboat disasters actually increased after its passage. By 1851, steamboat-related deaths in the United States were averaging more than two hundred per year, compared with roughly eighty deaths per year during the 1840s.[27]

When the *Henry Clay* exploded in July 1852, it was the year's twentieth steamboat disaster, raising the cumulative death toll to at least 428, more than twice the annual average. Newspaper accounts of these 1852 disasters observed what had become the standard narrative conventions for coverage of such events. Reports of the *Glencoe*, which exploded in St. Louis in April, for instance, lingered over the spectacle of "dreadfully mangled" bodies with "limbs in some cases being torn from the trunk" and "heads . . . mashed and disfigured," as well as more specific tableaux of "the body of a woman . . . stretched across a marble slab . . . every bone . . . broken" and "the body of a little girl, with the legs torn off," later fished out of the Mississippi River. Accounts of the *Henry Clay* revealed that forty-one women and fifteen children were known to have died, while only fourteen men were lost; sixty-one men were known to have survived the disaster, while the numbers of women and children among the survivors were twenty-four and ten, respectively.[28]

The death tolls of other recent steamboat explosions, a prime New York location, and some particularly compelling details altogether guaranteed the impact of the *Henry Clay* disaster, as coverage in the recently established *New York Times* shows. The *Times* reported that the ship's captain was racing with another ship, the *Armenia*, and that his recklessness terrified passengers even before the boiler's explosion engulfed the ship and its four to five hundred passengers in fiery chaos and people scrambled to escape the vessel, which had no usable lifeboats. No one knew for sure how many passengers were aboard the ship, but the *Times* reporter was "quite certain" that many bodies remained missing more than a week after the explosion. Equally certain was the fact that women and children numbered disproportionately among the casualties, and that many lives were lost due to a lack of lifeboats and life preservers. The dead included some well-known people, including a granddaughter of former president John Adams, Nathaniel Hawthorne's sister, a former mayor of New York, and the landscape architect Andrew Jackson Downing. Public committees angrily denounced the owners and operators of the *Henry Clay* and insisted that only the "indignant voice of the public" could ensure punishment for their "criminal recklessness." After a meticulously reported inquest, the coroner's jury quickly indicted those men for manslaughter, but they were all found not guilty in the US District Court, a verdict that helped steamboat owners and operators to recoup their losses via insurance while rendering it virtually impossible for victims' families to get restitution in civil court.[29]

In response to the wreck of the *Henry Clay*, public demands for new safety regulations included an unprecedented public petitioning effort, which focused on the need to enact more effective legislation to prevent future disasters and deaths by making steamboat travel safer. Support also came from leading insurance companies weary of compensating steamboat operators for their losses in the aftermath of disasters. Petitioners from New York City—more than 1,500 signers in all—expressly called on members of Congress to read "the published accounts" of the *Henry Clay* and other "fearful and appalling disasters" that had resulted in such a "dreadful waste of human life."[30]

The petitioners' efforts were ultimately successful in part because vivid accounts of steamboat disasters inspired public conversations about passengers' vulnerability and government's role in preventing disasters and protecting citizens' lives. The "dismal history" of seemingly endless steamboat explosions, averred one Boston clergyman, meant that anyone—indeed, everyone—should expect to lose loved ones in such a calamity.[31] Gender was at the center of that very "dismal history," with its graphic descriptions of mangled bodies of suffering ladies and their children and the men who tried, often unsuccessfully, to preserve their fragile lives.

Often overlooked by historians of disasters, exploding steamboats were the most consequential calamities of the antebellum era. By comparison, hurricanes and earthquakes received surprisingly scant newspaper coverage and had minimal presence in popular culture and negligible impact on public policy. Most Americans could perhaps imagine that they would be safe from these other sorts of disasters. They could dismiss deadly fires as urban problems and take comfort in knowing that earthquakes, tornadoes, and even hurricanes were relatively uncommon, at least in most places. Moreover, even as scientists learned more about the causes and consequences of hurricanes, earthquakes, and the like, these natural phenomena seemed comparatively impervious to human intervention or governance. By contrast, steamboats, which traversed every American waterway and were increasingly essential for the transportation of both goods and people, were created and controlled by human actors. For all these reasons, steamboat explosions captured Americans' attention and imagination and, powered by the larger cultural assumptions and biases of the times, resulted in early and important disaster prevention efforts.

NOTES

1. Morton J. Horwitz, *The Transformation of American Law, 1780–1860* (Cambridge, MA: Harvard University Press, 1977), 85–99, 203–4; Mark Aldrich, *Safety First: Technology, Labor, and Business in the Building of American Work Safety, 1870–1939* (Baltimore: Johns Hopkins University Press, 1997), 4–5, 79; Anthony F. C. Wallace, *St. Clair: A Nineteenth-Century Coal Town's Experience with a Disaster-Prone Industry* (New York: Knopf, 1987), 252–55, 265–66, 270–71; Jamie L. Bronstein, *Caught in the Machinery: Workplace Accidents and Injured Workers in Nineteenth-Century Britain* (Stanford, CA: Stanford University Press, 2008), 60–61, 68, 95–96.

2. Louis C. Hunter and Beatrice Jones Hunter, *Steamboats on the Western Rivers: An Economic and Technological History* (1949; New York: Octagon, 1969), 272–85; John G. Burke, "Bursting Boilers and the Federal Power," *Technology & Culture* 7 (1966): 1–23; R. John Brockmann, *Exploding Steamboats, Senate Debates, and Technical Reports* (Amityville, NY: Baywood, 2002); Paul F. Paskoff, *Troubled Waters: Steamboat Disasters, River Improvements, and American Public Policy, 1821–1860* (Baton Rouge: Louisiana State University Press, 2007), 28–36; "Steamboat Disasters," *North American Review* 50 (January 1840): 20; Cynthia A. Kierner, *Inventing Disaster: The Culture of Calamity from the Jamestown Colony to the Johnstown Flood* (Chapel Hill: University of North Carolina Press, 2019), 169–70.

3. Cynthia Owen Philip, *Robert Fulton: A Biography* (New York: Franklin Watts, 1988), 198–205, 270–81; James T. Lloyd, *Lloyd's Steamboat Directory, and Disasters on the Western Waters* (Cincinnati: James T. Lloyd, 1856), 17–41; Walter Johnson, *River of Dark Dreams: Slavery and Empire in the Cotton Kingdom* (Cambridge, MA: Harvard University Press, 2013), 6, 79; John Kennedy Brown, *Limbs on the Levee: Steamboat Explosions and the Origins of Federal Public Welfare Regulation* (Middlebourne, WV: International Steamboat Society, 1988), 10–11.

4. Benson John Lossing, quoted in George Rogers Howell and Jonathan Tenney, *Bi-centennial History of Albany [. . .] from 1609 to 1886* (New York: W. W. Munsell, 1886), 312.

5. William J. Showalter, "First Steamboat Explosion in the West," *Tallow Light* 47, no. 2 (2016): 41–43; *Washington (KY) Union*, June 21, 1816; Lloyd, *Lloyd's Steamboat Directory*, 55–57.

6. *New York Commercial Advertiser,* May 17, 1824.

7. *New York Commercial Advertiser,* May 17, 1824; *Albany (NY) Argus,* May 21, 1824.

8. *New York Commercial Advertiser,* May 17, 1824; *Trenton (NJ) Federalist,* May 24, 1824; *Ballston Spa (NY) Gazette,* May 25, 1824; John Stanford, *A Discourse, Delivered in the New-York City Hospital [. . .]* (New York: E. Conrad, 1824).

9. *New York Commercial Advertiser,* May 17, 1824; *Richmond (VA) Enquirer,* May 24, 1824.

10. *New York Commercial Advertiser,* May 17, 1824; *Baltimore Patriot,* May 18, 1824; *Ballston Spa (NY) Gazette,* May 25, 1824; *Trenton (NJ) Federalist,* May 24, 1824.

11. Isabelle Lehuu, *Carnival on the Page: Popular Print Media in Antebellum America* (Chapel Hill: University of North Carolina Press, 2000), 37–58. For a visualization, based on data from the *Chronicling America* project at the Library of Congress, see "The Growth of U.S. Newspapers, 1690–2011," https://www.youtube.com/watch?v=28TG2QJYSGc.

12. Will Mackintosh, "'Ticketed Through': The Commodification of Travel in the Nineteenth Century," *Journal of the Early Republic* 32 (2012): 61–89; Calvin R. Fremling, *Immortal River: The Upper Mississippi in Ancient and Modern Times* (Madison: University of Wisconsin Press, 2005), 168–73, 178; Martin Doyle, *The Source: How Rivers Made America and America Remade Its Rivers* (New York: Norton, 2018), 48–50. For assertions of the relative safety of American steamboats, see, for instance, *Memorial of the Sundry Proprietors and Managers of American Steam Vessels* (New York, 1840), 1, 47; *Report of the Secretary of the Treasury, of the Statistics and History of the Steam Marine of the United States [. . .]* 1852, *Proquest Congressional;* and Lloyd, *Lloyd's Steamboat Directory,* 57.

13. Karen Halttunen, *Murder Most Foul: The Killer and the American Gothic Imagination* (Cambridge, MA: Harvard University Press, 1988), chap. 3; *New Orleans Picayune,* November 16, 1849; *Richmond (VA) Enquirer,* November 27, 1849, *Wisconsin Democrat* (Madison), December 1, 1849.

14. Drew Gilpin Faust, *This Republic of Suffering: Death and the American Civil War* (New York: Knopf, 2008), 6–8; Gary Laderman, *The Sacred Remains: American Attitudes toward Death, 1799–1883* (New Haven, CT: Yale University Press, 1996), chap. 2.

15. *Cincinnati (OH) Whig,* April 25, 1838. See also *Richmond (VA) Enquirer,* May 1, 1838; *Salem (MA) Gazette,* May 4, 1838; *Newport (RI) Mercury,* May 5, 1838; S. A. Howland, *Steamboat Disasters and Railroad Accidents in the United States* (Worcester, MA: Dorr, Howland, 1846), 76–84; Lloyd, *Lloyd's Steamboat Directory,* 89–93.

16. Lloyd, *Lloyd's Steamboat Directory,* 139.

17. Lloyd, *Lloyd's Steamboat Directory,* 98–99, 124–25; Howland, *Steamboat Disasters,* 97–102.

18. Lloyd, *Lloyd's Steamboat Directory,* 124–25.

19. Howland, *Steamboat Disasters,* v–vi, 46–47; Kierner, *Inventing Disaster,* 41–50.

20. Lloyd, *Lloyd's Steamboat Directory,* 119, 143.

21. Mikael Elinder and Oscar Erixson, "Gender, Social Norms, and Survival in Maritime Disasters," *PNAS* 109 (August 2012): 13220–42; A. C. Addison, *A Deathless Story, or, The "Birkenhead" and Its Heroes* (London: Hutchinson, 1906); Steven Biel, *Down with the Old Canoe: A Cultural History of the Titanic Disaster* (1996; New York: Norton, 2012); Howland, *Steamboat Disasters,* 166–67.

22. *New York Herald*, January 23, 1840; *Pennsylvania Inquirer* (Philadelphia), January 21 and 24, 1840; *Baltimore Sun*, January 23, 1840; *New York Commercial Advertiser*, February 24, 1840; [C. Weild], *A Warning Voice from a Watery Grave!* (New York: Sacket and Sargent, 1840), 6–7; Howland, *Steamboat Disasters*, 177, 180–81, 207.

23. Lloyd, *Lloyd's Steamboat Directory*, 85; Thomas C. Buchanan, *Black Life on the Mississippi: Slaves, Free Blacks, and the Western Steamboat World* (Chapel Hill: University of North Carolina Press, 2004), 10–12. See also Jeremy Zallen, *American Lucifers: The Dark History of Artificial Light, 1750–1985* (Chapel Hill: University of North Carolina Press, 2019), 57–60, 91–92, 200–209; and Bronstein, *Caught in the Machinery*, 14–15, 68–73, 106–14.

24. Lloyd, *Lloyd's Steamboat Directory*, 127; Howland, *Steamboat Disasters*, 97–98; *Frederick Douglass's Paper*, November 3, 1854.

25. B. R. Burg, "'Women and Children First': Popular Mythology and Disaster at Sea, 1840–1860," *Journal of American Culture* 20 (1997): 8; Robin Miskolcze, *Women and Children First: Nineteenth-Century Sea Narratives and American Identity* (Lincoln: University of Nebraska Press, 2012), xvi.

26. "Loss of the Arctic," 1854, American Song Sheets, Library of Congress Rare Books and Special Collections, https://www.loc.gov/item/amss.as108060/. News reports include *Newburyport (MA) Morning Herald*, October 13, 1854; *Jersey City (NJ) Daily Telegraph*, October 17, 1854; *Daily National Intelligencer* (Washington, DC), October 18, 1854; and *Georgia Weekly Telegraph* (Macon), November 7, 1854. For a detailed account, see Alexander Crosby Brown, *Women and Children Last: The Loss of the Steamship* Arctic (New York: Putnam's Sons, 1961).

27. Burke, "Bursting Boilers and the Federal Power," 8–19; Brockmann, *Exploding Steamboats*, 124–26; Lloyd, *Lloyd's Steamboat Directory*, 228, 252, 294, 296–97. Lloyd counted 186 deaths in the West alone in 1851.

28. "Steamboat Accidents in the United States in 1852," *The Friend*, 25 (August 1852): 391; Lloyd, *Lloyd's Steamboat Directory*, 288; Kris A. Hansen, *Death Passage on the Hudson: The Wreck of the Henry Clay* (Fleischmanns, NY: Purple Mountain, 2004), 165–67.

29. *New York Times*, July 29 and 30, 1852; *New York Herald*, August 2, 1852. For a full account, see Hansen, *Death Passage on the Hudson*.

30. Petition of citizens of New York, August 2–13, 1852 [85 copies], House Committee on Commerce, 32nd Cong., HR 2A-G4.10, National Archives, Washington, DC.

31. William M. Rogers, *A Sermon, Occasioned by the Loss of the Harold and the Lexington* (Boston: Perkins and Marvin, 1840), 8–9.

SPRING FLOODS AND SETTLER COLONIAL AMBIVALENCE

A MICROHISTORY OF FRESHETS ON WRIGHT'S ISLAND IN THE MID-NINETEENTH CENTURY

TOM WICKMAN

Joseph Wright (1785–1864), a Yale-educated, fifth-generation farmer on a frequently flooded island in the Connecticut River, kept a detailed, year-round diary from 1837 to 1863.[1] While Wright owned a brick house on firm ground away from the river, on Main Street in Glastonbury, Connecticut, he spent many nights from late spring to fall in a farmhouse on Wright's Island, an island named for his seventeenth-century ancestors. Located within Wangunk territory, the island's name in Algonquian was Mannhannock.[2] Wright devoted several pages of the journal in most years to anticipation about the spring freshet (or flood), daily and hourly accounts of changing river conditions, detailed spatial descriptions of the water as it affected his island buildings and lands, regular comparisons of the latest flood to previous ones, and narratives of his family members' and hired laborers' daily and nightly responses to water that inundated the island.[3] The journal provides an extraordinarily detailed nineteenth-century engagement with the lived agroecology of flooding on the Connecticut River, one that evokes the experiences that previous generations must have experienced working regularly flooded land. Wright kept the diary to track natural patterns, to chart the rhythms of labor, to record revenue, and to reflect on divine providence. Continuity in the face of flux and uncertainty was his main priority. The recognition of subtle patterns in the floodplain landscape was crucial to his notion of improvement or mastery, but he worried that increasingly disastrous floods would ruin Wright's Island.

Wright's ambivalent diary entries about the freshet reveal something important about the persistence of settler colonialism in nineteenth-century New England. On the one hand, Wright viewed the floods as replenishing his farmland, and their regularity suggested intergenerational links stretching backward to his ancestors and forward to his descendants. Rather than seeing the American Revolution or the Industrial Revolution as exceptional events causing radical breaks in history, Wright saw continuities between his forebears' agrarian lives and his own. Certainly, he did not question the colonial displacement of Indigenous people that initially had given the Wrights access to the island. Indeed, in 1844 he included transcriptions of seventeenth- and eighteenth-century deeds, connecting himself by chain of title to the early colonists, and in 1851 he described approvingly Glastonbury's bicentennial celebrations.[4]

On the other hand, Wright worried that family control of the farm would not last forever, doubting the potential sustainability of settler colonialism, at least at that singular and personally meaningful place. He feared the destruction to agricultural infrastructure that could result from powerful floods, and he tracked the way that the river was eroding the island itself and how its unstable power disrupted individual property rights. Although Wright never put into writing explicit doubts about the settler colonial project that created those property lines in the first place, and though he did not mention the Wangunk or other Indigenous peoples of Connecticut, one clear function of his diary was to express his own claims to the land and to exorcise fears that his family's settler privileges would not last. Like the authors of contemporary local histories, Wright used the diary to imaginatively shore up his settler status.[5]

This essay's microhistorical study of Wright's material and discursive responses to flooding suggests that many nineteenth-century Americans experienced disasters as crises for the structures and processes of settler colonialism that had been established over several generations and that continued to privilege them. Rebuilding from recurrent disasters was an extension and repetition of settler colonial processes, whether at the small scale of Wright's farm or at the larger scales of a city, state, or nation. In some ways, Wright represented his family's possession and cultivation of land on the island within natural cycles that seemed almost ahistorical and apolitical, but in other ways Wright's diary evoked the material and intellectual fragility of settler colonialism, its historicity, and its need for continual reinforcement, rebuilding, and reinscription.[6]

Spring flooding was an ordinary occurrence on the Connecticut River, essential to the fertility of the land, but the highest and longest floods brought devastation.[7] At Wright's Island, if not managed carefully, the freshet season threatened human life, and floodwaters could disrupt farming for a time. For Wright, accepting some flood-related damage was part of the coping skills that allowed him to make a livelihood in the floodplain. Yet he was always haunted by "fears of a great freshet" that would take too great a toll. Freshets brought a mix of hazards and benefits, and Wright worked around the risks as best he could. That is, Wright lived with floods rather than battling or seeking to prevent them. Elsewhere along the lower Connecticut River, disastrous floods damaged houses, carried away bridges, dislocated residents, and took human lives, especially at recently reclaimed and developed riverside lands. Wright's grounded perspective on the precarity and promise of cultivating a floodplain just downriver from the city of Hartford presents a counterpoint to the urban views of river engineering that gained prominence and altered the river's flow at midcentury.[8]

Scholars of disaster studies have focused on large-scale catastrophes, disaster relief, vulnerability, inequality, and resilience, and new scholarship has called for studies of recurrent, small-scale but often cumulative disasters. Wright's journal reveals how one individual navigated uncertainty about the effects of each year's freshets and the cumulative consequences of many freshets over time. In the diary, Wright processed the long-term plight of his island house and of the island itself as a protracted, slow disaster, while also narrating sudden, fast-moving catastrophes such as the flood of 1854.[9]

On the island, Wright cultivated wheat, corn, rye, and potatoes; kept beef cattle and pigs; and managed grasses in his meadows. He sold corn (which he often referred to as "Indian corn"), broom corn, wheat flour, buckwheat, rye, potatoes, pork, beef, and hay, usually in Hartford, although he sold potatoes as far south as New York and Baltimore. He caught shad fish in nets as the floods subsided, which he sold in Hartford. Wright's economic worldview was consistent with the traditional ideal of a "competency," or comfortable independence that he could share with members of his hierarchical, patriarchal household and pass on to a subsequent generation. In his year-end assessments, Wright described first the quality and quantity of each harvest, crop by crop, and often noted the conditions that influenced these outcomes. He usually then gave the prevailing prices for each commodity. The fullest entries then multiplied quantities and prices, adding the results up to a single sum. His year-end meditation focused therefore on the land's productivity and on total revenue. He less frequently mentioned the costs of labor or commented on profits. The rhetorical separation of agroecology from prices allowed Wright to focus first on the farm's productivity, viewed providentially as the interaction of planning, labor, weather, the life cycles of plants, and God's grace, followed secondarily by the vagaries of economic markets. Notably, he used the terms "calamity," "failure," and "disastrous" on the one hand and the "productive," "abundant," and "prosperous" on the other to describe agroecological outcomes. The possible future loss of his island lands to the river troubled him not just in immediate financial terms, but because he viewed the island's house and farmland as part of his stewardship from past generations. In this sense, the freshets factored into his hopes, dreams, anxieties, and fears about settler sustainability and loss.[10]

Because the freshets, for all their troubles, had made his family lands productive for generations, Wright may have put his observations about floods on paper as instructive lessons to any descendants who would continue to work the land. Wright's immediate purpose in the journal was to track the nuances of all floods, so he could better live with, work around, and take advantage of the floodwaters. He registered his thoughts about floods annually, seasonally, monthly, weekly, nightly, daily, and even hourly. Wright's Island was located within what is now called the Connecticut River's Glastonbury reach, where the river had meandered back and forth within the floodplain for thousands of years.[11] Over the previous two centuries, successive human alterations of the Connecticut River watershed over its four-hundred-mile course, due to fur trapping, deforestation, damming, and river channelization, contributed

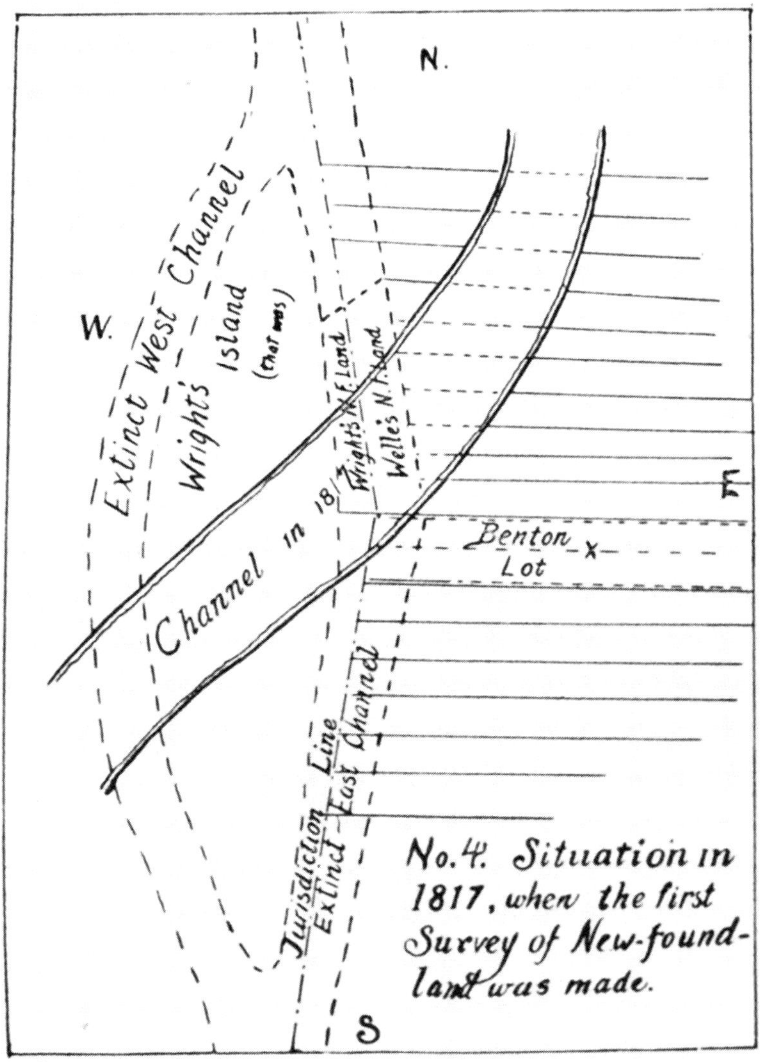

No. 4. Situation in 1817, when the first Survey of New-found-land was made.

to changes in patterns of water flow and may have made possible the most disastrous floods.[12]

In one sense, agriculture on annually flooded land had proven to be sustainable over several generations, but in another sense, Wright's island property was precariously close to going permanently underwater, because the river channel was shifting downstream and wearing away his land, turning it into river. Wright and his contemporaries still referred to Wright's Island as the "island," despite the fact that the river's main channel bisected the historical island during his lifetime rather than running in an east and west channel around an island as it had generations before. During flood times, however, water levels rose in the old eastern channel bed, restoring in some sense the insular geography that had given Wright's Island its name, and Wright could only reach his farm by boat. Not long after Wright's death, local writers began to refer to Wright's Island as having "disappeared."[13] That ultimate outcome resulted partly from the river's natural meandering but likely also from the increasingly powerful and disastrous floods of Wright's lifetime.

Opposite: "No. 4. Situation in 1817, when the first Survey of New-found-land was made," one of five maps first drawn by Sherman W. Adams in 1884, "Illustrative of the Gradual Changes in the Current of the Connecticut River, from 1639–1884, and the Consequent Alterations in the Form and Location of Mannhannock Island, now Known as the Island." The double lines show the banks of the river in 1817, entering the picture from the north and bending southwest. By 1817, the main stem of the Connecticut River bisected Wright's Island. The dotted lines show the river's course in the seventeenth century, when the main stem split at Wright's Island into two channels, labeled here "Extinct West Channel" and "Extinct East Channel." Looking back from 1884, the diagram refers to the island as "Wright's Island (that was)." From 1817 to 1884, the river channel continued to work downstream, crossing the historic island farther south. A Hartford judge and local historian, Adams was particularly interested in the way fluvial dynamics led to jurisdictional disputes between the towns of Glastonbury and Wethersfield and conflicts between individuals over private property including rights to "N.F. Land" or "New-found land." Like Joseph Wright, Adams expressed settler colonial nostalgia, crafting these maps on the 250th anniversary of Wethersfield's colonial founding. Sherman W. Adams, *The History of Ancient Wethersfield, Connecticut* (New York: Grafton, 1904), 2:874–75. Courtesy of the Watkinson Library, Trinity College, Hartford, Connecticut.

Wright understood each year's freshet as a naturally occurring regional phenomenon, resulting partly from snowmelt or rainfall upriver as far as Vermont. In mid-March, he awaited ice floes as signs that the river was breaking up abruptly farther north, and he was relieved (or "happily disappointed") when the thaw instead occurred gradually.[14] Around early April, he routinely noted that distant thaws caused the river to rise: what he formulaically registered as "the melting of the snow at the northward."[15] Wright informally gathered information from newspapers and word-of-mouth sources, using the phrase "it is said" to describe what he learned about northern snow depths or ice on the river.[16] But he seemed to read the weather and the river directly as well, as evident in an entry from early May 1852: "The weather is getting warm and the river begins to feel the snow and to rise again."[17] With hindsight after floods subsided, Wright often looked back and assessed the likely balance of contributing factors: in some years, freshets resulted "entirely or chiefly from snow"; in other years, floods were "produced from both snow and rain"; and, in rare cases, rising waters derived "entirely from rain."[18]

In April and early May, from the late 1830s to early 1860s, Wright anticipated the freshet with deep ambivalence. The freshets that brought the most disruption to Wright's Island and thus occasioned some of the lengthier descriptions occurred in 1837, 1843, 1847, 1850, 1852, and 1854.[19] For Wright, the flood of 1854 clearly constituted a full-blown disaster, but many other freshets were more ambiguous. The adjectives Wright used to describe potential or actual floods included gloomy, extraordinary, suspicious, unusual, and destructive.[20] Anticipating, viewing, or recalling a strong or prolonged flood, he felt fearful, apprehensive, anxious, "sadder still," astonished, appalled, and afraid.[21] His flood-time prospects became unpromising, discouraging, and "very dark."[22] He characterized life during a flood as "dully and dispiriting"; "anything but cheering"; "truly discouraging"; "in great confusion"; and "constantly apprehensive."[23] He expressed "fearful forebodings of a freshet."[24] One year when the roof blew off the cow house and floodwaters carried away 150 fence posts, Wright wrote, "Woes cluster."[25] But quite often, fear and grief were followed by relief. Wright's everyday style was watchful and empirical. He often reserved observations about God's providence until year's end. At the end of December 1847, for example, he reflected that although his farming business had not gone well, "we have been greatly blessed in the spared lives and health of our family and our exemption from destructive floods." Wright showed some awareness about the uneven exposure to hazard along the river, but his providential worldview largely flattened out that consciousness about how class, racialization, or other factors created unequal experiences of disaster.[26]

During strong freshets, Wright described almost in real time what occurred and estimated the hourly rate at which the river was rising over the course of a day. A minimum rate of one inch per hour was worthy of notation, and he recorded sustained rates as high as four inches per hour, though sudden rises could be even faster.[27] Over the extended course of a single freshet season, his daily entries tracked the erratic rise and fall of the river. In at least ten spring flooding seasons, Wright made ten or more entries about the rising and falling of the river, some series of entries spanning mid-March to early June.[28] Wright also noted when the water was "on a stand," a phrase he used frequently to express wonderment when the elevated river level paused during freshet season, neither rising nor falling.[29]

As a practical and modestly market-oriented farmer and fisherman, Wright viewed late spring floods with a mixture of hope for bumper crops of hay and exasperation about delays in planting corn or netting shad. The "unseasonable" flood in mid- to late May 1837 occurred after he had begun plowing and planting. Surveying floodwaters that nearly covered the island, Wright predicted, "The freshet will therefore throw me much behind in my farming business—but the flood will be worth a great deal to the grass in the meadow." Subsequent entries tracked the slow progress in his "backward" cornfield. Ultimately, the corn was not ready before the first frosts, and he had a poor harvest. Throughout that 1837 growing season, Wright had referred to the "May flood" and "most extraordinary spring." By October 26 he concluded, "My crop this year would have been good if I could have planted it at the usual time in May—but the water prevented my beginning."[30] At the same time, as predicted, the deep flood and ongoing rains in 1837 had been better for the hay crop. In early June, Wright had written that the ground was "exceedingly wet and the grass grows fast and looks very promising." In late June, the grass looked "finely in the meadows." By late summer, Wright marveled at the resilience of the grass and the fortuitous rise in prices for hay.[31]

With the right combination of factors, the freshet's fertilizing effects could produce lush meadow grass on Wright's Island. On March 29, 1845, Wright delighted in the color of early spring: "The weather for nearly week has been truly spring-like. The grass has sprung up green throughout the pasture and the water is running up the little river occasioned by the melting of the snow to the northward." By mid-July 1845, he rejoiced: "Grass commands a good price and is in demand. It never was as good in quantity and quality, I think, on Wright's Island."[32] When floodwaters covered the island for a long period in spring, and when early summer brought a balance of sunshine and intermittent rains, Wright seemed most optimistic. In 1847, he noted that a full river from local rainfall and northern thaw had produced promising results: "Grass looks exceedingly well on the Island."[33] In early July, 1850, he again marveled, "Grass has not looked better for many years owing to the high and long flood in spring."[34] The delicate balance was elusive, however. In late April 1852, Wright had predicted that the unusually high freshet would be "of great benefit to the meadow," but by early July, he wrote with disappointment, "It has been too dry for grass and the high and long spring freshet has greatly injured the fine grass."[35] Usually, though, sunny, warm "hay weather" in July and early August facilitated the cutting and drying of grass for hay.[36]

Wright managed his fences, barns, and other infrastructure around the year's natural cycles. Every spring Wright fenced in his pasture after the floods receded.[37] Around November he pulled up the fence before it froze into the soil and so that high water in winter or the following spring would not damage or carry away the fence.[38] Freshets not only directly fertilized his pastures and fields but also supported meadow grasses for hay that cattle turned into manure, another source of fertilizer for his fields. Because much of the manure was collected over the winter, spring floods could leach the stores of manure, if not raised above the likely crest of the flood.[39] In mid-May 1850, Wright wrote: "Began to drain out manure. Our manure has been excessively leached, the water having been in the barn yard for more than a week. We still thought it might have some strength in it and concluded to put it on the land notwithstanding its great weight and wetness."[40] Five years later, he drew out manure from an elevated spot he called "the 'Mount' at the press barn" in early May: "All of our manure would have been washed by the freshet if we had not moved it to the press barn hill."[41] Wright also commented on how receding floodwaters deposited mud within his two houses and his outbuildings and spread sand over his meadows, leaving him with remediation duties long after the freshet. The buildings could be cleaned, at least. In the wake of flooding in January 1841, Wright wrote, "We washed out the house, corn house, and the 2 barns which contained an unusual quantity of mud." In April 1843, when he went "to the island to clear and wash the house floors etc.," he "found a great abundance of mud, washed it out and cleaned out the press barn." Thanks to the practice of raising and storing the hay above likely flood level, he found that his five tons of hay had remained dry, despite evidence that the barn floor had held a foot of water.[42]

Thick sediment spread by a freshet over the meadows in excessive quantities or at the wrong time was more difficult to remedy. Surveying his meadows in May 1843, Wright lamented the "destructive effects" of the flood upon the fabric of the land: "The ground has been torn up and hollows made, and hollows filled up and more sediment deposited than I ever saw before. Many acres of mowing land will be nearly ruined the present season and I shall have several that will bear but a trifle of good grass this season."[43] Looking back at the flood season of 1856, Wright reflected on the mixed results: "Our rowing [or second-growth of grass] this year has turned out well though it was inundated by the flood. It grew chiefly after the freshet, the weather being warm & wet. But little of it was dusty after drying. The first cuttings after the flood were much soiled by the mud of the freshet."[44]

If the sediment dried out too quickly and was kicked up by winds, Wright increasingly used the word "sand" instead of "mud" to describe flood deposition and began complaining of silt in the air and choked pastures. In late July 1841, Wright wrote, "My pasture has been unexpectedly almost useless from the burying up of the flood and the dry weather." He later looked back at how dry summer weather had succeeded early floods: "So much sand was brought on by the freshet in January, that, in connection with the droughts I have had but little feed, so that I have fed my cattle almost every day since the 1st July." He had expanded the pasture range to no avail and had to compensate by providing feed directly.[45] Hay crops could fall short.[46] The sediment also diminished air quality on the island and created concentrations or drifts of sand.

Dry, windy weather in April 1845 led to "sand on the north end [of Wright's Island] by the river filling the air like a cloud."[47]

After the freshet, Wright turned part of his energy for several weeks to a seasonal fishing business. High water levels delayed or interrupted the late-spring shad fishing season. Wright employed several men and large nets during the fish runs of May and June for supplementary income. When the water levels were low, the fishing was good. If he could keep nets in the water for several weeks, Wright's fishing operation could haul in a few thousand shad, which he sold for a profit in Hartford.[48] But he repeatedly expressed impatience about water "too high for fishing,"[49] and he rued each day they were "obliged to quit" by rising waters. The income from the shad fishery hedged Wright against some of the risks of farming and was a longtime practice on the Connecticut River associated with the ideals of a competency.[50]

In most years from 1837 to 1849, Wright lived on the mainland for at least part of the winter and early spring, moving to the island full-time from late spring through fall.[51] By January 1848, Wright had lost family support for living on the island due to attritional effects of coping with each spring flood. His family members were "all averse to living here in winter," he wrote from the island. "I should be so too if we could live on the street as conveniently and economically as we can here," he added.[52] In the late 1830s and 1840s, Wright crossed floodwaters by boat from the island back to Main Street on Sundays to participate in church services as a deacon.[53] Glastonbury's first church had been founded in 1692 so that farmers on the river's east bank would not have to cross over to Wethersfield on Sundays, but in freshet season Wright's Island still required occasional short crossings to Glastonbury's mainland.

Wright studied the river's meander process over the years, watching attentively as private property returned to the river and as the island as a whole changed shape and diminished in size. In March 1846, he noted the pressure points on the north tip of the island and estimated the annual lateral change in one embankment due to floods, "The river is wearing away the bank in the meadow above the point of the island and below at an alarming rate. Last season in freshet time it wore on the meadow bank from 1 to 4 rods, at least."[54] Wright and his neighbors charted the accompanying property losses: "The N.W. end of Mr. Plummer's lot went into the river in the freshet of 1844.

Last year, '45, the whole width of the lot went off at the west end. This year (22 March 1846) more than one half of the west end of George Hale's lot has gone into the river."[55] Recent events had pushed the freshet's thrust from the main channel over the island and over the piers that connected the island to the mainland at low water. For example, Wright thought that "ice lodging on the flats on the west side of the river" just upriver and opposite the island in the winter of 1844–45 had displaced the river current. As a result, the freshet "came down with great force" in the spring of 1845 "close by the East bank till it arrived at the head of the island when it cut between the shore and the pier at the N. end of the island and kept on making a deep channel on this side till it got down to the lower pier where it pressed hard almost cutting a channel between the long pier and the East shore, greatly to my detriment."[56] In August 1846, when the river was very low, Wright read the patterns in the "extensive flats making from my shore in the river westward."[57] He continued: "The ground between the bank and the Island west of the press barn is rapidly filling up and young trees and bushes are fast coming forward. The flats making below have extended quite half across the river." Nature worked quickly, turning river to land and land to river.[58]

By the end of 1849, Wright decided that living on the island for half the year was no longer tenable. On November 27, 1849, he wrote ruefully: "Got up most of our remaining articles of household use and finally quitted the island house at about dusk in the evening with the intention of permanently living at the street hereafter. It makes me sad to quit the island."[59] The Wright family had owned land on the island since the seventeenth century. He feared that the changing channel of the Connecticut River was reclaiming his insular inheritance. Within the island's microgeography, he could see how the "old eastern bank of the river" remained on the landscape, and he knew the current channel was dynamic.[60]

Wright's study of the meander process contributed to his decision over the winter of 1849–50 to move his family permanently back to the mainland. His entries about the changing river channel became dour. In August 1850, Wright observed "a great crevasse between the end of the long pier and the bank, made by the freshets this season which I fear, will in the end ruin the Island."[61] Weeks later, the river had "considerably washed away the bank at the crevasse by the long pier."[62] In December 1853, the pattern on the floodplain was all too clear: "Our land is wearing away very fast from every freshet and according to present appearances, the greater part of our farm will be in the river or on the other side within 50 years!"[63] Wright imagined that some of his "descendants" would still be on the land in 1903 to see if his "prophecy" would "prove true or false."[64] He often referred to his farming business with the first-person singular possessive, "my," but here he switched to the plural "our" to evoke the intergenerational dimensions of the farm as a shrinking and precarious inheritance. In 1848, he had surveyed his property on Wright's Island to be seventy-nine and three-quarters acres.[65] In five years, the acreage had decreased to seventy-five.[66]

By 1854, Wright had described dozens of freshets but was not prepared for the catastrophic magnitude of that spring's flood. Wright awoke on the morning of Sunday, April 30, "appalled" by "unparalleled" overnight change in the height of the river. The water had risen three feet in the roughly ten hours "from Sun to Sun." By 4:00 a.m., the water reached "the house floor" and continued at that pace of "3½ and 4 inches an hour." The rising waters brought destruction to his mainland home lot: "Our picket fence is all up, several stable doors and corn house doors gone and every thing fragile gone to pieces." Wright saved his livestock before water entered the press barn by asking neighbor Philo Phelps to carry away the animals on his scow, a simple flat-bottomed boat. Wright preserved the "rails and posts" by pulling them up and piling them in the same barn from which the cattle had been rescued. By 4:00 p.m., the water was "reaching the lower windows in the house" and still rising four inches per hour.[67]

Wright was aware of the river's history and knew how his contemporaries measured flood stages and compared each new flood to the historical record. Over the past two decades, the floods seemed to Wright to be increasing in height and duration. Wright had described the height of the water as "unprecedented" in 1837 and "unexampled" and "unparalleled" in 1843.[68] In both 1843 and 1854, Wright looked for historical precedents, referring to floods in 1692 and 1801, two floods also mentioned by newspaper reports. Notably, these questions about floods caused him to reflect on early colonial processes and events, searching for continuities with the struggles of previous farmers who had persisted in working land along the river. By May 6, 1854, Wright declared the past week's freshet to be "the Greatest flood on the river that is known to History."[69] Modern sources agree that the 1854 freshet reached the highest flood stage at Hartford of the nineteenth century, though it was exceeded by four floods in the twentieth century.[70]

Wright's journal gave a rural view of the 1854 freshet as the floodwater interacted with land, buildings, plants, and animals, not unlike downtown Hartford writers and artists, who depicted the 1854 flood from atop a hill or rooftop, six miles north of Wright's Island.[71] In Hartford, residents suffered property damage, including to homes and private possessions. Wright was not as vulnerable as many urban wage workers, including those living in Hartford's Irish and Black communities, many of whom lived by the river lowlands. The *Hartford Times* reported "DAMAGE TO POOR FAMILIES. Many families living in the river precincts were taken entirely by surprise, and the amount of damage done to them is very large." Samuel Colt was in the process of building a dike to protect his new firearms factories in the floodplain of Hartford's South Meadows when the 1854 freshet occurred. Simultaneously, as he imagined conquering the freshets and improving riverside lands, Colt invoked colonial history explicitly and appropriated Indigenous names in the planning of his factory village. Many of Colt's workers had been living in new or temporary housing in the floodplain and were displaced by the floodwaters. Pigs belonging to working families were drowned. The *Hartford Courant* reported two Hartford deaths by drowning in the flood and pointed to one-story homes and businesses as particularly vulnerable. The flood disrupted new forms of infrastructure such as railroad tracks, telegraph lines, and gas works delivering fuel to light fixtures. Total property damage in Hartford was estimated to be $100,000; dozens of displaced residents were housed in city hall and other downtown buildings; and at least a thousand people suddenly became unemployed.[72]

By May 6, 1854, Wright reported, the water finally fell and brought "to view the desolations of the Greatest flood on the river that is known to History." From the mainland, he catalogued the flood's effects structure by structure: "Every thing is swept from its foundation except our house proper and the two barns. The W. barn is in a weak and unsupported condition and must one day be taken down or fall. The Corn house is not worth moving back. The attached wood house and hay pen we shall get back as soon as we can." At the conclusion of 1854, in his December 31 entry reflecting on the year past, Wright recalled that year's freshet as "the highest and most destructive ever known." Assessing the flood's long-term consequences, however, together with a drought over the summer, the "farming business" turned out "better than usual." In other words, given nature's cycles of destruction and replenishment, it paid to rebuild in the floodplain.[73] Even after 1854, Wright continued to work the island's pastures, meadows, and fields, but eventually the family had the island house removed to the Glastonbury mainland rather than let the river carry it away. Upriver at Hartford, the construction of a dike expanded permanent access to riverfront land, but in this rural stretch of the river, temporary or permanent withdrawal from the floodplain were the likely options.[74]

Wright's journal indicated that he knew all too well the ways the Connecticut River could give and take away. At a time when other farmers invested in fertilizers and machinery, Wright mainly persisted in working the floodplain for grains and grasses and fishing for shad. Yet the freshet-based competency did not last forever, at least within the static bounds of private property. In his case, the river's natural meander process may have been accelerated by human activity upriver. At the same time, the eventual movement of the river bend downstream, though disastrous for barns and other outbuildings, was entirely predictable. Wright farmed the island in some ways that differed from Indigenous uses of Connecticut's riverside lands, especially his dedicating of meadows and pastures to feeding livestock. His patriarchal approach to agriculture also contrasted with Wangunk women's traditional role in horticulture.[75] By highlighting the land's natural fertility and by foreshadowing the endpoint of the Wright family's control of a parcel of farmland, the diary implicitly acknowledged how foundational the initial colonial acquisition or theft of land had been.

Wright's recurrent struggles with floods, his family's strategic retreat from his island in the wake of disasters, and the ultimate disappearance of the island itself have striking parallels to the twenty-first-century loss of coastal and riverside lands and dilemmas about whether to rebuild in areas vulnerable to disaster. The repeated occurrence of small-scale disasters leading to displacement harms residents, already vulnerable from social injustices, who often lack the resources to recover, but this kind of slow disaster over time also destabilizes the power and privilege of wealthier residents. One argument in favor of gradual, government-supported withdrawal from some coastal or riverside areas of overdevelopment, rather than rebuilding from disasters, is that in the long term, policies funding retreat from coastline and floodplain areas could contribute to rolling back settler colonial control of lands, shorelines, or rivers and redressing historical and ongoing injustices. Critical dismantling of settler colonial discourses about such places is equally necessary. In postindustrial communities of New England, public discussions about the future of rivers or coasts often invoke a preindustrial history as a natural alternative to nineteenth- and twentieth-century uses of these waterfront spaces. The long histories of settler colonial control over coastal and riverside lands are seldom critiqued as part of these discussions, and nostalgic colonial-themed names and imagery are often used to promote the reclaiming of the waterfront. Settler colonial structures and processes have been reproduced and reinscribed in response to disasters, whether in adaptive rebuilding, in flood control, or in restoration projects that make safe recreational access to rivers possible. Such ongoing development should be conceptualized as materially and discursively recolonial, and critical disaster studies might suggest alternative, decolonial responses.[76]

NOTES

1. The original manuscript journal and a full transcription can be found at the Historical Society of Glastonbury. The manuscripts are bound by year. Below, individual entries are cited by date. The author would like to thank Phyllis Reed and other staff members at the Historical Society of Glastonbury (hereafter HSG).

2. Jean Greene, lecture on Joseph Wright at the Wright House, Glastonbury, CT, June 10, 2007, five-page typescript, HSG; Peter Molk, "Joseph Wright: A Study into the Life of a New England Farmer," 2001, unpublished paper, HSG; Sherman Wolcott Adams, *The History of Ancient Wethersfield, Connecticut*, vol. 1, *History*, ed. Henry R. Stiles (New York: Grafton, 1904), 1:32, 82, 84, 92, 318, 544; 2:874–880.

3. The regional term "freshets" was of relatively recent, local coinage, being used commonly by the early nineteenth century in New England to describe spring floods (see *Oxford English Dictionary Online, s.v. "freshet, n.,"* accessed February 26, 2020).

4. December 31, 1844; May 18, 1853. Wright wrote surprisingly little about his wife, Sarah Lockwood Wright, with whom he had six children, and whose unpaid work was seldom mentioned in connection to the farm. One of his sons, Henry, stayed in Glastonbury and worked the

land with him, but he employed several other men on the island over time, at times noting their wages or describing the quality of their work in the diary. In a few cases, he noted workers' Irish or African American ancestry: November 21, 1849; April 20, 1852; April 11, 1854; August 5, 1854; December 31, 1854.

5. Jean M. O'Brien, *Firsting and Lasting: Writing Indians out of Existence in New England* (Minneapolis: University of Minnesota Press, 2010).

6. Patrick Wolfe, "Settler Colonialism and the Elimination of the Native," *Journal of Genocide Research* 8, no. 4 (2006): 387–409.

7. J. S. Taber, "Thinking Like a Floodplain: Water, Work, and Time in the Connecticut River Valley, 1790–1870" (PhD diss., University of Kansas, 2016); Lowell Duckert, *For All Waters: Finding Ourselves in Early Modern Wetscapes* (Minneapolis: University of Minnesota Press, 2017); James Scott, "In Praise of Floods," Social Sciences Research Council, Albert O. Hirschman Prize Ceremony and Lecture, December 4, 2020, https://www.youtube.com/watch?v=YzUP9Mjm16Y.

8. April 29, 1854.

9. Fiona Williamson and Chris Courtney, "Disasters Fast and Slow: The Temporality of Hazards in Environmental History," *International Review of Environmental History* 4, no. 2 (2018): 5–11, esp. 8–9; Eric Hsu, "Must Disasters Be Rapidly Occurring? The Case for an Expanded Temporal Typology of Disasters," *Time and Society* 28, no. 3 (2017): 904–21, esp. 915; Andy Horowitz and Jacob A. C. Remes, eds., *Critical Disaster Studies* (Philadelphia: University of Pennsylvania Press, 2021).

10. December 31, 1844; December 31, 1847; December 31, 1850; December 31, 1851; December 31, 1853; December 31, 1855; December 31, 1856; December 31, 1860; Greene typescript, 1–2. Daniel Vickers, "Competency and Competition: Economic Culture in Early America," *William and Mary Quarterly* 47, no. 1 (1990): 3–29; Richard Bushman, "Markets and Composite Farms in Early America," *William and Mary Quarterly* 55, no. 3 (1998): 351–74; Brian Donahue, *The Great Meadow: Farmers and the Land in Colonial Concord* (New Haven, CT: Yale University Press, 2004); Richard W. Judd, *Second Nature: An Environmental History of New England* (Amherst: University of Massachusetts Press, 2014).

11. On the free meander process within Glastonbury Reach, see Robert M. Thorson, Daniel Forrest, and Brian Jones, "Hydraulic Back-Flood Model for the Archaeological Stratigraphy of the Connecticut River Alluvial Lowland, Central Connecticut, USA," *Quaternary International* 342 (2014): 173–85, esp. 176; James Grant Macbroom, *The River Book* (Hartford: Connecticut DEP, 1998), 40–41; *The Flooding River: A Study in Riverine Ecology*, dir. Jonathan C. Huberth, DVD (1972; New York: DuArt, 2009); Jaime Grant, "Geomorphology of the Connecticut River, Glastonbury Reach, as a Spatial-Temporal Context for Understanding Pre-Contact Settlement Patterns" (PhD diss., University of Connecticut, 2015); Daniel T. Forrest, Brian Jones, and Robert Thorson, "The Adriaen's Landing Project and the Development of the Connecticut River Floodplain at Hartford," *Bulletin of the Archaeological Society of Connecticut* 70 (2008): 5–16; and Thomas R. Lewis, *Near the Long Tidal River: Readings in the Historical Geography of Central Connecticut* (Washington, DC: University Press of America, 1981).

12. William DeLoss Love, "Navigation of the Connecticut River," *Proceedings of the American Antiquarian Society* 15 (1903): 385–441, esp. 399, 401; Strother Roberts, *Colonial Ecology, Atlantic*

Economy: Transforming Nature in Early New England (Philadelphia: University of Pennsylvania Press, 2019).

13. Adams, *The History of Ancient Wethersfield*, 1:84.

14. March 15, 1844; March 16, 1846; March 12, 1848; March 11, 1852.

15. April 13, 1843; April 6, 1844; March 29, 1845; April 23, 1847; April 21, 1862.

16. January 30, 1840; January 23, 1855; April 21, 1862.

17. May 6 and 7, 1852.

18. April 30, 1850; April 25, 1852; February 7, 1847. See also May 11 and 31, 1847.

19. Wright also wrote about strong floods at other times of year in 1839, 1841, and 1856, to give three examples.

20. August 9, 1837; February 26, 1840; February 5, 1847; January 21–22, 1856.

21. August 16, 1839; February 15, 1840; January 12 and 13, 1841; October 9, 1843; February 23, 1845; April 10, 1847; April 30, 1854; February 8, 1857.

22. May 2 and 9 1840; April 17, 1843; May 7, 1850; August 21, 1856.

23. May 19 and 22, 1837; May 8, 1841; April 20 and 29, 1843; May 1, 1843; February 25, 1843.

24. July 22, 1857.

25. May 1, 1843.

26. December 31, 1847.

27. May 17, 1837; April 16–18, 1843; May 2, 1843; June 11, 1843; March 15, 1844; April 1, 1845; March 14, 1846; April 24–25, 1847; April 30, 1850; May 7, 1850; April 21, 1852; April 29–May 1, 1854; February 16, 1855; April 18, 1855; February 10, 1857.

28. 1837, 1840, 1841, 1843, 1844, 1845, 1847, 1850, 1852, 1854.

29. May 21, 1837; April 27, 1843; April 7, 1844; March 22, 1846; May 2 and 10, 1850; March 16, 1852; May 12–14, 1852.

30. May 18, 22, 25, and 29, 1837; June 26, 1837; July 11, 1837; August 1, 1837; October 26, 1837.

31. July 11, 1837; August 1, 1837.

32. March 29, 1845; July 17, 1845. See also May 2, 1843; June 30, 1843; May 20, 1844; July 13, 1854; August 20, 1856; May 15, 1862.

33. May 31, 1847; June 19, 1847.

34. July 4, 1850.

35. April 25, 1852; July 5, 1852.

36. July 15 and 31, 1843; August 2–4, 1843. See also August 7, 1841; and July 19, 22, and 26–27, 1843.

37. May 12, 1837; May 8, 1841; May 5, 1847. Wright tried to time it just right but did not always succeed (see May 1, 1843; April 29, 1854; April 20, 1862).

38. November 16 and 18, 1837; October 10, 1838; November 22, 1839; December 1, 1840; November 14 and 22, 1843; November 27, 1844; December 3, 1845; November 20, 1847; November 20, 1848; November 10 and 30, 1849; November 20 and 27, 1852; November 13, 1853; November 13, 1854; October 24, 1857. Wright's picket fence around his mainland house also was vulnerable to flood damage, even though it was on higher ground (see April 20 and 27, 1843; April 26, 1847; May 9, 1850; April 25, 1852; April 30, 1854).

39. May 29, 1843.

40. May 16 and 17, 1850.

41. May 4, 1855.

42. January 12, 1841; April 21, 1843.

43. May 6, 1843. See also May 14, 1850; July 26 and 29, 1850; November 13, 1853; May 8, 1854.

44. November 24, 1856; *Oxford English Dictionary Online, s.v.* "rowen, *n*.," accessed May 2, 2021.

45. July 30, 1841; August 17, 1841.

46. June 1, 1862.

47. April 30, 1845; May 28, 1850; March 31, 1851; May 31, 1855.

48. April 8, 1839; May 12, 1840; May 8, 1841; May 5, 1843; April 22, 1844; April 13, 1846; April 15, 1848; April 28, 1851; May 12, 1855.

49. May 3, 1837; May 14, 1853; May 14 and 28, 1857; April 26, 1858.

50. April 29, 1840; May 17, 1850. See also June 9, 1838; April 21, 1841; May 22 and 30, 1850; and May 13, 1854. See also Daniel Vickers, "Those Dammed Shad: Would the River Fisheries of New England Have Survived in the Absence of Industrialization?," *William and Mary Quarterly* 61, no. 4 (2004): 685–712.

51. April 24, 1837; March 28, 1840; May 23, 1843; May 2, 1849; November 20 and 25, 1848.

52. January 1, 1848.

53. May 8, 1837; June 11, 1838; November 11, 1838; April 7, 14, and 21, 1844; April 27, 1845; March 29, 1846; April 11 and 25, 1847; May 2 and 9, 1847; December 5, 1847; May 7, 1848; November 11, 1849.

54. March 22, 1846.

55. March 22, 1846.

56. March 22, 1846.

57. August 21, 1846.

58. August 21, 1846.

59. November 27, 1849.

60. January 16, 1841.

61. August 2, 1850.

62. August 27, 1850.

63. December 27, 1853.

64. December 27, 1853.

65. January 7, 1848.

66. December 27, 1853.

67. April 30, 1854.

68. May 22, 1837; April 17–18, 1843; May 6, 1843. Several times after 1843, he compared subsequent freshets to the 1843 benchmark: April 25, 1847; May 2 and 8, 1850; July 22, 1850; April 25, 1852; May 1, 1854.

69. May 6, 1854.

70. April 19, 1843; May 6, 1843; May 1, 1854. For newspaper reports, see "The First Great Flood," *Hartford Courant,* March 22, 1859, 2. For tables comparing flood stages, see "Historic Crests for Connecticut River at Hartford," https://water.weather.gov/ahps2/crests.php?wfo=lwx&gage=hfdc3&crest_type=historic; M. T. Thomson, W. B. Gannon, M. P. Thomas, and G. S. Hayes, *Historic Floods in New England,* Geological Survey Water Supply Paper 1779-M (Washington, DC: US Department of the Interior, 1964), M85. See also Adams, *The History of Ancient Wethersfield,* 1:713; Taber, "Thinking Like a Floodplain," 280; and Love, "Navigation of the Connecticut River," 400.

71. William Hosley, *Colt: The Making of an American Legend* (Amherst: University of Massachusetts Press, 1996), 108, 115; Herbert Houze, *Samuel Colt: Arms, Art, and Invention,* ed. Elizabeth Mankin Kornhauser (New Haven, CT: Yale University Press, 2006), 233–39; *Hartford Courant,* May 2, 1854, 2.

72. Hosley, *Colt,* 98, 101, 107–8; Houze, *Samuel Colt,* 171; *Hartford Courant,* May 1, 1854, 2; *Hartford Courant,* May 2, 1854, 2; *Hartford Times,* May 6, 1854, 2; Taber, "Thinking Like a Floodplain," 293–98.

73. December 31, 1854.

74. The brick house remains at 2033 Main Street. The "island house," after being relocated, was lost to a fire in the 1920s (Adams, *History of Ancient Wethersfield,* 2:879; Donald M. Smith, "A Lost Island That Lingers in Glastonbury's Memories," *Hartford Courant Magazine,* April 14, 1943).

75. Timothy Ives, "Wangunk Ethnohistory: A Case Study of a Connecticut River Indian community" (master's thesis, William and Mary, 2001).

76. Margaret Bruchac, "Historical Erasure and Cultural Recovery: Indigenous People in the Connecticut River Valley" (PhD diss., University of Massachusetts, Amherst, 2007), 4.

RICHMOND'S YEAR OF DISASTERS

RELIEF, RECONCILIATION, AND THE END OF RECONSTRUCTION

ALYSSA TOBY FAHRINGER

In 1870, the approximately fifty-one thousand inhabitants of Reconstruction-era Richmond, Virginia—the second-largest city of the Confederacy and also its capital—were recovering from wartime desolation. In the final months of the Civil War, Confederates abandoned the city and ordered soldiers to set fire to bridges, armories, and warehouses, so large portions of the city had to be rebuilt in the years following the war's end in 1865.[1] During this period, Black Richmonders—almost half of the city's residents—voted in large numbers for Republicans and other politicians supporting Reconstruction policies. In 1867–68, twenty-four Black politicians were among the 104 delegates who attended the convention that crafted the new state constitution, which voters ratified, along with amendments to the US Constitution that abolished slavery, recognized Blacks Americans as citizens, and enfranchised freedmen. Congress approved these actions and readmitted Virginia to the Union in January 1870.[2]

Despite the formal end of Reconstruction in Virginia, political and social upheavals and uncertainties continued to plague Richmond throughout the remainder of 1870. Notwithstanding political changes made throughout Reconstruction, a Conservative opposition party still maintained significant political power and attempted to block Republican policies. Specifically, the city was reeling following the passage of the Enabling Act in March, which allowed the governor to remove militarily appointed officeholders and replace them with other officials, generally less supportive of federal Reconstructions reforms and policies, who would serve in their capacity until the next election. The governor-appointed Council for the City of Richmond elected Henry K. Ellyson, a Conservative, mayor of Richmond. George Chahoon, whom Major General John M. Schofield had appointed mayor in 1868 during Radical Reconstruction, found the authority of the Council illegitimate and refused to give up his office. The conflict over the mayoral seat devolved into violence, and both Chahoon and Ellyson developed their own police forces. Richmonders had hoped that the case would be resolved on April 27, when the city suffered the first of three ruinous disasters.

On April 27, 1870, citizens of Richmond and visitors from across Virginia were at the Capitol Building, awaiting the verdict in the Chahoon-Ellyson disputed mayoral election case. Reporters, lawyers, and members of the public filled the courtroom and its gallery beyond capacity. At eleven o'clock, the large girder that held the gallery snapped, causing the supports to loosen and separate from the wall. The gallery fell onto the courtroom floor, which collapsed and fell into the legislative chamber beneath the courtroom. Some spectators were crushed to death; others suffocated from inhaling the dust of the crumbled plaster. Clouds of dust and debris poured from the Capitol's windows, and people in the Capitol Square thought the building's boiler had exploded or that the building was on fire. Bells rang throughout the city to alert everyone to the catastrophe, and the fire department arrived and began rescue operations. The dead and wounded were pulled from the debris and placed in the Senate Chamber or outside in the Capitol Square, where city physicians attended to their injuries. Approximately sixty people died, and hundreds more were injured.[3]

Five months later, on September 30, a ruinous flood engulfed the city when the James River rose six feet as a result of heavy rainfall. Throughout the afternoon, the river continued to rise at a rate of one foot every half hour. The storm downed many telegraph lines, so some Richmonders lacked the advance notice they needed to adequately prepare for the approaching deluge. The following day, floodwaters engulfed the riverside community of Rocketts, and approximately two hundred families fled their homes. No one in the city died as a result of the flood, but initial estimates of damages were profound, estimated at $500,000.[4] A bar, feed store, toy and confectionary shop, grocery, pharmacy, harness shop, and fertilizer store were some of the businesses that sustained

"The Richmond Calamity—Interior of the Hall of Delegates—Getting Out the Dead and Wounded," *Harper's Weekly*, May 14, 1870. This illustration of the scene inside the Capitol following the collapse conveys a sense of chaos and destruction. Rescuers and survivors are pictured attempting to extricate the wounded and dead from piles of debris. Having circulated in a widely read national publication, this image may have enticed some readers to contribute to relief efforts. Courtesy of the American Antiquarian Society.

major water damage. Other businesses fared better: Haxall, Crenshaw, and Company's flour mills were not too badly damaged and resumed operations after a few days, and Tredegar Iron Works sustained minimal damage in the form of rusted tools. The proprietors of Morriss, the sugar refinery, reassessed their initial estimate and confirmed that the cost of damage was less than they had originally thought. Elsewhere in Virginia, the flood destroyed several bridges of the Chesapeake and Ohio Railroad and washed away a mile of track, resulting in roughly $100,000 worth of damage. In Albemarle County—approximately seventy-five miles northwest of Richmond—at least fourteen people died, and the flood destroyed fifty mills and dams.[5]

Less than three months later, a third costly disaster befell the former Confederate capital. On Christmas Day at about two in the morning, the night watchman at the Spotswood Hotel noticed smoke coming from a crevice in the weatherboarding surrounding the pantry. When he broke the pantry door down, he discovered that the entire pantry was on fire. In less than half an hour the fire had expanded to every one of the five floors of the hotel. Occupants evacuated and stood outside in freezing temperatures. The fire destroyed the office of the Southern Express Company, located on the ground floor. Strong winds moved the flames to the west, and adjoining buildings also caught on fire. The fire burned for three hours. The following day, workers dug through the debris to recover the bodies of the eight people who died. The *Richmond Daily Dispatch* called for an inquest into the cause of the fire. It was the custom of hotels to have only one clerk and two servants on the ground floor of the hotel after midnight, leaving the remainder of the floors unsupervised. Following the disaster, state legislators planned to introduce a bill requiring all hotelkeepers in the state to have a watchman or watchmen visit each floor of a hotel every ten or fifteen minutes throughout the night to ensure the safety of the hotel's occupants, but these efforts were unsuccessful.[6]

As in the case of most contemporary American disasters, relief for suffering Richmonders in 1870 came from nongovernmental sources. While the federal government was undoubtedly becoming more involved in disaster relief efforts—demonstrated in one instance in 1867 by Congress appropriating $500,000 to the Freedmen's Bureau to provide famine relief to all southerners under its purview, not just freedpeople—Richmonders did not anticipate or expect aid from the federal government following the disasters.[7] Nor were state governments generally involved in disaster relief efforts. Fiscal or material assistance after calamities was not yet the remit of organizations like the Red Cross, which became a private organization focused on disaster relief in 1881. In 1870, relief efforts were typically ad hoc, private, and often local. As Cynthia Kierner notes, "relief committees scrambled to bury the dead and collect donations of money, provisions, and expertise to aid the injured, hungry, and homeless."[8] Following the disasters in Richmond in 1870, residents of cities throughout the country—particularly northern metropolises—contributed money to their city's informal, ad hoc relief fund, and those contributions were then sent to Richmond. In many ways, the external response to Richmond was typical of the time.

Residents of northern cities became aware of Richmonders' suffering and financial needs via newspaper reports. Newspapers published outside Virginia covered the disasters in Richmond in 1870—particularly the Capitol calamity—and the press inspired and then reported northerners' outpourings of sympathy and relief. Richmond publications discussed local relief efforts following the disasters, which included the creation of a Committee on Visitation and Relief by the Chamber of Commerce after the collapse at the Capitol, but those efforts were not widely reported outside of Virginia.[9] Print media outside Virginia played a significant role in describing the disasters, and it was due to such coverage that some Americans felt compelled to provide aid. Residents of major cities throughout the North read about the Capitol, flood, and fire in widely circulating publications such as the *New York Herald* and the *Boston Daily Advertiser.* News of these disasters also spread rapidly to smaller cities and towns via local papers. Whereas readers of the *New York Times* first heard news of the Capitol disaster on April 28—the day after it occurred—readers of Little Rock, Arkansas's *Morning Republican* and the Indiana-based *Evansville Journal* received word only one day later. There was also coverage of the calamities in the Black press, such as the *New Era,* a national newspaper based in Washington and edited by Frederick Douglass.[10]

The narratives created by these publications and the actions of some white northerners in their locales in the wake of the three disasters that occurred in Richmond in 1870 demonstrate that these calamities provided the impetus for white northerners to demonstrate feelings of goodwill and sympathy for defeated southerners a mere five years following the end of the Civil War. The disasters created opportunities for Americans outside of the South to express sympathy, financially contribute to the rebuilding of the former capital of the Confederacy, and provide aid to its residents. In the case of the Richmond calamities, disasters and disaster relief became a part of the process of reconstruction and reunification. Publications frequently described mourning rituals, collective grief, and funerals to optimistically suggest that the disasters facilitated unity among Richmonders themselves—particularly in regard to political affiliation and race—despite their years of political and social conflict during the Civil War and Reconstruction. The sad stories of Richmonders' suffering also helped to initiate the process of reestablishing friendly relations between white northerners and southerners. In part because of the city's postwar poverty and desolation, sympathy and aid from the North were imperative in getting Richmonders the relief they desperately needed following each calamity.

Most scholars date reconciliation between the North and South to the 1880s and 1890s, although the yellow fever epidemic that struck the South in 1878 was another prior example of white northerners who were weary of war and Reconstruction showing sympathy for defeated southerners.[11] During that epidemic, northerners sent money, goods, and medical professionals to the southern states, demonstrating collective feelings of reunion. According to one historian, the epidemic "stood at a pivotal moment in postwar national reconciliation and the marginalization of African Americans."[12] The disasters in Richmond—eight years before the epidemic—led to an even earlier outpouring of assistance from northerners to southerners.

Many newspapers outside Virginia published sympathetic descriptions of suffering Richmonders in the wake of the 1870 calamities. After the flood, a Vermont-based *Burlington Weekly Free Press* journalist noted that "all the desolation" Richmond experienced during the Civil War "has been exceeded by . . . many days of destructive storm."[13] The suffering of the region "not yet fully recovered from the desolations of war, is dreadful to contemplate."[14] A writer for the *Baltimore Sun* said that Richmond had been "scourged by water as well as by fire"—referencing the fire Richmonders set themselves during the evacuation of the city in 1865.[15] The *New York Herald* referenced Richmond's history as the capital of the Confederacy when describing the Spotswood Hotel as a building that "saw the brunt of our civil war and heard within its walls the secret consultations of the rebel chiefs in their days of glory and their days of disaster."[16] While noting that leaders opposed to the Union held those conferences—the "rebel chiefs"—the *Herald* reporter managed to evoke the history of the city and of the building itself in a relatively ambivalent and ambiguous way. These papers did not depict Richmond as deserving of these disasters, which suggests that many of their northern readers were at least potentially sympathetic to the plight of the city's residents.

Other publications described the sympathy Americans outside Virginia felt for Richmonders who were suffering in the wake of the disasters. Such sympathy foreshadowed the eventual rapprochement that would take place between white northerners and southerners. The *New York Times* reflected that its city's residents felt "deep and sorrowful sympathy" for those affected by the Capitol collapse, a sentiment shared "in every part of the Union."[17] Similarly, the *Boston Daily Advertiser* noted that disasters "may happen any where and at any time," and as such, Richmond "will have the sympathy of the whole country."[18] The Capitol disaster seemed to annihilate "time and space . . . the sad affair seems to be at our own doorsteps."[19] From Washington, DC, even some Republican newspapers with both white and Black readers also declared their sympathy for Richmonders. Frederick Douglass's *New Era* reported, "every heart has been moved with sorrow, sympathy and condolence over the Richmond calamity," while the *Daily National Republican* stated, "the sad news fell with great force in this community and cast a deep gloom over all classes."[20]

Not all northerners showed sympathy and support for distressed Richmonders. For instance, one publication that was extremely critical of Richmond was the Republican *Chicago Tribune*, a publication that advocated the abolition of slavery prior to the Civil War, supported Abraham Lincoln in his bid for the presidency in 1860, and continued to push a Radical Republican agenda during and after the war. After the Capitol disaster, one writer for the paper observed that "from the battle of Bull Run . . . until the present accident, there has been one long succession of horrors enacted in [Richmond's] streets."[21] Referencing Richmond's ties to slavery, the journalist noted that the Capitol was the site at which "the whole collective genius of slavery met by choice, to make bondage, enforced labor, and the withholding of wages, righteous by statute . . . [in the] most Christian and most democratic century, they set the figures of the dial back."[22] The writer foresaw a bleak future for the city following the disaster, remarking, "The dusk of poverty lies over Richmond."[23] Despite the criticism, another *Tribune* writer reported that the Illinois Constitutional Convention, which was currently meeting in Springfield, "adopted resolutions of regret at the calamity," which demonstrated that "Virginians have friends where once they had enemies."[24] Coverage of the Richmond disasters in the *Chicago Tribune* demonstrated that not all northerners felt equally sympathetic, particularly writers for and readers of a staunchly Republican paper.

According to much of the coverage in the northern press, the Capitol disaster also precipitated a reestablishment of peace and order in the city. While there is a chance that Richmonders did manage to overcome their significant differences—or at least set them aside for a short period following the calamities—that seems unlikely given the volatile state of local government, most clearly evidenced by the conflict over the mayor's election and the fact that the city had two competing police forces at the time of the disasters. War weariness likely colored reports from Richmond. Most white northerners, including newspaper editors and writers, were less concerned with the postwar circumstances of Black southerners than they were with ensuring that the tumultuous Civil War years were over.

In their accounts of the Richmond disasters, sympathetic northerners characterized death as an equalizer that afflicted Richmonders regardless of class, race, or political affiliation. According to the *Boston Daily Advertiser*, "the falling floor at Richmond, hurling black and white, rich and poor, those of both parties and of every rank, together into the jaws of death, has for a time obliterated the prejudices even of that proud city."[25] The calamity spared "neither Rebel nor Radical," and "beyond a general expression of disgust at local politics, nobody was brutal enough to rejoice over any partisan enemy's affliction."[26] The day after the Capitol disaster, Governor Gilbert Walker gave a speech to a crowd of Richmonders assembled in front of the ruined Capitol. Those in attendance came from "all classes of the community and every shade of public opinion" and included white and Black members of both houses of

Virginia's legislature.[27] Both police forces of Chahoon and Ellyson, the candidates vying for the mayoralty, met and adopted resolutions in memory of those who died, and both forces agreed to participate in the funeral ceremonies. "All late political feeling is forgotten," proclaimed the Little Rock, Arkansas–based *Morning Republican.*[28]

Another way in which the press depicted Richmonders as coming together was over the death of James Bland, a Black state senator for Charlotte and Prince Edward Counties who died at the Capitol.[29] Bland was an accomplished politician: he had participated in all of the Republican conventions since 1867; was a member of the Constitutional Convention, where he served on the Committee on the Elective Franchise; and a large majority elected him to serve in the state senate. In 1869, Bland worked as assistant assessor of internal revenue for Charlotte and Appomattox Counties—the first Black person appointed to such a position.[30]

Bland's friends unsurprisingly penned laudatory obituaries that depicted him as a competent and successful politician, but their references to his goals for Black equality were surprising given his comparatively moderate views, which included support for the reenfranchisement of former Confederates and, not long before his death, the possibility of his abandoning the Republicans for the more conservative Democratic Party. In Frederick Douglass's *New Era*, J. Wesley Cromwell reported that Bland's death was untimely for the African American community, as Bland worked toward elevating "his race to a possession of all the privileges and immunities enjoyed by other citizens."[31] He predicted Bland's death would have detrimental effects on the "just, peaceable, and permanent reconstruction" of Virginia.[32] P. J. Mintor, another friend, appreciated Bland's "noble traits of character," which included his "pure motives" and earnestness.[33] Noting his relative youth and potential for future political success, Mintor reported, "With the broad field of life before him, I could almost see the very paths of glory and fame which fortune had laid out for his feet to tread in."[34] Mintor noted, "Virginia has lost a good citizen and the race a promising son."[35] Given that readers of *New Era* were primarily Black, it is to be expected that obituaries written by friends of Bland highlighted his significant accomplishments.

Yet, because of his relative conservatism, white publications' coverage of Bland ranged from fleeting mentions of his death to praise of his accomplishments and characterizing him as a model Black American.[36] The *Little Rock (AR) Morning Republican* and *Evansville (IN) Journal* perfunctorily reported that both Black and white members of the legislature mourned Bland's death, including Conservatives, and that white and Black senators followed his hearse at his funeral.[37] The *Baltimore Sun* noted that Bland "is spoken of as the ablest of the colored delegation in the Virginia Legislature. . . . He was withal of a liberal and conciliatory temper."[38] A tribute to Bland printed in the *Richmond Enquirer,* a conservative-leaning local publication, said Bland's death resulted in "universal regret"—further cementing the idea that both Blacks and whites mourned him—and condescendingly opined, "no one of pure African blood on this continent has gained so enviable a reputation."[39] The reporter for the *Enquirer* believed Bland to be a "superior" member of the Black race because he was smart, displayed fine manners, and had a promising future. It is evident that northern editors held the same beliefs as their southern counterparts as to what made Black men respectable in the eyes of whites.

In addition to reporting the news from Richmond, the northern press also played a crucial role in inspiring disaster relief efforts. Publicizing disasters and spurring relief efforts had been common practice for newspapers since the late eighteenth century. Monetary support from places outside of Richmond—particularly northern cities—was imperative to recovery efforts, as the South was still recovering from the economic, political, and social devastation following the war and established government sources of relief did not exist at the time. Newspapers throughout the United States reported the disasters, which led people to organize fund drives and other relief projects, and then press reports detailed such efforts.

Sometimes Richmond residents used the press to appeal directly to northerners for help. Elizabeth Van Lew, a Richmonder famous for spying for the Union during the Civil War, was perhaps uniquely well-positioned to appeal to northerners for financial aid after the Capitol disaster.[40] The *Chicago Tribune* published one of her pleas, in which she noted that such aid would "[invoke] the spirit of charity in its broadest sense, without any reference to political or social diversities."[41] She made a similar appeal to Daniel Fox, the mayor of Philadelphia. Van Lew pledged "the money shall be used only for the needy and destitute sufferers."[42] While the *Chicago Tribune* never reported whether Chicagoans sent Van Lew money directly, Mayor Fox sent her a $1,000 check.

Van Lew went to the newly formed Committee on Visitation and Relief in Richmond, presented them with the check, and said that if the board members accepted it, they must also allow her to serve on the committee. The *Petersburg Index* reported that the "gentlemen of the Board told her they would accept the money, but could not agree to the other part of the proposition, as it would not be proper to place a lady on the committee."[43] Instead of capitulating to their demands, Van Lew created her own committee that included "gentlemen of both political parties" who would "distribute under her supervision such funds as she may receive" from her appeals to northerners.[44] While this episode not only demonstrates the generosity of one local northern political leader, it is also an example of how one woman used her own fundraising efforts to wield power and how residents of Richmond, as in other American communities, formed committees to dispense aid locally in the aftermath of disasters.

The local press was instrumental in orchestrating disaster relief efforts for Richmond in other cities. In Boston, journalists and newspaper editors urged residents to turn their sympathy into "a material form which will indicate [their] sincerity and result in providing the means for relieving much of the distress" following the Capitol collapse.[45] They expressed their hopes that Bostonians of all classes would assist in raising a significant sum so as to reflect well on the city. Residents formed a relief committee, and on May 28 the *Boston Daily Advertiser* reported that the fund had already raised approximately $20,000.[46] Ultimately, Bostonians contributed much to the relief of the Richmond sufferers; by August they had contributed about $78,000 to the relief fund for the Capitol disaster.[47]

In other northern cities, individuals led efforts to solicit and receive monetary donations for the victims of the Capitol disaster. In Chicago, W. A. Butters—a former resident of Richmond—sent a check to assist suffering families in the former Confederate capital. The editor of the *Richmond Dispatch* thanked Butters and said that while the suffering was worse than anticipated, Richmonders were "much consoled by the kind feeling of our Northern friends."[48] The editor's words demonstrated that Richmonders gratefully acknowledged and needed the help of northern benefactors to fully recover from the disaster and likely inspired Butters to appeal to Chicagoans and residents of the Midwest for contributions.[49] On May 9, the paper reported that the amount

Chicagoans contributed was "thus far under $4,000," indicating that the amount of funds collected, while substantial, was lower than anticipated.[50]

Perhaps because of the extensive business ties between Richmond and New York and the fact that Confederate sympathies had been widespread in this northern metropolis, New York–based businesses, individuals, and the local government were generous in their financial assistance to Virginians after the Capitol collapse and flood. A. W. Dunn sent a $100 check from the Brooklyn Life Insurance Company to Virginia governor Gilbert Walker, writing, "As a Virginian and a soldier in the late war, I am proud to represent a Northern Company whose officers have the sympathy to contribute to the relief" of those who were "rendered destitute" by the Capitol disaster.[51] The bank of Glendenning, Davis, and Amory sent $100 to Walker.[52] An unnamed New York merchant authorized Richmond authorities to "draw on him for $1,000," while both James T. Soutter and Benjamin Hart each sent $1,000 to the governor.[53] On May 2, the New York Chamber of Commerce met and appointed a committee of fifteen men to solicit funds for relief. By May 8, the committee had raised $8,000.[54] New Yorkers continued to financially assist Virginians after the flood that affected the entire state in the fall of 1870. The New York Gold Exchange sent $2,000; the Stock Exchange donated $25,000; and the Gold Exchange raised $10,000.[55]

In Philadelphia, ordinary Philadelphians, businesses, and the mayor provided material and fiscal assistance to Richmonders. After the Capitol disaster, a former Richmond resident who had since moved to Philadelphia sent crutches and "a quantity of excellent port wine" to the sufferers.[56] Tobacco merchants Woodward, Bro. and Company contributed $75 to the Richmond relief fund. On April 30, the mayor of Philadelphia established a relief fund, and by May 11 Philadelphians had donated $5,589.75.[57] After the flood, Philadelphians again offered their assistance to Virginians. Jacob Semon donated $50, Thomas A. Scott offered $1,000, and the president of the Philadelphia Board of Bankers gave $250 to Governor Walker.[58]

Baltimoreans' efforts to raise money took several different forms. In Baltimore, former residents of Richmond banded together and created a committee of twelve who collected contributions—either monetary relief or supplies—and sent them to the mayor of Richmond. One columnist thought that Baltimoreans would respond "warmly and liberally, to the voice of suffering and distress" and "not be behind in the good work."[59] One committee member collected $3,000, and residents seemed to be attuned to the great need of Richmonders.[60] Churches took up collections; the Firemen's Insurance Company appropriated $1,000 for the relief fund; and the Right Worthy Grand Lodge of Maryland of the Independent Order of Odd Fellows collected $100.[61] Newspaper editors established subscription lists: the day the editor of the *American* opened their list he received $1,000 in donations; the *Gazette* was similarly successful, raising $1,157.50 in one day.[62] Two men collected $1,450 from merchants in Baltimore in the course of a morning.[63] J. H. Adams and Wilson Brunslee both sent $100 checks to Governor Walker.[64]

In a few northern cities, theaters held benefit performances to raise money for the Richmond sufferers, but these were not always successful ventures. At the Chestnut Street Theatre in Philadelphia, no one seemed to have attended the benefit performance, and the *Philadelphia Press* opined that it was "difficult to understand why our charitable public, which is usually so liberal, failed to respond."[65] In Baltimore, the Front Street Theater and the Holliday Street Theatres held benefit performances. The latter raised $3,470.[66] On May 7 in Washington, Laura Keene reprised her starring role in *Our American Cousin*—the play in which Keene herself was performing when John Wilkes Booth assassinated Lincoln—in a benefit show, and proceeds went to the Richmond sufferers. *Our American Cousin* was a popular play throughout the latter half of the nineteenth century, but given its historical significance, it might have been surprising to contemporary audiences that the theater company found that particular play to be an appropriate fundraiser for inhabitants of the former capital of the Confederacy. Additionally, the Choral Society of Washington held a benefit performance at Lincoln Hall. The musicians volunteered to perform, a large crowd attended, and the organizers were able to donate $700 to Richmond.[67]

While the press played a significant role in enticing Americans to contribute to the relief of Richmonders, there was scant reporting on how those donations were disbursed, the extent to which such aid was helpful, or how the racialized politics of the period might have affected the distribution of relief. Following the Capitol calamity, the *Petersburg Index* reported that the Richmond relief committee had received $5,000 in donations from northerners but gave no indication as to when or how that money would be distributed.[68] Richmond businesses recovered quickly after the flood, so a relief committee was not established to provide aid to those who required it. As fires in urban areas were a common occurrence in the nineteenth century, newspaper coverage of the Spotswood Hotel fire was brief and relatively perfunctory in comparison to the Capitol disaster, and there was no report of a relief committee being formed to assist those sufferers.

The Capitol disaster, James River flood, and Spotswood Hotel fire devastated Richmond in 1870. White northerners were instrumental in helping Richmonders recover from these calamities. White northern publications facilitated and reported outpourings of sympathy and feelings of goodwill toward their southern counterparts. Northerners—including local politicians, businessmen, and ordinary individuals—provided monetary support to aid the suffering, formed relief committees, and put on theatrical performances. Ultimately, the feelings of sympathy and goodwill and the provision of fiscal relief demonstrate that these disasters were the prelude to the full-fledged reconciliation between northern and southern whites that would take place in the decade to come. White Americans erased their former sectional divisions, embracing white supremacy and annihilating the political, legal, social, and economic advances Black Americans made during Reconstruction.[69]

NOTES

1. Megan Kate Nelson, *Ruin Nation: Destruction and the American Civil War* (Athens: University of Georgia Press, 2012).

2. Louis Moore, "The Elusive Center: Virginia Politics and the General Assembly, 1869–1871," *Virginia Magazine of History and Biography* 103, no. 2 (1995): 221; George Chahoon, Mayor 1870, p. 1, George Chahoon Papers, 1870–1934, Library of Virginia, Richmond; Edwin J. Slipek, "The Mayor Time Forgot," *Style Weekly*, November 2, 2005, 2; Richard G. Lowe, "Virginia's Reconstruction Convention: General Schofield Rates the Delegates," *Virginia Magazine of History and Biography* 80, no. 3 (1972): 341–42.

3. George Chahoon, Mayor 1870, pp. 2–3, George Chahoon Papers; "The Frightful Calamity at Richmond, Va.," *Frank Leslie's Illustrated Newspaper*, May 14, 1870; "The Richmond Calamity," *Harper's Weekly*, May 14, 1870; "The Scene Outside," *Petersburg (VA) Index*, April 29, 1870. The

number of dead and wounded varies according to source: *Frank Leslie's Illustrated Newspaper* reported that more than 60 people died and 125 were wounded; *A Full Account of the Great Calamity* (Richmond: Ellyson & Taylor, 1870) reported 58 people died; Edwin J. Slipek wrote that 62 people died and 310 were wounded.

4. According to the US Bureau of Labor Statistics Consumer Price Index Inflation Calculator, $500,000 in January 1913 (the earliest date available) equals $13,514,132.65 in March 2021 (see https://www.bls.gov/data/inflation_calculator.htm).

5. "Destructive Flood in Virginia," *Alexandria (VA) Gazette*, October 1, 1870; "The Rising James," *Richmond Daily Dispatch*, October 1, 1870; "The Great Flood," *Alexandria (VA) Gazette*, October 3, 1870; "The Flood Fallen," *Richmond Daily Dispatch*, October 4, 1870; "The Losses by the Flood," *Alexandria (VA) Gazette*, October 4, 1870. In the *Alexandria (VA) Gazette*'s column "The Great Flood," the writer noted the following about Rocketts residents: "The families who had removed in the houses, hoping the flood would subside, commenced crying from the upper windows for help. Boats were brought and they were saved. . . . Two hundred families in that portion of the city are houseless to-night." There was no indication, in the *Alexandria Gazette* or elsewhere, about who rescued those families.

6. "Disastrous Fires," *Alexandria (VA) Gazette*, December 27, 1870; "Our Last Disaster," *Richmond Daily Dispatch*, December 28, 1870. My search of *Acts Passed at a General Assembly of the Commonwealth of Virginia* for the years 1870/71 and 1871/72 provided no evidence of such a bill being passed (see https://catalog.hathitrust.org/Record/008885427).

7. Gareth Davies "The Emergence of a National Politics of Disaster, 1865–1900," *Journal of Policy History* 26, no. 3 (2014): 307. Davies argues that during the postwar period a "*national* politics of disaster" emerges, "with Washington far more to the fore than had been the case in the earlier nineteenth century," but this period of disaster relief "cannot reasonably be seen as having clearly anticipated the modern world of federal disaster politics" (306).

8. Cynthia A. Kierner, *Inventing Disaster: The Culture of Calamity from the Jamestown Colony to the Johnstown Flood* (Chapel Hill: University of North Carolina Press, 2019), 201, 206–7.

9. "The City. The Great Disaster. Action of the Chamber of Commerce. Proceedings of Meetings, Etc.," *Richmond Daily Whig*, April 30, 1870.

10. See "About *New Era* (Washington, DC) 1870–1870," and "About *New National Era* (Washington, DC) 1870–1874," on the Library of Congress website *Chronicling America*: https://chroniclingamerica.loc.gov/lccn/sn84024437/ and http://chroniclingamerica.loc.gov/lccn/sn84026753/.

11. David Blight, *Race and Reunion: The Civil War in American Memory* (Cambridge, MA: Harvard University Press, 2001). Blight argues that race was "the central problem in how Americans made choices to remember and forget their Civil War" and posits reconciliation between the North and South did not begin until the mid-1870s (98).

12. Edward Blum, *Reforging the White Republic: Race, Religion, and American Nationalism, 1865–1898* (Baton Rouge: Louisiana State University Press, 2005), 147.

13. [No title], *Burlington (VT) Weekly Free Press*, October 14, 1870.

14. [No title], *Burlington (VT) Weekly Free Press*, October 14, 1870.

15. "Flood and Drought," *Baltimore Sun*, October 5, 1870.

16. "The Richmond Disaster," *New York Herald*, December 26, 1870.

17. "Killed by Careless Architects," *New York Times*, April 30, 1870.

18. [No title], *Boston Daily Advertiser*, April 30, 1870.

19. [No title], *Boston Daily Advertiser*, April 30, 1870.

20. "The Richmond Calamity," *New Era*, May 5, 1870; "Death—Stroke! Heartrending Accident in Richmond. The City of Terrible Calamities. Men Crush and Crippled. A Horrible Scene of Suffering," *Daily National Republican*, April 28, 1870.

21. "Washington. The Great Accident at Richmond. Scenes and Reminiscences. A Talk with a Spectator," *Chicago Tribune*, May 2, 1870.

22. "Washington. The Great Accident at Richmond. Scenes and Reminiscences. A Talk with a Spectator," *Chicago Tribune*, May 2, 1870.

23. "Washington. The Great Accident at Richmond. Scenes and Reminiscences. A Talk with a Spectator," *Chicago Tribune*, May 2, 1870.

24. "Evening Funerals," *Chicago Tribune*, April 29, 1870; "Virginia. Condition of the Survivors of the Richmond Calamity—Testimonials from Abroad—The Decision in the Mayoralty Case in Favor of Ellyson," *Chicago Tribune*, April 30, 1870.

25. [No title], *Boston Daily Advertiser*, April 30, 1870.

26. "Washington. The Great Accident at Richmond. Scenes and Reminiscences. A Talk with a Spectator," *Chicago Tribune*, May 2, 1870.

27. "The Richmond Calamity. Expression of Grief and Sympathy with the Sufferers. A Vast Meeting in Front of the Fatal Edifice. A Succession of Funeral Processions to the Churches. A Day of Humiliation and Prayer Appointed. Descriptions of the Fearful Fall by Survivors," *New York Times*, April 29, 1870.

28. "Latest by Telegraph! Midnight Dispatch. The Richmond Disaster! Over 60 Persons Killed, and 200 Wounded," *Little Rock (AR) Morning Republican*, April 29, 1870.

29. Ervin L. Jordan Jr., "J. W. D. Bland," *Encyclopedia Virginia*, last modified November 2, 2015, http://www.encyclopediavirginia.org/Bland_James_William_D_1844-1870#start_entry.

30. J. Wesley Cromwell, "The Late Senator Bland," *New Era*, May 12, 1870.

31. J. Wesley Cromwell, "The Late Senator Bland," *New Era*, May 12, 1870.

32. J. Wesley Cromwell, "The Late Senator Bland," *New Era*, May 12, 1870.

33. P. J. Mintor, "The Late Senator Bland," *New Era*, May 12, 1870.

34. P. J. Mintor, "The Late Senator Bland," *New Era*, May 12, 1870.

35. P. J. Mintor, "The Late Senator Bland," *New Era*, May 12, 1870.

36. Brent Tarter, *The Grandees of Government: The Origins and Persistence of Undemocratic Politics in Virginia* (Charlottesville: University of Virginia Press, 2013). Bland promoted reconciliation and economic recovery, and did not seek to disenfranchise former Confederates. Conservatives endorsed this agenda (238).

37. "Latest by Telegraph! Midnight Dispatch. The Richmond Disaster! Over 60 Persons Killed, and 200 Wounded," *Little Rock (AR) Morning Republican*, April 29, 1870; "The Richmond Disaster—Greatest Calamity since Burning of Theatre in 1811—Richmond in Mourning—Funerals of the Victims—Reported Death of Ex-Governor Wells a Mistake—He is Expected to Recover," *Evansville (IN) Journal*, April 29, 1870.

38. "The Calamity at Richmond, VA," *Baltimore Sun*, April 28, 1870.

39. "Personal," *Chicago Tribune*, May 6, 1870; [No title], *Manchester (VT) Journal*, May 10, 1870.

40. Elizabeth R. Varon, *Southern Lady, Yankee Spy: The True Story of Elizabeth Van Lew, a Union Agent in the Heart of the Confederacy* (New York: Oxford University Press, 2003).

41. "Virginia. An Appeal for Aid to the Sufferers by the Late Richmond Calamity," *Chicago Tribune*, May 14, 1870.

42. "The Late Calamity in Richmond," *Petersburg (VA) Index*, May 3, 1870.

43. "Our Richmond Letter. The Approaching Election—Dismissal of Wrenn for Shooting Ben Scott—Crutches for the Capitol Sufferers—Condition of the Wounded—The Fatal List—The Funeral of W. C. Dunham—The Architects and the Capitol—Additional Wounded—The Philadelphia Subscription—Other Items," *Petersburg (VA) Index*, May 3, 1870.

44. "Our Richmond Letter. The Approaching Election—Dismissal of Wrenn for Shooting Ben Scott—Crutches for the Capitol Sufferers—Condition of the Wounded—The Fatal List—The Funeral of W. C. Dunham—The Architects and the Capitol—Additional Wounded—The Philadelphia Subscription—Other Items," *Petersburg (VA) Index*, May 3, 1870.

45. [No title], *Boston Daily Advertiser*, May 17, 1870.

46. "In General," *Boston Daily Advertiser*, May 28, 1870.

47. [No title], *Boston Daily Advertiser*, August 1, 1870.

48. "Railroad Election—Sympathy for the Richmond Sufferers," *Chicago Tribune*, April 30, 1870; "The Richmond Disaster," *Chicago Tribune*, May 1, 1870.

49. Wm A. Butters, "The Richmond Disaster," *Chicago Tribune*, May 4, 1870.

50. "Aid for the Richmond Sufferers," *Chicago Tribune*, May 9, 1870.

51. Secretary of the Commonwealth Executive Papers, Library of Virginia, Richmond.

52. "The City. The Great Disaster. Action of the Chamber of Commerce. Proceedings of Meetings, Etc.," *Richmond Daily Whig*, April 30, 1870.

53. "Latest from Richmond. Funerals of the Victims—Houses in Mourning—Flags at Half Mast—Sympathy from Abroad—Illinois Sympathy—Business Suspended in Fredericksburg, &c," *Petersburg (VA) Index*, April 29, 1870; Secretary of the Commonwealth Executive Papers, Library of Virginia, Richmond; "The Great Calamity. Large Meetings of Citizens on the Capitol Square. Proceedings of Other Meetings. Additional Facts and Incidents," *Richmond Daily Whig*, April 29, 1870.

54. "Our Richmond Letter," *Petersburg (VA) Index*, May 2, 1870; "Relief for the Richmond Sufferers," *Petersburg (VA) Index*, May 2, 1870; "The News," *Petersburg (VA) Index*, May 3, 1870; "Meeting in New York to Aid the Sufferers by the Richmond Calamity," *Petersburg (VA) Index*, May 3, 1870; "New York Subscription for the Richmond Sufferers," *Petersburg (VA) Index*, May 10, 1870.

55. Executive Papers of Governor Walker, box 1, folder 3, Library of Virginia, Richmond; "New York Subscriptions to the Virginia Sufferers," *Virginia Herald*, October 13, 1870.

56. "Our Richmond Letter. The Approaching Election—Dismissal of Wrenn for Shooting Ben Scott—Crutches for the Capitol Sufferers—Condition of the Wounded—The Fatal List—The Funeral of W. C. Dunham—The Architects and the Capitol—Additional Wounded—The Phila-

delphia Subscription—Other Items," *Petersburg (VA) Index*, May 3, 1870; "Substantial Sympathy," *Virginia Herald*, May 5, 1870.

57. "Our Richmond Letter. The Approaching Election—Dismissal of Wrenn for Shooting Ben Scott—Crutches for the Capitol Sufferers—Condition of the Wounded—The Fatal List—The Funeral of W. C. Dunham—The Architects and the Capitol—Additional Wounded—The Philadelphia Subscription—Other Items," *Petersburg (VA) Index*, May 3, 1870; "The City. The Great Disaster. Action of the Chamber of Commerce. Proceedings of Meetings, Etc.," *Richmond Daily Whig*, April 30, 1870; "[Second Dispatch] Funerals—Offers of Assistance from Abroad—Mayor Chahoon Yields up the Position to Mayor Ellyson, &c.," *Petersburg (VA) Index*, April 30, 1870; "Relief for the Richmond Sufferers," *Petersburg (VA) Index*, May 11, 1870; [No title], *Virginia Herald*, May 16, 1870.

58. Executive Papers of Governor Walker, box 1, folder 3, Library of Virginia, Richmond.

59. "The Richmond Calamity. Meeting of Native Virginians and other Citizens of Baltimore—Aid and Sympathy for the Sufferers—Action of the Board of Trade and Corn Exchange—City Council Resolutions," *Baltimore Sun*, May 3, 1870; "Meeting in Behalf of the Richmond Sufferers," *Baltimore Sun*, May 2, 1870.

60. "Local Matters," *Baltimore Sun*, May 5, 1870.

61. "Local Matters," *Baltimore Sun*, May 5, 1870; "Local Matters," *Baltimore Sun*, May 4, 1870; [No title], *Virginia Herald*, May 12, 1870; "Letter from Richmond," *Baltimore Sun*, May 11, 1870.

62. "The Late Calamity in Richmond," *Petersburg (VA) Index*, May 3, 1870; "The Richmond Calamity. Facts, Incidents, &c.," *Petersburg (VA) Index*, May 4, 1870.

63. "Richmond Calamity! Maryland Joins Virginia in Humiliation and Prayer. Sympathy and Liberality of Baltimore," *Petersburg (VA) Index*, May 4, 1870.

64. Secretary of the Commonwealth Executive Papers, Library of Virginia, Richmond.

65. "Philadelphia and the Richmond Calamity," *Virginia Herald*, May 9, 1870.

66. "Local Matters," *Baltimore Sun*, May 5, 1870; "Local Matters," *Baltimore Sun*, May 4, 1870; [No title], *Virginia Herald*, May 12, 1870.

67. [No title], *Daily National Republican*, May 7, 1870; "An Appeal for the Richmond Sufferers," *Daily National Republican*, May 2, 1870; "The Choral Society's Concert," *Daily National Republican*, May 5, 1870; "The Choral Society's Concert," *Daily National Republican*, May 9, 1870.

68. "From Richmond. Circular from the Distributing Committee," *Petersburg (VA) Index*, May 6, 1870.

69. David Blight, *Race and Reunion: The Civil War in American Memory* (Cambridge, MA: Harvard University Press, 2001); Jane Dailey, *Before Jim Crow: The Politics of Race in Postemancipation Virginia* (Chapel Hill: University of North Carolina Press, 2000).

THE SLOW DISASTER OF JIM CROW AND LOWCOUNTRY HURRICANES, 1893–1940

CAROLINE GREGO

Hurricanes ushered Jim Crow into the Lowcountry of South Carolina. Three particularly dangerous hurricane seasons of 1893, 1911, and 1940 collided with the political, social, and economic currents of the Lowcountry, a region along the southeastern coast of the United States where waterways and marshes separate the coastal plain from a matrix of islands. Through these three storm seasons, a clearer picture emerges of how the most emblematic natural phenomenon of the southeastern coast—the hurricane—coalesced with a regime of racial injustice to reveal the environmental valences of Jim Crow.

This intense series of hurricanes, which began with the deadliest recorded hurricane in South Carolina history in August 1893, battered the sea-edge of the region, inundating ocean-facing barrier islands, swamping salt marshes, reshaping beaches, and washing salt far up intertidal waterways. These hurricanes killed thousands of Black residents of the coast, who had been held there by slavery and, after emancipation, sustained there by their hard-won traditions of landownership, political participation, and cultural practices. The hurricanes reduced tens of thousands to a level of penury in which the white elite rejoiced, as a renewed means of control over the Black residents' land and labor. The hurricanes served as a push factor during the Great Migration to expel African Americans from the region. Just as this spate of storms moved ocean and land to sculpt the coast, so did they change the lives of the African Americans who had made the Lowcountry their homeland.

At the same time, the story of these three hurricane seasons is not just one of decline and failure. The history and the environment of the Lowcountry preclude easy categorization. Black residents of the region, first as African captives forcibly brought to the Lowcountry as enslaved workers and later as free people who advocated for education, landownership, and property rights, developed understandings of the region that brought together the environmental and historical forces that shaped their varied experiences there. African Americans, throughout the troubled decades from 1893 to 1940, persisted in cultivating their own narratives, which interwove their centuries-long struggles for political rights, economic autonomy, and cultural and spiritual meaning. These narratives, while sometimes tragic, defy any sense of historical inevitability.

The hurricanes of 1893, 1911, and 1940, in their destruction to coastal agriculture and industry, damaged the white elite's prospects for economic ascendance, even as they worked to wield the storms' damage against African Americans to secure their own power and wealth. The hurricanes inflicted grievous wounds upon African Americans in the Lowcountry with their high death tolls and damage to property, while Black sea islanders regrouped after these storms to bolster their communities against white-led assaults. This contentious discourse between white and Black residents of the Lowcountry will be explored through the archive that Jim Crow–era hurricanes left behind. Within transcribed interviews, fictionalized accounts, newspaper articles, organizational documents, and personal letters, we can locate not only white South Carolinians' hunger for Jim Crow but also African Americans' efforts after the storms to nurture their communities and to object to racial injustice under a new legally prescribed system of debasement and segregation. A full account of Jim Crow in the Lowcountry cannot be written without hurricanes, and the hurricanes of those years cannot be understood without facing up to Jim Crow. The hurricanes and Jim Crow comprised cycles of destruction and violence that were simultaneously chillingly familiar and profoundly disruptive to Black residents of the Lowcountry, even as they resisted capitulating to them. The hurricanes and Jim Crow were intertwined disasters that unfurled over the course of decades.

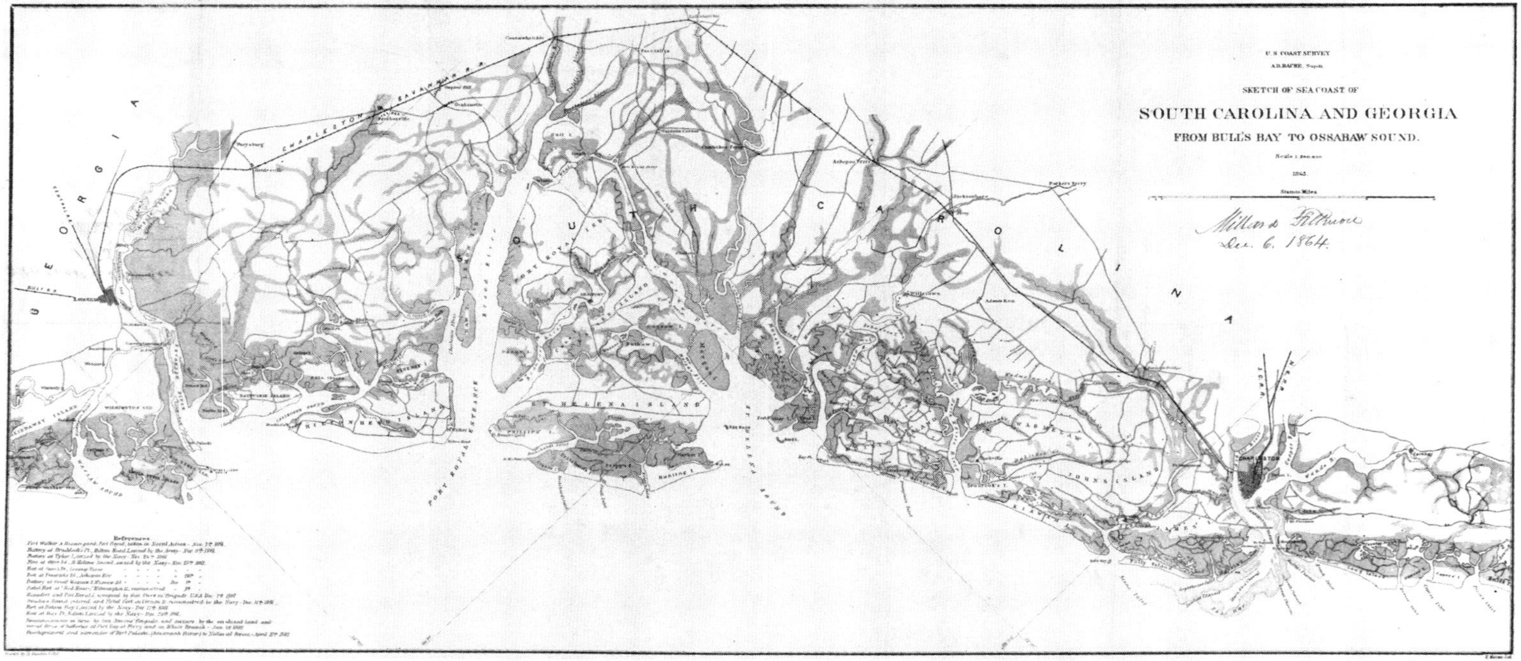

"Map of the Lowcountry, from Bull's Bay to Ossabaw Sound." This map from 1863, though slightly dated to the events at hand, is nonetheless one of the finest maps of the Lowcountry: the cartographer shaded in the salt marshes and floodplains and thus showcased the coastal areas most vulnerable to hurricane storm surges and damage. Library of Congress, Prints & Photographs Division.

* * *

The deadliest hurricane in recorded South Carolina history struck on the full-moon night of August 27, 1893.[1] Called the Great Sea Island Storm, the hurricane dragged a massive storm surge ashore, inundating entire sea islands and pouring ten to twenty feet of water into the streets of Beaufort and Charleston. At least 1,500 people died that night—though some speculated that as many as 5,000 may have perished in the roiling waters. All but a couple dozen were African American. Black residents of the region, 30,000 of whom had lost their houses and crops, struggled through their grief to organize relief efforts that would prioritize rebuilding their communities and used the American Red Cross's substantial offer of rations, tools, and supplies to do so. Some white residents, mostly Republicans in Beaufort, mobilized to assist the Red Cross's emissaries in their work and to collaborate with Black sea islanders in a rare moment of interracial solidarity. Most white South Carolinians, from Lowcountry landowners and politicians to local officials, however, cast doubt upon the degree of African American suffering, planted rumors that Black sea islanders sought to manipulate the relief efforts to spur a second Reconstruction, and plotted to obstruct the Red Cross recovery.

Without the Red Cross's presence in the Lowcountry from September 1893 to July 1894, the winter of 1893–94 would have likely been much deadlier—no less because, in mid-October 1893, a second hurricane, smaller than its August predecessor but quite powerful, swept ashore on the coast north of Charleston, killing a couple dozen people and wrecking homesteads and farms around Georgetown and along the Grand Strand.[2] The Great Sea Island Storm and its October sibling, known as the Flagg Storm for the name of the white family who perished in it, had a powerful impact upon the material conditions of the coast, wrecking thousands of homes, rice fields, the booming phosphate industry, the cotton crop, and the waterfronts of Beaufort and Charleston.

The hurricane season of 1893 thus signaled a turning point in Lowcountry history, and it loomed large in how Lowcountry residents shaped their understanding of the early years of Jim Crow. White South Carolinians in the wake of the hurricanes shaped narratives for Jim Crow, in which Black sea islanders had died because they were not fit to live independently of white rule and the white elite deserved to reclaim the ground lost since emancipation. At the same time, Black residents of the Lowcountry crafted their own counternarratives that gave voice to the exploitation and extraction that they and their ancestors had faced.

Two accounts demonstrate how white and Black South Carolinians viewed the inextricability of the so-called natural world from their own histories and ideologies. Elisabeth Carpenter Satterthwait, a white woman who married into a wealthy South Carolina family in 1884, wrote a novel in which the Great Sea Island Storm is the dramatic climax of the tale, *A Son of the Carolinas: A Story of the Hurricane upon the Sea Islands.*[3] In Satterthwait's loosely autobiographical romance novel, published in 1898, the hurricane triggers the reconciliation and reunion between the North and the South. Pauline Pyatt, a young Black woman living in Murrell's Inlet, recounted a parable of the Flagg Storm for a Works Progress Administration (WPA) interviewer in 1937 that wove together elements from an African-descended spiritual world, the history of slavery, and the present of Jim Crow.[4]

Elisabeth Carpenter Satterthwait's maudlin late-Victorian novel brought the Great Sea Island Storm firmly into the realm of white supremacist literature that smoothed over the grave wounds of slavery and the white North's postwar betrayal of the formerly enslaved. This popular genre of the late nineteenth and early twentieth centuries brought reconciliation between the former Confederate South and the northern United States into the realm of popular cultural consumption. In Satterthwait's novel, a well-educated, quiet young Quaker woman named Margaret Hallowell arrives at the gracious sea island home of Rachel Dare, a middle-aged matron who took in sickly white northerners. (Satterthwait was herself a Quaker.) Margaret's sufficiently amorphous illness quickly dissipated so she could enjoy the balmy air and sea views, as well as the attentions of Dare's dashing nephew Robert Dare.[5] Satterthwait interspersed the romance with picaresque vignettes of the island's African American residents, who served merely as stereotyped, crudely rendered props for the lives of well-to-do whites.[6] Against this backdrop, Robert and Margaret fell in love, and Satterthwait saw their attachment as a proper reunion of the United States and the former Confederacy: "There they sat, hand in hand. He a sunny-haired South Carolinian, an Episcopalian and a Democrat, whose father had shouldered a musket and gone to battle against the very principles her father had been taught to uphold. She was a dark-haired New Yorker, a staunch Republican, a Friend, and shuddered at the very thought of war. And yet God had drawn their hearts together."[7] However, the young lovers' union could never be so simple as that. An anonymous letter informed Margaret that Robert fathered a child with a Black woman who had lived on his parents' land, and the distraught maiden fled to her uncle's home in Philadelphia before Robert could speak with her.

But then the Great Sea Island Storm struck. Satterthwait described the storm in accurate detail, likely due to either firsthand knowledge or from carefully studying friends' or newspaper reports from her husband's home state. Robert soldiered heroically into the storm to help others to safety and was listed as missing within newspaper reports, which made their way north to the heartbroken Margaret. Ashamed that she had "judged [him] by the past," Margaret found it within her heart to forgive him. Practically in the same moment, a letter arrived from a Black maid named Betty, who confessed that a romantic rival with Margaret for Robert's heart bribed her to write the damning epistle and that the terror of the storm as a manifestation of God's wrath compelled her to admit the truth. In fact, it was Robert's father who had impregnated the young woman, and Robert covered for his father to spare his dying mother. The letter also revealed that Robert was alive and well.

Margaret returned to South Carolina, and there the two were wedded after granting each other "forgiveness born of the love that had drawn them together" that had "passed through trials and come forth triumphant."[8] Satterthwait rendered the hurricane and the Civil War as two faces of the same coin. In Satterthwait's narrative, the tribulations of the Civil War and the hurricane inflicted injuries, but none so grave that could not be healed with love and a mutual pledge to a greater good. Wealthy white southerners' refusal to relinquish slavery and their precipitation of the Civil War were only a "misunderstanding." Slavery was "the sin of the dead" that served only "to make trouble for the living," for both Robert and Margaret were too young to have any real memory of that era.[9] It would do no good to assign blame to the descendants of the enslavers or to obsess over the brutality of the Civil War, and Satterthwait deliberately, blissfully concealed the widespread racist violence and oppression that had plagued Black southerners in the decades since. Satterthwait used the deadly hurricane as an opportunity to peddle this shallow narrative of reconciliation between white southerners and the United States, which ignored the ongoing violence and legacies of slavery in the South and cast aside the struggles of Black southerners as irrelevant.

In contrast, Pauline Pyatt's parable laid bare how the wounds that slavery inflicted were kept raw by Jim Crow. African Americans experienced the 1893 hurricane season as yet another trial to endure. The hurricanes comprised part of the grinding cycles of crisis in which reliance on one's immediate community constituted the primary avenues of recourse for African Americans living in the Lowcountry. At the same time, Pyatt's account of the October hurricane, which she relayed during a visit from a white woman writer collecting interviews for the Federal Writers' Project, rejected that dispossession, disenfranchisement, and suffering were their fate.[10] She suggested a world off-kilter from God's plan, which was centered on justice rather than the racial oppression and economic marginalization that African Americans faced. It did not have to be this way. Indeed, the brutality that white South Carolinians enacted against African Americans proved that the world was horrifically askew. Pyatt's account was also infused with the mystical, though its magical qualities mingled with the sticky web of historical context. Elements of this story may be outside reality, but its message revealed the political realities of Black life under Jim Crow and warned against the deadly consequences of white hubris. And it all began with a mermaid.

Pyatt blamed Dr. Joshua John Ward Flagg, a rich white landowner whom she called "Dr. Ward" to distinguish him from his father, and a blue-tailed mermaid for the Flagg Storm.[11] Then thirty-three years old, he had lured the mermaid into a bathing house on the beach, using bread as bait—because as Pyatt asserted, "They sho' eat bread." The mermaid had a forked tail like a shark, blue scales like a catfish, and appeared as "pretty a white woman as you ever lay your eye on."[12] After her capture, it rained for thirty days, and Dr. Flagg's "storm ball"—a rudimentary barometer—kept ebbing and rising unsteadily. Pyatt's kin cautioned Dr. Flagg that the storm ball's unsettled movements, the biblical rainfall, and the imprisoned mermaid indicated that a hurricane would hit the coast, for Dr. Flagg had violated the mermaid's free rein. But Dr. Flagg did not listen. Instead, he dismissed with curses the African Americans who took those signs as warning. As the story goes, the mermaid's anger and sorrow summoned a hurricane to liberate her. The southern coast was collateral damage for her freedom, and Dr. Flagg's father, mother, and several other family members were the price that Dr. Flagg paid for his transgression.

But to dismiss Pyatt's story as superstition or a quaint yarn does Pyatt a disservice. This seemingly fanciful story seethed with racial tension. Dr. Flagg and Pyatt coexisted in a strange space: Dr. Flagg was born in 1860, too young to be an enslaver, and Pyatt was too young to have been enslaved, but he benefited from his family's wealth, and she knew her family's past. Besides, Dr. Flagg's ancestors had not just been any southern enslavers. Dr. Flagg's grandfather, Joshua John Ward, enslaved thousands of people near Murrell's Inlet. He died in 1853 with 1,092 enslaved workers deeded to his descendants in his will, and in 1860, his estate's human property had increased to 1,130 souls.[13] Pyatt's family was almost certainly among those he and his descendants enslaved.

It is not clear how, precisely, the story of the mermaid emerged. Pyatt recollected that when Dr. Flagg spoke about the hurricane, "he eye get full o'water."[14] His attitude was one of grief for the loss of his family. But he did not mention the mermaid, nor the role that African Americans ascribed to him in capturing the mermaid who drew the hurricane to the coast. The story most likely originated with Pyatt's community—no less because the mermaid resembles tales of the cymbee. These spirits inhabited Lowcountry springs, pools, and waterways, the African American cousin of West African nature spirits called "simbi," who existed within the cosmology of Kongo-speaking peoples. The mermaid of Pyatt's story, with its Kongo origins, is a keen reminder of how she and her ancestors adapted cultural, linguistic, agricultural, and religious practices from their West African heritage and their new Lowcountry roots into an identity known as Gullah-Geechee. The cymbee, like the mermaid, were powerful spirits who adopted a variety of forms and inspired a fearful respect in African-descended peoples. Just as the mermaid conjured a hurricane to rescue her and wreak vengeance on the man who trapped her, the violation of a cymbee's autonomy and power could incur terrible retribution.[15]

Pyatt may have been placing the hurricane and Dr. Flagg's role in it, as a selfish, profane man eager to trap a creature that should have been left alone, within a larger framework of how she and other African Americans understood white supremacy in the post–Civil War South. Dr. Flagg's birth at the dawn of secession did not exempt him from culpability for slavery's lingering cruelties. After all, Dr. Flagg's place in the southern hierarchy was assured. The fall of the Confederacy did not see a parallel permanent collapse of the white landed gentry: Dr. Flagg, a wealthy landowner in his own right, was proof of that. He may have lost his family in the hurricane, but he maintained his land and his class status. Viewed this way, Pyatt's parable becomes subversive, suggesting that Pyatt understood all too well how she lived within a new iteration of the old white supremacy that had underlain slavery.

Pyatt used the story of the mermaid and the hurricane as part of a tradition of resistance among southern African Americans, in which they used folkloric stories to deflect the watchful eye of white supremacy. With a measure of distance from a certain kind of "reality," Pauline could express how her kin really felt about white southerners, especially those in positions of power over them. Pyatt only lightly concealed her discontent with the racial hierarchy to which she had been chained her whole life. She found wealthy white southerners at fault for all sorts of maladies. She knew whom to blame not only for the storm but for the political, economic, and social conditions that worsened its impacts. It was impossible to separate the history from the hurricane.

Hurricanes battered the Lowcountry relentlessly in the years that followed, in September 1896, August 1898, September 1904 and 1906, and October 1910.[16] Worst of all was a hurricane that struck on August 28, 1911. Rossa Cooley, the principal of the historic African American Penn School on St. Helena Island, wrote of the "terrible storm," which blew down houses, flooded three-quarters of the island, and destroyed "crops which had promised to surpass" those of the several previous years.[17] Along the coast, a journalist reported, "the entire long cotton crop has been destroyed, and the loss to the short cotton crop will approximate 75 per cent."[18] The damage to the crops, houses, and businesses seemed to nearly equal that of the Great Sea Island Storm, though the loss of life was much less: twenty people died in the Lowcountry.[19] But as always, the death toll was never limited to the hours of the hurricane alone. On islands like St. Helena, an "unusually severe and wet winter followed," which resulted in "suffering and death among the old people and very young children."[20]

The unusual frequency of hurricanes heightened the political and economic turmoil of South Carolina in the 1890s and early 1900s. A constitutional convention passed South Carolina's "Jim Crow" constitution in 1895, and the five African American delegates from Beaufort County walked out of the convention and refused to sign the disenfranchising document.[21] White South Carolinians strove to institute Jim Crow, an array of laws enforcing segregation and African American disenfranchisement, economic practices that relegated African Americans to exploitative labor arrangements including sharecropping and low wages, and violence against African Americans that ranged from lynching to incarceration to everyday humiliations. After hurricanes, Jim Crow also meant an intentional lack of institutional and governmental support for African Americans in need.

Economic attrition also impacted the Lowcountry. The hurricanes irrevocably broke the banks of the region's rice fields, sounding "the death-knell of rice planting in South Carolina."[22] White landowners who had comforted themselves on the land they inherited from their enslaver ancestors began to sell their properties to wealthy northerners as winter retreats. African Americans had relied both on their small farms' ability to produce a few bales of cotton and subsistence crops and on a meager wage from work in rice fields, the phosphate mines, and other small industries—but those opportunities, and the thin topsoil on their farms, washed away in the storm surges that roiled the coast.[23] While the white elite consolidated political power over the region, turned to their Charleston townhouses, and profited from the healthy prices they netted for family properties, African Americans in the Lowcountry had no such recourse.[24]

A key to white supremacy was apathy in the face of disaster, which prolonged suffering and worsened poverty among African Americans. White residents of the Lowcountry therefore took deliberate steps to block outside aid. They retained such resentment against the Red Cross's work after the 1893 hurricane, which supported Black autonomy, that, as one resident of St. Helena Island wrote, "A great deal has been said against the aid coming from [the Red Cross]," so much so that the organization "was turned back" when it offered aid.[25] A. C. Kaufman, the acting president of the South Carolina State Board of the American Red Cross, clarified that no aid was forthcoming because the mayor and city council of Charleston rejected the organization's overture of assistance.[26] Local journalists also dismissed need for relief, arguing: "Abundant work for the negroes is at hand. Planters still have their acres. . . . Nobody will starve in a land of plenty."[27] Even the white leadership of Beaufort was compelled to admit that, despite some initial questions as to whether "the Red Cross could not do something for colored sufferers of the storm," they would not formally request aid because the twenty dead were so few in comparison to the August 1893 storm.[28] What African Americans may have wanted did not matter, and the Red Cross may not have wished to wade into another fraught recovery effort against the explicit, immediate disapproval of the white Lowcountry elite.

African Americans who lost everything in the 1911 hurricane could only rely upon their communities. Between 1893 and 1911, even once-sympathetic white Beaufortonians had largely turned on their African American neighbors, emboldened and habituated to the practices of white supremacy that enriched them and dulled what impulses to interracial cohesion that they may have once felt. Satterthwait's prediction of the Great Sea Island Storm's social impact—that it could cultivate unity among whites, at the expense of African Americans—seemed to have come true. In response, Black farmers on St. Helena Island banded together to advocate for help from the Penn School. In the absence of state assistance and in the presence of Jim Crow, African Americans on St. Helena fomented solidarity and turned to each other to survive.

In 1911, as it had been since its founding in 1862 during the Port Royal Experiment, the Penn School's management was mostly white, and its donors were wealthy white northerners—but despite the paternalism that characterized its upper levels, it was an institution still answerable to and in service of Black residents of St. Helena Island.[29] There, multiple generations of African American families received an education; African Americans could find employment as teachers, administrators, and groundskeepers; and instruction focused on inculcating practical lessons in agriculture, health care, and homemaking. The Penn School also became a nexus of community organizing and mutual aid. The Eustis Memorial Fund, established in 1911 after the storm

The Penn School, pictured here, has been a nexus of African American organizing, community activities, and mutual aid on St. Helena Island, South Carolina, since it was founded during the Port Royal Experiment in 1862—including after many hurricanes. Library of Congress, Prints & Photographs Division.

prompted pressure from Black residents on St. Helena, provided "weekly rations in small amounts" to 277 people, wages to 200 people in exchange for "sewing," "work on the roads, the wood-pile and on the new Industrial Building," and lumber for 234 houses to be rebuilt and repaired.[30] Even with that aid, twice the number of patients than usual required medical care, which kept a Penn School graduate who had recently completed his course of study at the Medical Department of Howard University in Washington, DC, very busy.[31]

Black sea islanders recognized from long experience that sustained mutual aid would be necessary as a bulwark against any more coming storms—so African Americans on St. Helena Island also organized the St. Helena Cooperative Society, which operated from 1912 well into the 1920s. J. E. Blanton, the African American superintendent of the Penn School, selected eight community members to form a committee to oversee the establishment and operation of the Society.[32] The committee borrowed $1,000 from the School Relief

Fund, agreed to a reasonable rate of interest, and set a membership fee at one dollar per annum. Blanton wrote that the Society also functioned through "buying supplies in bulk, giving the small farmer low prices, also loaning . . . to the farmers on short terms notes" to carry them through crises.[33] The most common bulk purchase seems to have been, strategically, fertilizers and seed, valuable and expensive goods that were a frequent entry point into debt owed to merchants and wealthy landowners for Black southerners. The members of the society also sold their crops collectively.[34] The Society nurtured solidarity and lent support to small African American freeholders in an era when Black independence was a threat to the status quo of sharecropping and white-controlled land.

Environmental and political circumstances only worsened in the years after the Society's founding. The arrival of the boll weevil to Beaufort County in the growing season of 1919 crashed cotton production.[35] This catastrophe shifted the needs of Black farmers on St. Helena Island. The amount that the Black farmers of St. Helena Island requested in loans unsurprisingly increased between its first year in 1912 and the early 1920s, and what they asked for in the loan applications changed as well. Requests for loans increased from fifteen and twenty dollars, more common in 1915 to 1916, to twenty-five and fifty-dollar notes a few years later—a shift from roughly four hundred to eight hundred dollars in contemporary currency.[36]

Amid the boll weevil years, as the small beetle devastated southern cotton crops, most farmers borrowed money to raise sweet potatoes and peanuts rather than cotton, with a significant interest in rice and corn. The year with the highest average requested loan, at forty-three dollars (or about six hundred dollars in 2022 USD), was 1920, right as cotton production in Beaufort County dove to zero. They were able to do so because of the Society's funds.[37] The Black farmers on St. Helena Island had founded the Society as a form of long-term assistance after the 1911 hurricane because they knew that the Jim Crow state would engineer their suffering and then watch them starve. Without the Red Cross, there was no other disaster relief alternative available, so Black sea islanders had to make their own.

Since 1893, the white elite had learned to cut African Americans off from any avenue of outside assistance. Stripped of white allies (no matter how imperfect), surrounded by an ossifying Jim Crow regime, battered by hurricanes, Black residents of the Lowcountry were supposed to sell their farms to white landowners and submit to white employers as permanent sharecroppers or wage laborers. The white elite may have lost their position as rice and sea island cotton "planters" and lost control of the coastal environment—but they had nonetheless consolidated white supremacy statewide and watched as thousands of African Americans drowned and lost their homes during a generation of hurricanes. It should be no surprise that Pauline Pyatt felt no more kindly toward the descendants of enslavers than enslavers themselves.

Through the 1920s and 1930s, Black sea islanders diverged on their approach to the economic, political, and environmental conditions that constricted their choices and held them down. Many stayed on their land. Many left for northern cities like New York and Philadelphia. The reduction in population was immense. St. Helena Island, for example, lost 45 of its population from 1900 to 1928.[38] African Americans cited the exploitative practices of Jim Crow that left them "disgusted and discouraged," eager "to better [their] condition," and desperate to escape "the white people of the South" who "[kept] their feet on the necks of the blacks."[39] Though the ocean and atmosphere quieted in those decades, with only two minor hurricanes making landfall in the Lowcountry between 1916 and 1940, the hurricanes had done their damage, and Jim Crow carried their mantle forward. Many African Americans pointed to that generation of hurricanes as doing irrevocable damage to their livelihoods and as combining with the dire economic and political situation in the Lowcountry to push them out.[40] Viola Ware, a young Black woman who moved to New York to work as a maid in 1899, recalled that "the situation on [St. Helena] Island that caused me to leave more than anything else was the 1893 storm."[41]

A hurricane in 1940—the last before the stirrings of the civil rights movement, before the second Great Migration, before bridges spanned intertidal waterways to connect remote sea islands to the mainland—prompted Black sea islanders to reflect on the decades since 1893. "The storm came to me on Wassaw Island early Sunday morning August 11th," sixteen-year-old Harriet Taylor wrote.[42] As "the tide began rising" with the "waves . . . climbing and dashing to the shores," Harriet was separated from her family as they ran for higher ground and "was caught up by the tide from two sides." In what must have been a terrifying experience, she nearly drowned; "the water got deeper and deeper," she recalled, "and began going over my head and everytime I tried to breathe the water went down my throat. I couldn't move until the wind stopped blowing a little." When the storm was over, Harriet said, "the Island looked very strange," for "some of the houses were crushed, some leaning and tops were blown off," and worst of all, the hurricane had swept away nearly everything that her family owned and covered the rest in a thick sludge. Harriet was a student at the Penn School, where Rossa Cooley still served as principal. Cooley had given the students an assignment to write about the hurricane that struck the sea islands in August 1940.

A new generation reflected on the impact of a hurricane and looked to their elders to contextualize their experiences. The letters, written by African American students aged eight to nineteen, show at once how much and how little had changed since 1893. A few letters referred to warnings that no one could have received in the late 1800s and early 1900s. Virginia Wrotten, fourteen years old, "heard on the radio that the storm was coming," and Lillian Fields wrote that "about nine-thirty a white man came and told the people in our community to cut lo[o]se all the cattle and horses that were tied, and gather all boats, because a storm is on its way, and may be on the Island about noon."[43] Agnes Robinson, age seventeen, described how she and her sister turned on their radio "to see if we could hear if a storm was really coming. The radio announced that a hurricane was coming on the southern coast making 95 miles an hour."[44]

In many ways, African Americans relied on the same means of survival that they always had: the students wrote of strategies very similar to those that sea islanders deployed in 1893, like boring holes in the floor so that the floodwaters would weigh the house down rather than sweep it out to sea, or fleeing for higher ground with their families.[45] Lillian described how the chimney in her house crumbled under the pressure of the wind and water, so her family had to "struggle through the wind and rain" for a nearby schoolhouse, where they found other refugees and "cuddled together on benches until morning."[46] Outside, Eleanor noted, "watermelons, boats, tomato crates, chickens, turkeys and parts of people's houses went floating by."[47]

When the children emerged from their shelters, Lillian thought that "it looked like 'No Man's Land.' Trees fell, houses were all tattered and torn up. All the crops were washed away."[48] Rosa, a ten-year-old, told her teacher that "the storm was terrible and I was frightened to death."[49] Eleanor spent the day fearing that she might die, writing that "it was so fierce that people could only wait for the worst to happen."[50] Helen Grant, nine years old, wrote to her teacher that "If that storm had come in that night most all of us would be drowned."[51] Perhaps some of Helen's relatives told her about the 1893 hurricane, when the storm did come in at night, and drowned thousands more than the ten people killed during the 1940 hurricane.[52] Willie Smalls mentioned the 1893 hurricane directly: "The people on my plantation said that this storm was worse than the 1893 storm, only the tide didn't come as high."[53]

The Great Sea Island Storm of 1893 was on everyone's mind in 1940. One white St. Helena Island resident, F. R. Ford, wrote to a friend that, except for one of the ten, "all the other deaths were on Eustis plantation where so many were drowned in '93. The old timers say that this storm was the equal of '93 in all respects, except the tide didn't cover the land as long. My observation is that it was more destructive than the 1911 storm."[54] Ford, traveling to Beaufort, found "the waterfront completely demolished," as it had been during the 1893 hurricane. Another St. Helena Islander, writing to the absent Principal Cooley, also characterized the hurricane as "the worse [*sic*] storm that has been here since 1893."[55] Philip Seabrook, an attendant at the Penn School, told Principal Cooley that "many of the farmers have lost their poultry, crops and livestock as a result of the high tide. This indicate*[s]* a great reduction in food supply for the Islanders."[56] Even fifty years later, the loss of a single year's crop could seriously harm Black sea islanders' chance at survival.

There to assist the sea islands, like in 1893, was the Red Cross. The trustees of the Penn School had sent a request for Red Cross aid to bypass hostile local and state politicians, outlining the "need for immediate and generous aid."[57] Two days after the storm blew through the sea islands, the organization had set up "a depot with food, and clothing" on St. Helena Island.[58] The Red Cross, one of its representatives telegraphed to a Penn School employee, had a "Disaster Unit" in the area ready to provide "food, clothing and shelter rehabilitation assistance in repairing and rebuilding homes, replacing necessary household furniture or any other disaster-caused needs beyond the ability of the families."[59] The Red Cross had returned to the field of recovery on the sea islands, made possible by local action on the part of the Penn School trustees, perhaps by faded memories among white politicians of 1893, and by an expansion of federal government intervention in southern states under the New Deal. Laborers from the Works Progress Administration, for example, joined the Red Cross and assisted in cleaning up roads and filling in a washed-out causeway.[60] While the State of South Carolina yielded no assistance, the Red Cross asserted its presence in the region once more, and new glimmers of federal assistance appeared in the form of the WPA workers—despite the efforts of white southern lawmakers to bar Black southerners from most New Deal benefits.

But any recovery was marginal. The African American population of the region had been hollowed out by the last few decades, and the communities that remained had done so despite the material conditions around them. Beaufort County, for example, saw its population move from a post–Civil War high in 1900 of 35,495 people to a low of 21,815 in 1930. Some already knew what was coming: one young Black man predicted that "thirty years from now, [St. Helena] Island will be owned by the white people."[61] Bridges, corporate developers, and tourists would, within the next generation, carry a new era of dispossession and white domination into the Lowcountry. The hurricanes and Jim Crow had paved the way.

For Black residents of the Lowcountry during the early decades of Jim Crow, the concept of "recovery" rang hollow. Jim Crow *was* the disaster. After all, the white elite stonewalled recovery in any meaningful sense, because true recovery for African Americans would entail the destruction of white supremacy—even when that meant an end to their status as rice and cotton "planters," and a shift in land use and to new economies. African Americans sought reprieve in their communities, on their small farms, and in the stories that they told to explain how the natural world, spiritual forces, and the political realm fit together. Hurricanes could introduce new elements of tragedy and loss into their lives, and the generations of storms from 1893 to 1940 were a crushing weight upon many of them.

For all the theorizing that academics do now over the meaning of disaster, Pauline Pyatt in 1937 demonstrated that she and her kin understood what it meant with the clarity of lived experience and lifelong knowledge. Even if hurricanes inflicted some wounds upon the white elite, they inevitably retrenched to their wealth and power. African Americans in the Jim Crow Lowcountry saw these circulations of wind and power for what they were: ongoing and mutually reinforcing.

NOTES

1. The title's use of "Slow Disaster" is attributed to Scott Gabriel Knowles, who developed this concept. See his website, Slow Disaster, https://slowdisaster.com. The hurricane is described in a few studies. The most recent and thorough is Caroline Grego, *Hurricane Jim Crow: How the Great Sea Island Storm of 1893 Shaped the Lowcountry South* (Chapel Hill: University of North Carolina, 2022). Older ones include William and Fran Marscher, *The Great Sea Island Storm of 1893* (Macon, GA: Mercer University, 2004); and Lawrence Sanders Rowland and Stephen R. Wise, *Bridging the Sea Islands' Past and Present, 1893–2006: The History of Beaufort County, South Carolina* (Columbia: University of South Carolina Press, 2015). For academic treatments, see Robert D. Bland, "'A Grim Memorial of Its Thorough Work of Devastation and Desolation': Race and Memory in the Aftermath of the 1893 Great Sea Island Storm," *Journal of the Gilded Age and Progressive Era* 17 (2018): 297–316; Marian Moser Jones, *The American Red Cross from Clara Barton to the New Deal* (Baltimore: Johns Hopkins University Press, 2013); and Caroline Grego, "Black Autonomy, Red Cross Recovery, and White Backlash after the Great Sea Island Storm of 1893," *Journal of Southern History* 85, no. 4 (2019): 803–40.

2. For more on the Flagg Storm, see Walter J. Fraser Jr., *Lowcountry Hurricanes: Three Centuries of Storms at Sea and Ashore* (Athens, GA: Wormsloe, 2009), 184–87.

3. Elisabeth Carpenter Satterthwait, *A Son of the Carolinas: A Story of the Hurricane upon the Islands* (Philadelphia: Henry Althemes, 1898), 191, online at the Hathi Trust, https://babel.hathitrust.org/cgi/pt?id=wu.89098007586;view=1up;seq=7.

4. Pauline Pyatt's story, in "Uncle Ben Horry," interview by Mrs. Genvieve W. Chandler, Murrell's Inlet, Georgetown County, in *Federal Writers' Project: Slave Narrative Project*, vol. 14, *South Carolina*, pt. 2, Eddington-Hunter, 1936, Manuscript/Mixed Material, 298–322, https://www.loc.gov/item/mesn142/.

5. Satterthwait, *A Son of the Carolinas*, 19.

6. Satterthwait, *A Son of the Carolinas*, 5.

7. Satterthwait, *A Son of the Carolinas*, 191.

8. Satterthwait, *A Son of the Carolinas*, 268.

9. Satterthwait, *A Son of the Carolinas*, 263.

10. The writer Genevieve Chandler is the subject of astute analysis in the introduction by Kincaid Mills, Genevieve C. Peterkin, and Aaron McCollough, eds., *Coming Through: Voices of a South Carolina Gullah Community from WPA Oral Histories, Collected by Genevieve W. Chandler* (Columbia: University of South Carolina Press, 2008), xvii—xli.

11. Mermaid stories appear elsewhere in Gullah folklore. Ras Michael Brown explores the mermaid in in *African-Atlantic Cultures and the South Carolina Lowcountry* (Cambridge: Cambridge University Press, 2012). He traces connections between mermaids and West African spirits from Kongo-speaking peoples called "simbi," which became "cymbee" in the Lowcountry. Brown includes Pauline's story on page 257.

12. Pyatt's story, in "Uncle Ben Horry," 320.

13. From the 1850 and 1860 US slave schedules; data obtained from the Historical US Census Browser.

14. Pyatt's story, in "Uncle Ben Horry," 322.

15. See Brown, *African-Atlantic Cultures*, chap. 6, "Mermaid Histories and Power," for a discussion of the simbi/cymbee as "avengers of the enslaved" (253).

16. See Fraser, *Lowcountry Hurricanes*, 164–210; and Wise, *Bridging the Sea Islands' Past and Present, 1893–2006*, 184.

17. Rossa Cooley, "Report of the Principal," in *Annual Report of the Penn Normal, Industrial and Agricultural School of St. Helena Island Beaufort County South Carolina, Forty-Ninth Year, 1910–1911*, p. 13, folder 446, "Annual Reports (Bound Volume), 1908–1912," box 51, "Annual Reports, 1890–1907—Annual Reports, 1908–1912," #3615, Penn School Papers, University of North Carolina at Chapel Hill.

18. "Ruin Was Wrought on the Sea Islands," *Charleston (SC) News and Courier*, August 31, 1911, 1.

19. See Fraser, *Lowcountry Hurricanes*, appendix, "Chronology of Lowcountry Hurricanes."

20. Cooley, "Report of the Principal," 13.

21. For a description of those events, see Michael Perman, *Struggle for Mastery: Disenfranchisement in the South, 1888–1908* (Chapel Hill: University of North Carolina, 2001), chap. 5, "South Carolina, 1895."

22. Duncan Clinch Heyward, *Seed from Madagascar* (Chapel Hill: University of North Carolina, 1937), 245.

23. The conclusion of many scholars; but see Wise, *Bridging the Sea Islands' Past and Present, 1893–2006*, 184; and Clyde Vernon Kiser, *Sea Island to City: A Study of St. Helena Islanders in Harlem and Other Urban Centers* (1932; New York: Atheneum, 1969).

24. See Mart Stewart, *"What Nature Suffers to Groe": Life, Labor, and Landscape on the Georgia Coast, 1680–1920* (Athens: University of Georgia, 1996), 237.

25. Unnamed author on Penn School letterhead, October 12, 1911, folder 1, box 32, 1863–1911, Penn School Papers.

26. "Mr. Kaufman Finds That Society's Aid Is Not Required," *Charleston (SC) News and Courier*, September 5, 1911, 3.

27. "The Sea Islands and the Storm," *Charleston (SC) News and Courier*, August 31, 1911, 4.

28. "Mr. Kaufman Finds That Society's Aid Is Not Required."

29. For a history of the school, see Orville Vernon Burton and Wilbur Cross, *Penn Center: A History Preserved* (Athens: University of Georgia, 2014).

30. *Annual Report of the Penn School, 1910–1911*, 15.

31. *Annual Report of the Penn School, 1910–1911*, 14.

32. A letter from L. Hollingsworth Wood to Rossa B. Cooley describes some recommendations for the formation of the Society, October 31, 1911, folder 5, "1910–1911," box (folders 1–5), 1863–1911, Penn School Papers.

33. See the Penn School Papers, 1915–1923, on reel 2, at the South Caroliniana Library, which contains applications to the Society scattered throughout the microfilm.

34. Barnwell, "Annual Report, 1920," on the page labeled "COOPERATIVE BUYING AND SELLING ORGANIZATIONS."

35. See the map on page 7 of Mary Fletcher Stackhouse's master's thesis at the South Caroliniana Library, "*A Study of the Boll Weevil Conditions of South Carolina*" (University of South Carolina, June 1922); and for the cotton numbers, see Kiser, *Sea Island to City*, 110.

36. Calculated using the US Bureau of Labor Statistics online calculator at https://www.bls.gov/data/inflation_calculator.htm.

37. C. L. Baxter, "Annual Report, 1922," on roll 9, p. 4, "Annual Narrative & Statistical Reports," mentions the abandonment of cotton and the eagerness of farmers for other crops.

38. Kiser, *Sea Island to City*, 104.

39. All quotes from Kiser, *Sea Island to City*, in this order: 121, 120, 135.

40. Kiser, *Sea Island to City*, 100.

41. Kiser, *Sea Island to City*, 99.

42. Harriet Taylor to Miss Cooley and Miss House, September 24, 1940, folder 97-A "Student Letters, Sept. 1940," box 12, "August 1939–October 1940," Penn School Papers. All of the following citations pertaining to children's letters are in that folder.

43. Virginia Wrotten to Miss Cooley, September 24, 1940; Lillian Fields, "The Storm of Nineteen Hundred Forty," September 25, 1940.

44. Agnes Robinson, "My Experience during the Storm of August 1940," September 27, 1940

45. Rosa Bell Gadson to Miss House, September 24, 1940; Julia Sherman to Miss House, September 23, 1940; Ella Mae Chaplin to Miss House, September 25, 1940.

46. Fields, "The Storm of Nineteen Hundred Forty."

47. Eleanor Barnwell to Principal Cooley, September 26, 1940.

48. Fields, "The Storm of Nineteen Hundred Forty."

49. Gadson to Miss House, September 24, 1940.

50. Barnwell to Principal Cooley.

51. Helen Grant to Miss House, September 24, 1940.

52. Death count mentioned in F. R. Ford to Dr. Arthur W. Elting, August 13, 1940, 2, folder 95c.

53. Willie Smalls to Principal Cooley, September 26, 1940, folder 97-A.

54. F. R. Ford to Dr. Arthur W. Elting, August 13, 1940, p. 1, folder 95c.

55. B. L. Boyd to Principal Cooley, August 13, 1940, p. 1.

56. Philip Seabrook to Principal Cooley, August 13, 1940, p. 1, folder 96.

57. Francis R. Cope, Jr. to Rossa B. Cooley, August 17, 1940, which included a copy of the telegram sent to the National Red Cross, folder 96, box 12, August 1939–October 1940, Penn School.

58. Ford to Elting, August 13, 1940, p. 2.

59. Francis R. Cope Jr. to Rossa Cooley, August 17, 1940, p. 1.

60. J. P. King to Rossa Cooley, August 14, 1940, p. 1.

61. Kiser, *Sea Island to City*, 135.

LAYERS OF VIOLENCE

SLOW DISASTER IN THE CANCER ALLEY ANTHROPOCENE

SCOTT GABRIEL KNOWLES AND ASHLEY ROGERS

The history of southern Louisiana as a disastrous land has been often marked out by individual storms or by conventional dividing lines such as the opening of colonial settlement, the founding of the United States, the Louisiana Purchase, or the end of the Civil War. This essay takes a different approach, applying an Anthropocenic frame of analysis and thus taking a much longer historical view as a method by which to bring socioeconomic systems that were previously analyzed separately into the same narrative of disaster history: intensive, extractive plantation capitalism; unfree and unhealthy labor; structured violence and inequality. From the slave system of the eighteenth and nineteenth centuries, to the Jim Crow system of racialized labor after 1865, to the industrial system of petrochemical production in the current era, the flow from system to system forms a remarkable, disastrous, slow, Anthropocenic continuity.

On January 8, 1811, the largest uprising of enslaved people in the history of the United States began on plantations in St. John the Baptist Parish, on the so-called German Coast of southern Louisiana. The path of the freedom fighters wound through the wealthiest sugar production lands of the United States and, given the intensity of its slave labor system, also one of the most violent byways in America. Inspired by the revolution in Haiti, which overthrew the slave power in 1804, almost five hundred enslaved persons participated, before being met and defeated by federal forces and local militia two days later, near present-day Kenner, Louisiana. Over the course of the revolt, two white men were killed. Estimates vary, but at least thirty of the enslaved individuals involved were killed in the attack, and another forty-five were executed by January 15, with about two dozen more captured and executed later. Severed heads of those executed were exhibited in New Orleans and along the Mississippi River levee, where, according to historian Leon Waters, "a display of heads placed on spikes stretched over 60 miles."[1]

In a place like Louisiana, disasters are known only through the deep and ongoing entanglements of the land, agriculture, humans and animals, water, race, labor, and violence.[2] In this sense, the German Coast Uprising was a disaster that overwhelmed the local population—enslaved and free—as surely as any hurricane or epidemic. For enslaved people, enslavers' brutal killing of dozens of revolutionaries was not only a personal tragedy for family and community members, but seeing their decomposing heads on pikes daily was an ongoing trauma. Not only a source of immense pain for loved ones, the display of bodies was itself an act of suppression. Each body part served as a warning, reinforcing the disastrous outcome for attempting revolution. Commodore John Shaw, a leader of the military suppression force, reflected the position of the local white population when he wrote that had "not the most prompt and energetic measures been thus taken, the whole coast would have exhibited a general sense of devastation; every description of property would have been consumed; and the country laid waste."[3]

Control of the disaster's aftermath was crucial to enslavers fearful of new uprisings, and also to territorial governor William Charles Cole Claiborne, who was eager to play down the event and maintain public confidence in the slavery system in a territory poised to enter the Union as a state in 1812.[4] Money and power were on the line. In an early form of disaster relief, the Louisiana territorial government appropriated emergency funds to compensate planters three hundred dollars for every enslaved worker killed in the uprising.[5] From the enslavers' perspective, the disaster recovery succeeded. Enslaved people remained in bondage, illiterate, and isolated. They were not invited to write the history of their attempt at liberation; the full impact of this revolt—on a micro or macro level—is unknowable when the story is maintained only through a lens of white supremacy. And so the German Coast Uprising remained mostly a local disaster story, fading into near legend over time. It has not been widely taught or studied and barely exists in American history textbooks.[6]

In November 2019, the German Coast Uprising came to life once again, this time orchestrated as a meticulous reenactment performance by artist and activist Dread Scott. Marching through the same byways, the performers and their audience found themselves in a radically altered landscape from the one their predecessors had passed through two centuries earlier. Equally wealthy and productive, more so even, the sugar plantations had in the intervening years been replaced—on the same lands—with the facilities of the world's most profitable petrochemical companies.[7] The violence of enslavement is now gone, replaced by a different type of violence, rank environmental racism causing a public health crisis of epic proportions. Factories built on former

Dread Scott, *Slave Rebellion Reenactment, Still #1*, 2019. This reenactment of the German Coast Uprising proceeded twenty-four miles over two days through the River Parishes and culminated in New Orleans. It was timed to mark the four-hundredth anniversary of the arrival of enslaved Africans in North America. Image reproduced courtesy of Dread Scott.

plantations spew and spill toxins on the homes, schools, and bodies of the predominantly African American residents who live there today. In this "Cancer Alley," the descendants of the German Coast Uprising suffer the highest cancer rates in the United States.

Ending their performance in New Orleans's Congo Square, the reenactors read the names of their historical antecedents and hosted a celebration of music and dance, "transforming the violent suppression of the freedom fighters into a joyous recognition of their courage and achievement."[8] Here was a long-deferred recognition, name by name, for the martyrs amid the slow disaster of American slavery. Dread Scott's goal in this confrontational history action was clear: bring out of obscurity "the most radical vision of freedom on the North American continent" in a performance that would "highlight the disquieting continuity between Louisiana's plantation past and its petrochemical present."[9] These seemingly disparate disasters in one parish—a slave revolt, sugar plantation violence, high cancer rates, environmental racism, and then high rates of COVID-19 infection—are in reality plot points on a continuous line.

This disastrous historical continuity is not unlike that one finds in a core sample, a geological extraction that one of the oil companies so active in Louisiana might perform to deduce the viability of drilling in a new location. Layer upon layer, the geological record explains to the trained eye the environmental history of a place. Individual bands in the record tell the tale of disastrous times, of volcanic eruptions and floods. But characterizing the geological history of a place involves much more than isolating a single disastrous event. Longer-term phenomena such as global cooling or warming, atmospheric changes, sea level rise and fall, mark out the longer spans in which species thrive and evolve, or decline and face extinction. Geoscientists now believe we have entered a new geologic era, an Anthropocene era, defined as a period in Earth's history when human industrial activity is for the first time the most dominant force shaping the planet. The Anthropocene is known in the atmosphere, for example, by the increasing concentration of carbon dioxide. The "human signatures" in the rock record include radioactive particles, plastics, and chemicals associated with intensive industrial agriculture and petrochemical production.

Historical scale is crucial to discussions of the Anthropocene, and so too is an understanding of the ways that disasters like a slave revolt, or Hurricane

Katrina, or the *Deepwater Horizon* oil spill gather and hoard attention to the exclusion of slower and steadier processes of predatory capitalism, and of violence.[10] By reaching across a longer span than usual in the social history of a place like the Mississippi Delta, we embrace an "Anthropocenic" point of view. Strong economic and political forces are at work in the portrayal of a slave revolt or an oil spill as an aberrant event, unconnected from the normal flow of time, somehow separate and operating according to the logics of chance, or acts of God, or the madness of men. The idea of a "slow disaster" is a way to expose and explore the political investments in disaster event thinking, an invitation to analyze disasters not as disconnected, unwanted events but as long-term processes linked across time.

Framing a disaster as a single event leaves us with a comfortable certainty. We can sort the victims and the survivors. We can count and index. But what about the uncertainties: the long-standing mental and physical health impacts of racial violence and segregation, or the mental distress of living in an unhealthy land, with an unreliable government? These, too, are attendant features of a slow disaster. The obscured layers, the stories untold, are themselves extensions of the violence that gave enslaved persons a subhuman status—a violence that today leaves the residents of Cancer Alley unsure of their own exposures to cancer-causing toxins. These unknowns are not usually accidents but reflect a deeper commitment to the ignorance of certain facts appropriate to a power structure that might, for example, count a Black American as three-fifths of a person; or one that might frame a cancer diagnosis as indicative only of a person's lifestyle choices, and not their environment.[11]

Not only were enslavers successful in their suppression of the German Coast Uprising and its history, but they thrived in the decades that followed. After the United States' participation in the international slave trade came to an end in 1808, Louisiana became the heart of the domestic slave trade in the Deep South. Investors and speculators streamed south, buying land to plant with cotton and sugarcane, and enslaved people to work it. Propped up by a tariff on foreign sugar, Louisiana sugar planters expanded their holdings of land that hugged the river between Baton Rouge and New Orleans. They grew phenomenally wealthy from the labor of the enslaved, building ever more opulent and fantastical plantation homes to showcase their success. These homes sat facing the levee one after another, each one with attendant, orderly rows of cabins for the enslaved people and vast fields tended by hundreds of enslaved workers.

Louisiana's sugar plantations had some of the highest populations of enslaved people anywhere in the country. The stately homes, set off by lush gardens and stands of oak and pecan trees, obscured and softened the industrial-scale labor and violence in the fields and sugar factories. Mark Twain famously wrote in 1883 that Louisiana's plantation homes on either side of the river sat "so close together, for long distances, that the broad river lying between the two rows, becomes a sort of spacious street."[12] The homes were only a grim showpiece. The real purpose of the plantations was industrial extraction, with enslaved laborers processing sugarcane in a highly technical process inside of on-site factories. The Mississippi River connected these businesses to global demand. By the time that Edmond Bozonier Marmillion, a prominent Louisiana planter, began building his fanciful San Francisco Plantation in St. John the Baptist Parish in the 1850s, the great slave revolt of 1811 must have felt like a distant memory of hard times long gone—sugar planters were wealthier than ever, their success resting on the brutal, violent control of enslaved workers.

San Francisco Plantation is now a major tourist destination in the middle of what is known as New Orleans Plantation Country. Tourists from around the world come to southern Louisiana to experience the culture, food, and history of this once wealthy enslaving society. As with many plantation museums, the enslaver's home is the prize of San Francisco Plantation. The "big house," with its ornate facade painted in rich Caribbean blues and yellows, is prominently featured in regional promotional materials and advertisements. A visitor might be forgiven for being captivated by this spectacle of antebellum architecture—that was the very purpose of its construction, after all. But it is hard to see the complex truth with your gaze fixed, myopically, on the house. Widening the scope reveals the architectural context of this 1853 mansion. It is surrounded today on all sides by petrochemical tanks and machinery belonging to the Marathon Oil Company, which owns the mansion and until 2021 operated a museum there. Beside, behind, and throughout the property there are ugly, unsettling reminders of the economic imperative for the home's existence: in the nineteenth century, agricultural slavery; in the twentieth, petroleum.

San Francisco Plantation, which was at one time known as Saint-Frusquin, is rare in how well documented it is as a site of violence. After Edmond Bozonier Marmillion died in 1856, his son Valsin Bozonier Marmillion took over the plantation. Multiple sources confirm the conditions enslaved people endured under Valsin's ownership. "The cruelest master in St. John the Baptist Parish during the time of slavery was Mr. Valsin Mermillion" [*sic*], recalled Mrs. Webb, a woman who had been formerly enslaved by Marmillion. "One of his cruelties was if a slave was disobedient, to put him standing in a box with nails in it, and make him stand in a way that he could not move and could not swat the flies and ants that crawled on him."[13] Marmillion seemed to relish the ownership of his human chattel, so much so that he burned his own initials into their flesh. During the Civil War in 1864, out of Marmillion's 210 enslaved laborers, 205 fled the plantation to Union lines.[14] Of those, thirty had been branded with the initials "V.B.M."—most on their chests and shoulders, but some on their foreheads.[15]

Marmillion's practice of branding his enslaved workers became widely known during the war. One man who was enslaved at San Francisco Plantation, Wilson Chinn, sat for photographs along with several other Louisiana freedpeople. In Chinn's portrait, he demonstrated the instruments of plantation torture, including leg irons and a bell collar. Keloids forming the initials of his former enslaver can be plainly seen across his forehead, a gruesome reminder of the violence that enslaved people endured. This photo, commissioned by Union Colonel George Hanks and sold as a carte de visite to raise funds for schools, remains one of the most famous images of an enslaved person in the United States.[16]

Marmillion was deeply committed to recovering the property he lost during the Civil War—namely, the 205 enslaved people who fled to freedom. After the River Parishes came under Union control during the Civil War, Marmillion "took the oath of allegiance, but refused to work his plantation unless he could have *his own negroes* returned to him."[17] Many of Marmillion's formerly enslaved laborers were nearby, working in Union encampments in New Orleans. When a Union official attempted to get them to return to work the plantation, they all refused to return. "I will go anywhere else to work," one man said, "but you may shoot me before I will return to the old plantation."[18]

M. H. Kimball, photographer, *Wilson Chinn, a Branded Slave from Louisiana*. Library of Congress, Prints & Photographs Division.

* * *

Plantations like San Francisco needed river access to move their sugarcane to market—a global market that was intensifying over the eighteenth and nineteenth centuries through industrial-scale plantation agriculture and the brutal "management" of slave-labor forces. The plantations marked out long, skinny plots of land, with "big houses" fronting the river; today the houses are hidden behind the Mississippi River levee system. Docks stood along the river, the houses of the enslaved stretched back into the cane fields toward the towering smokestacks of the sugar mills, and swampy woods made up the rear. After the Civil War—the moment of an expected liberation for the freed population of the German Coast—the economy carried on largely unchanged, with sons and daughters of enslaved people, and grandsons and granddaughters, working the land. They were tied to this land by Jim Crow laws and customs that prevented free movement and locked African Americans in debt, unrepresented and in constant fear of racial terrorism. In the early twentieth century, the land use of the Gulf Coast region began to change, and a new industry developed alongside centuries-old plantations.

The first reserves of Gulf oil were discovered at Beaumont, Texas, in 1901. This was quickly followed by a strike in Jennings, Louisiana, just a few months later. Investors brought refineries to the state in short order. Standard Oil bought 225 acres of a plantation in Baton Rouge in 1909, establishing a precedent for dozens of companies.[19] Chemical manufacturing to serve markets for fertilizers, pesticides, plastics, and the manifold additives for petroleum manufacture settled in to stay. The long, skinny plantation holdings were now assembled for industrial uses, perfectly situated for the purposes of petrochemical manufacturing with their river access points, once again tying the land and the factories to a toxic global market. As international companies bought up Louisiana's sugar and cotton lands, refineries, tank farms, and pipelines began to share space with plantations, many of which did not cease operations until the late twentieth century. The intensification of petrochemical manufacturing along this stretch of river delta is heralded as one of the defining features of American economic development through and following the Second World War. Environmental impacts—manifest in the air, the water, the senses of the residents and workers—were ignored in the absence of any regulations or restraint. Sugarcane still grows along the edges of the industrial plants, and cattle graze along the fence lines.

In Louisiana's oil refineries and petrochemical plants, workers were (and continue to be) mostly white, and skilled positions for college graduates are plentiful. The neighborhoods surrounding the plants are largely African American communities, made up of the descendants of the sugarcane slavery system. Their communities have become "sacrifice zones," rained on by the pollutants emitted night and day by the plants. In LaPlace, situated on the east bank of the Mississippi River in St. John the Baptist Parish, the manufacture of plastics at the Denka Performance Elastomer plant has resulted in chloroprene emissions that are tied to cancer, skin conditions, dizziness, and headaches. Today residents of LaPlace, Reserve, and Garyville are fighting to enhance air-quality monitoring and to find the funds to move an elementary school that sits on the Denka chemical company fence line. Continuous agitation from community members, supported by environmental chemist Wilma Subra and the Louisiana Environmental Action Network, has led to some hope for the school's relocation, but there is no hope that the plant will close.[20] Pollution is the slow disaster of everyday life in St. John Parish.

The discovery of oil in Louisiana in the early twentieth century and subsequent growth of the petrochemical industry is often heralded as the beginning of industrialization in the state, but a larger scope reveals the continuous lines between industrial-scale sugar production in the nineteenth century and oil extraction in the twentieth. The presence of oil did more than just add another industry to the state; it changed the nature of sugar production. In 1951, Esso Standard Oil's Baton Rouge employees proudly proclaimed in their company newsletter that "petroleum power and petroleum products have changed the face of agriculture." Problems that had long vexed plantation owners could be solved by oil's many miraculous products. "Petroleum has become a treasure trove of derivatives [*sic*] and compounds for agriculture—herbicides, insecticides, fungicides, fertilizers, sprays, waxes, specialty products to hasten or delay ripening of fruits and vegetables, and scores of other things."[21]

After World War II, a variety of pesticides derived from oil gained widespread use on American farms. One insecticide, a highly toxic chlorinated naphthalene called endrin, was particularly favored by sugar plantation owners. Among the many organisms it kills, endrin is especially destructive to lepidopteran pests and thus was sought-after in the planters' fight against the larvae of *Diatraea saccharalis*, also known as the sugarcane borer. Endrin's more famous cousin, DDT, pales in comparison in terms of toxicity. Endrin is "15 times as poisonous as DDT to mammals, 30 times as poisonous to fish, and about 300 times as poisonous to some birds."[22]

Since the nineteenth century, Louisiana's sugar industry had been helmed by leaders who obsessively sought scientific ways to improve their techniques and increase yields.[23] In the 1920s, Louisiana's sugar industry nearly collapsed when it was crippled with a suite of problems—bad weather; sugarcane borer infestations; red rot fungus; root rot caused by snails; and an outbreak of the mosaic virus, which is carried by aphids. Between 1921 and 1924, these combined problems caused a decrease in yield per acre from 18.5 tons to just 7.2.[24] With no synthetic pesticides yet available in the 1920s, planters turned to new species of cane with resistance to certain insects and fungi. By the time of World War II, sugar planters were eager to try pesticides that might prevent wholesale loss of crops. The use of endrin in Louisiana mirrors the rapid expansion of industrial chemical manufacturing worldwide after World War II.

Sugar planters in the Mississippi Valley began to deploy endrin to combat the sugarcane borer in 1957. It was endrin alone that allowed sugar planters to wrest control over this moth that had infested fields and caused fungal infections since the 1850s.[25] The principal method of endrin application in sugar fields was by aerial spraying. In the 1950s, though some aspects of sugarcane plantation labor had been mechanized, plantations still largely relied on manual labor by field hands, especially in planting. When the pesticide planes came, workers were sent into the fields to mark the boundary lines with handheld signs, making sure that the planes knew exactly where to go.

Remembering his life growing up at Whitney Plantation in St. John the Baptist Parish, where his parents and grandparents were field workers, John Howard said that he did not understand the danger of these planes as a child: "A lot of people died from, I guess you could say, got poisoned, now that I look at it, you know. Used to make some of the workers hold up signs in the fields so the airplane could know where to spray. . . . They ended up with all kinds of disease. . . . I guess they thought it was right. And at the same time, I don't know." Though John was a child and did not have to stand in the fields himself, he remembered watching as it happened to his family. "My parents and uncles and them," he said, "I remember when they went out there."[26]

In the 1960s, when the plantation compelled John Howard's family to stand in the fields without wearing any protective gear while planes sprayed them with endrin, plantation owners imperfectly understood its dangers. Contemporary studies of aerial sprayers indicated that people exposed in the workplace in high concentrations might be most at risk. Endrin, like other pesticides in its class, causes neurological problems such as convulsions and seizures. Because it is stored in fat, it can be released and cause recurring seizures months after exposure as well—these recurrences are heightened by emotional stress.[27] Field workers, who lived in substandard housing, suffered from food insecurity and poverty, and often had inadequate medical care, would have experienced high levels of stress.

Though endrin exposure may have caused health problems in cane workers, it would have been difficult for the average plantation owner to link cause and effect. If Whitney Plantation's managers had paid close attention, however, they may have noticed what it did to marine life. One manager's child remembered seeing the effects of endrin in the canals that fed the rice fields: "When they sprayed, the next day? You had dead fish all over the place."[28] Whitney Plantation was not the only site of fish kills. Between 1963 and 1964, five million fish turned up dead in streams and bayous as a result of endrin spraying on sugar plantations.[29]

When Valsin B. Marmillion burned his initials into the flesh of slaves on San Francisco Plantation, the violence was immediately visible. Slaves carried the trauma of plantation violence on their bodies in scars and keloids. The violence exacted upon enslaved laborers in the nineteenth century was a matter of capitalistic production; it ensured acquiescence and hard labor from a class of people who feared for their safety. When John Howard's parents and uncles, the grandchildren of enslaved people, stood in the rows of cane while planes dusted them with endrin, the violence of fieldwork was not gone; it had just changed shape. Their bodies, too, were abused for capitalistic production and efficiency. Its invisibility is the most insidious feature of this violence. Unlike Wilson Chinn, who knew for certain what his owner's brand had done to his skin, twentieth-century workers were left to wonder. Which case of cancer, which early death, which birth defect, was caused by the plantation owner's poison that rained down and coated their skin?

Early in the deadly COVID-19 pandemic month of April 2020, the *New York Times* first reported startling results from a public health study performed by researchers at the T. H. Chan School of Public Health at Harvard University. "Coronavirus patients in areas that had high levels of air pollution before the pandemic are more likely to die from the infection than patients in cleaner parts of the country . . . higher levels of the tiny, dangerous particles in air known as PM 2.5 were associated with higher death rates from the disease."[30]

Intuitively, Beverly Wright, director of the Deep South Center for Environmental Justice, knew what this meant: "When they first showed the statistics . . . it showed that St. John Parish had the highest death rate for COVID. I was like, what in the world is going on? Why would this little town you know, have such high rates? And then the Harvard study came out, which absolutely told us why. . . . [T]hey live in Cancer Alley right across from polluting facilities with extreme exposure to PM 2.5 over long periods of time. So they fit the description."[31]

Wright's observations were apt, and by mid-April St. John the Baptist Parish was for a time reporting some of the highest COVID-19 infection rates in the United States. People with underlying lung distress were acquiring the disease at higher rates, and those with comorbidities like asthma and other chronic pulmonary disease were suffering a worse course of the virus. The everyday slow disaster of Cancer Alley predisposed these victims to the disaster of COVID-19—an interlacing of disasters moving at different speeds, torturing slowly and then killing fast. The many funerals of the springtime told the tale.

The slow disaster of pollution and racial violence was again punctuated by a rapid-onset disastrous event in Louisiana. This time it was a disaster event unlike any seen in our lifetimes, a pandemic with contours still mostly unrecognizable in April 2020, spreading especially quickly in communities of color across the United States, communities with poor access to health care. "It reminds me so much of [Hurricane] Katrina," Wright remarked at the time, "because you know, the same thing happened, the people who are least able to fight a flood or have some disaster, get it piled on to them at a time when they are less able to overcome the conditions that they live with every day. So it's like a piling-on effect. You know, it's like, how do we get out of this?"

Beverly Wright's question is Dread Scott's question, just as it was the question of the German Coast martyrs of 1811—how can the powerless and disaffected amid powerful industrial systems break the trend and disrupt the cycle of disasters? No easy answer is forthcoming today, nor has there been an easy answer for more than two hundred years in one of the most disaster-prone places in North America. Perhaps, though, by linking the disasters of slavery, structural racism, and pollution across an Anthropocenic stretch of time, we can begin to account fully for the disaster impacts on the people of this region. Maybe then, but only then, could a pathway leading away from the plantation truly begin to emerge.

For disaster historians the method of Anthropocenic analysis opens the way to a correlate revolution in the temporal frames we use. Too often disaster histories present hurricanes, fires, or disease epidemics as single events or episodes, fascinating microcosms of the politics of their time and place, but somehow unmoored from the deeper historical structures of their making. Take Cancer Alley, for example, a place known for seasonal hurricanes and riverine flooding. These disasters comport to an event-driven analysis, but the temporal bounds of a single storm or season leave the reader groping to understand the deeper questions: Who lived on the high ground and who on the low? Who suffered and whose suffering went unnoticed? Who profited by the conditions that made this event? If the disaster history of the lower Mississippi Delta is one limited to storms, then we have failed to account for disasters moving at different time scales, the disasters of enslavement and plantation agriculture, of petrochemical industrialization and its attendant environmental and public health wreckage, of climate change. An Anthropocenic approach enhances our understanding of individual events while simultaneously opening up a broader analytical vista.

NOTES

1. Leon A. Waters, "Jan. 8, 1811: Louisiana's Heroic Slave Revolt," Zinn Education Project, https://www.zinnedproject.org/news/tdih/louisianas-slave-revolt/; "The 1811 Slave Revolt," Whitney Plantation, https://www.whitneyplantation.org/history/slavery-in-louisiana/resistance/.

2. For discussion of the historical construction of disaster categories, see Scott Gabriel Knowles, "Learning from Disaster? The History of Technology and the Future of Disaster Research," *Technology and Culture* 55, no. 4 (October 2014): 773–84.

3. Commodore John Shaw, quoted in Daniel Rasmussen, *American Uprising: The Untold Story of America's Largest Slave Revolt* (New York: Harper Perennial, 2011), 148–49.

4. Rasmussen, *American Uprising*, 167–70.

5. Nathan A. Buman, "Historiographical Examinations of the 1811 Slave Insurrection," *Louisiana History* 53, no. 3 (Summer 2012): 325.

6. On the German Coast Uprising, see Albert Thrasher, *On to New Orleans! Louisiana's Heroic 1811 Slave Revolt* (New Orleans: Cypress, 1996); and Daniel Rasmussen, *American Uprising: The Untold Story of America's Largest Slave Revolt* (New York: HarperCollins, 2011).

7. Leila Fadel and Emma Bowman, "Hundreds March in Reenactment of a Historic, but Long Forgotten Slave Rebellion," NPR, November 9, 2019, https://www.npr.org/2019/11/09/777810796/hundreds-march-in-reenactment-of-a-historic-but-long-forgotten-slave-rebellion. The reenactment coincided with the opening of the Anthropocene River Campus, a multiday exploration of the Anthropocene, history, and environmental justice based in New Orleans and sponsored by the Haus der Kulturen der Welt (HKW), Berlin. Parts of this chapter were published online by the HKW and appear here by permission (https://www.anthropocene-curriculum.org/contribution/layers-of-violence).

8. Fadel and Bowman, "Hundreds March in Reenactment."

9. Julian Lucas, "Dread Scott's Rebellion," *Vanity Fair*, October 2019, https://www.vanityfair.com/style/2019/09/dread-scott-slave-rebellion-reenactment.

10. For discussion of the Anthropocene and historical method, see Christophe Bonneuil and Jean-Baptiste Fressoz, *The Shock of the Anthropocene: The Earth, History, and Us*, trans. David Fernbach (New York: Verso, 2016); Donna J. Haraway, *Staying with the Trouble: Making Kin in the Chthulucene* (Durham, NC: Duke University Press, 2016); Gabrielle Hecht, "Interscalar Vehicles for an African Anthropocene: On Waste, Temporality, and Violence," *Cultural Anthropology* 33, no. 1 (2018): 109–41; Scott Gabriel Knowles and Zachary Loeb, "The Voyage of the Paragon: Disaster as Method," in *Disaster Studies: New Perspectives on Disaster Risk, Vulnerability, and Resilience*, ed. Andy Horowitz and Jacob Remes (Philadelphia: University of Pennsylvania Press, 2021); Jason W. Moore, ed., *Anthropocene or Capitalocene? Nature, History, and the Crisis of Capitalism* (San Francisco: PM, 2016); Will Steffen, Asa Perrson, Lisa Deutsch et al., "The Anthropocene: From Global Change to Planetary Stewardship," *Ambio* 40, no. 7 (2011): 739–61; and Meera Subramanian, "Humans Versus Earth: The Quest to Define the Anthropocene," *Nature*, August 6, 2019, https://www.nature.com/articles/d41586-019-02381-2.

11. Slow violence, a related but distinct concept, is articulated in Rob Nixon, *Slow Violence and the Environmentalism of the Poor* (Cambridge, MA: Harvard University Press, 2011).

12. Mark Twain, *Life on the Mississippi* (Boston: Osgood, 1883), 247.

13. Mrs. Webb, interview by Michinard, August 17, 1940, translated from the Creole French by Whitney Plantation, Watson Memorial Library, Cammie G. Henry Research Center (folder 19 of FWP), Northwestern State University of Louisiana.

14. "Emancipated Slaves, Brought from New Orleans by Col. George H. Hanks," *Findlay (OH) Jeffersonian*, March 4, 1864.

15. "The Young White Slaves," *New York Tribune*, quoted in "The Romance of a Radical," *New Orleans True Daily Delta*, February 18, 1864, 6.

16. M. H. Kimball, photographer, *Wilson Chinn, a Branded Slave from Louisiana / Photographed*

by Kimball, 477 Broadway, N.Y., 1863, Library of Congress, https://www.loc.gov/item/2018664120/.

17. "The Freedmen and the Ex-Slaveholders," *Liberator* (Boston, MA), July 29, 1864, 4; emphasis in the original.

18. "The Freedmen and the Ex-Slaveholders," 4.

19. "The Standard Oil Co. Will Build a $2,000,000 Refinery at Baton Rouge, La. Which Is to Be a Distributing Point for Products of Company," *St. Tammany Farmer* (Covington, LA), April 17, 1909, 1.

20. Julie Dermansky, "Photos of the Struggle for Environmental Justice in Louisiana's Cancer Alley in 2020," *Desmog Blog*, December 30, 2020, https://www.desmogblog.com/2020/12/30/photos-struggle-environmental-justice-louisiana-s-cancer-alley-2020.

21. "Today and Yesterday," *Stanocolan*, May 18, 1951, Special Collections, East Baton Rouge Parish Public Library.

22. Rachel Carson, *Silent Spring* (Boston: Mariner, 2002), 25.

23. John Alfred Heitmann, *The Modernization of the Louisiana Sugar Industry, 1830–1910* (Baton Rouge: Louisiana State University Press, 1987).

24. Eugene Chapel Tims, "Studies on Sugarcane Mosaic in Louisiana," *LSU Agricultural Experiment Station Reports* (1935); Claude Wilbur Edgerton, "The Sugar Cane Disease Situation in 1923 and 1924," *LSU Agricultural Experiment Station Reports* (December 1924).

25. "The Integrity of Science: A Report by the AAAS Committee on Science in the Promotion of Human Welfare," *American Scientist* 53, no. 2 (June 1965): 186; *Proceedings of the American Society of Sugar Cane Technologists* 9, Papers for 1962 (February 1963): 47.

26. John Howard, Oral History Interview, April 30, 2016, Collection of Whitney Plantation Museum, Wallace, LA; Watson Aviation Inc. Receipts, 1964, Collection of Whitney Plantation Museum, Wallace, LA.

27. Alvin M. Revzin, *Some Acute and Chronic Effects of Endrin on the Brain*, report for the Department of Transportation, Federal Aviation Administration, Office of Aviation Medicine (July 1970), 7–8.

28. Percy Paul Zeringue, Oral History Interview, July 10, 2017, Collection of Whitney Plantation Museum, Wallace, LA.

29. Craig E. Colten, ed., *Transforming New Orleans and Its Environs: Centuries of Change* (Pittsburgh, PA: University of Pittsburgh Press, 2000), 150.

30. https://www.nytimes.com/2020/04/07/climate/air-pollution-coronavirus-covid.html; https://projects.iq.harvard.edu/covid-pm.

31. *COVIDCalls*, April 17, 2020, Karen Gadbois, Andy Horowitz, and Beverly Wright, https://podcasts.apple.com/us/podcast/covidcalls/id1516341147.

A COLLISION OF DISASTERS

COVID-19 AND DIABETES

RICHARD M. MIZELLE JR.

Atlanta's Hartsfield International Airport was eerily quiet on the last Sunday afternoon in late February 2020. In one of the busiest airports in the world, travelers eyed each other suspiciously and attempted to leave distance between themselves and others in spaces that normally create intimacy, wanted or not. Some passengers refused to sit in the seating areas and just wandered about, whereas others tried to find a secluded corner of the airport to await boarding their flight. Sniffles, coughs, and sneezes garnered disapproving stares, and those wearing masks were met with a combination of envy, fear, and contempt. There was a sense of disaster in the air that perhaps people could not fully articulate. As passengers navigated this suddenly unusual space, it was clear something was about to change. The COVID-19 pandemic was in the early stages of what would be a long and torturous journey of death, despair, uncertainty, and the politicization of public health and health care. Scholars who work on race and disparities were painfully aware of what the pandemic would mean for marginalized and disadvantaged groups that always suffer the most during disasters. The coming public health disaster would serve as yet another window into the lives of America's racially stigmatized and the underclass that disproportionately shoulders both the burden of disaster and suffering that comes along with it. From pandemics centuries ago to those in more recent memory, the lessons brought forth by the current COVID-19 pandemic are both old and new, yet the will to change the environmental and societal circumstances that cause disproportionate suffering remains shockingly shallow.

This essay is about what happens when disasters collide, in this case the SARS-CoV-2 (the scientific term for what is generally known as COVID-19) pandemic and diabetes, a chronic disease whose complications and suffering have become endemic to poor and marginalized groups. One has transformed our notion of normalcy, death, healing, recovery, and social vulnerability; the other brings about chronic pain, disability, and suffering in ways so routine as to be ignored. I argue in this essay that COVID-19 represents a long continuum of suffering for people with chronic disease, in particular the chronic epidemic of diabetes. Historians of medicine continue to pay more attention to drastic and seemingly sudden diseases and epidemics to the detriment of chronic and long-term diseases that impact ever-greater numbers of people over a sustained period.[1] What if a similar amount of attention and resources were aimed at diabetes and the oft-ignored complications/disabilities of retinopathy, kidney failure, chronic headache, and peripheral arterial disease that is causing an epidemic of limb amputations in the United States? Perhaps for some Americans the threat of COVID-19 will eventually subside, but for others their suffering did not begin and will not end with COVID-19. By analyzing the seemingly sudden rise of COVID-19 with the chronic experience of diabetes, we can come to a better understanding of both in time and space.

Our common usage of the word "pandemic" dates to the late nineteenth and early twentieth centuries and the transportation of goods, people, and germs across the globe via modernizing transportation systems. Diseases that were once considered endemic and seasonal to regions could circulate the globe along with bodies and lead to outbreaks in the far reaches of the earth. Where usage of the term "pandemic" in the seventeenth century might imply a local disease that plagues an entire population, by the late nineteenth century pandemics were considered epidemics that reached far beyond local environments.[2] Yet pandemics are both biological and social phenomena. Scholars have revisited Charles Rosenberg's influential 1989 essay "What Is an Epidemic? AIDS in Historical Perspective," published during the height of the HIV/AIDS crisis, where he makes the case of epidemics being akin to a drama in three stages.[3] Feigned ignorance of illness and disease represents the early stage where societies dismiss the growing epidemic to protect the reputation and economic interests of society or assuage fears. The slow acknowledgment of an epidemic leads to the second act and a desire to place moral blame on certain groups or individuals for the pain and suffering of the whole.[4] Jews were blamed for the fourteenth-century bubonic plague, eastern and southern European immigrants blamed for nineteenth-century cholera epidemics, suspicious and unknown strangers blamed for yellow fever epidemics of the nineteenth century, and homosexuals, Haitians, drug users, and a single flight attendant blamed for the HIV/AIDS epidemic in the 1980s.[5] The third act is the public and public health response to an epidemic, which itself provides a unique window into societal levels of xenophobia, racism, caste, class, and gender, all before the epidemic seemingly sinks away suddenly and in nondramatic fashion.[6] Since the publication of Rosenberg's essay, scholars have increasingly focused on the question of epidemic endings, suggesting that epidemics do not often fall away in nondramatic fashion but continue indefinitely.[7]

Both environmental and public health disasters bring about a breakdown of local, state, and federal services and protections, which in turn provides an unadulterated glimpse into which citizens are considered worthy of assistance and charity and which are deemed unworthy and expendable. During the 1927 Mississippi River Flood, Black sharecroppers were systematically locked out of resources and charity provided by the American Red Cross by local planters and landowners who devalued their lives and marked them as unworthy of benefitting from the same resources provided to help others.[8] From the 1900 Galveston hurricane to the present, Black people, minorities, and the poor endure what I have called a "Double-Environmental Burden" of race and disaster where they must deal with the power of nature (hurricane and pandemics, for instance) and the power of racism, gender, caste, and class. Historian Theodore Steinberg has called this burden the "unnatural history" of disasters.[9] In his seminal work on the 1995 Chicago Heat Wave, sociologist Eric Klinenberg described a social autopsy that revealed the multifactorial causes of death and suffering among the mostly elderly, poor, and Black victims. Those individuals who lacked resources and social networks were the most vulnerable, particularly elderly residents who could not afford high utility bills caused by extended air-conditioning use, mostly lived alone, and whose feebleness made them unable or wary to seek help outside their homes in degraded neighborhoods. Out of sight and forgotten, these residents were neglected to death by city officials.[10] In many cases their deaths were not made visible until the rent was past due, prompting a visit from the apartment complex management, or the bodies decomposed to the point that someone notified authorities.

In times of environmental and public health disaster, society often leans on military metaphors to suggest a beginning, middle, and end.[11] But like some wars, the ravages of epidemics extend well beyond the battlefield. During the COVID-19 crisis, public commentators and academics dubbed the "working poor" as America's "frontline" workers, forced out of necessity to toil for wages in service industries for the benefit of all—supermarkets, post offices, public transportation, food industries. During the early months of the disaster, as shelves of meat products were depleted from stores all over the country, meat factory workers risked starvation and termination if they did not come to work. By early May 2020, as the country was moving into the height of the pandemic, roughly seven hundred workers at a Tyson Meat Processing Plant in Perry, Iowa, tested positive for COVID-19, representing over 58 percent of the company's workforce. Two workers died, and close to eight hundred others tested positive before a Smithfield Foods plant was closed in Sioux Falls, South Dakota. Then presidential candidate Joe Biden remarked that plants and nursing homes are the "most dangerous places there are right now. . . . [T]hey designate [employees] as essential workers and then treat them as disposable."[12]

Women in the workforce continue to face additional burdens from the pandemic. Long-standing social and economic-based gender inequalities have been reinforced and exacerbated by the global disaster. From the earliest days of the pandemic, home nurses, health aides, and nursing home workers were among the most vulnerable in our society. Caribbean immigrants and Black women make up a sizable portion of nursing home workers, and many were forced to work long hours in multiple facilities while taking care of their own families. The elderly population and lack of uniform health standards make nursing homes particularly vulnerable spaces. Many of the same criticisms of leadership that emerged from nursing home deaths following Hurricane Katrina reemerged during the pandemic.[13]

Women have been more likely to lose jobs and work-related opportunities in comparison to men across the globe, according to a report in the *Guardian*.

Institutions of higher learning have reported higher dropout rates and petitions for leave among women. While "frontline" workers are valued in certain industries, the pandemic shook other industries to the core. In the United States and across the globe, women disproportionally suffered wage losses from the shutdown in various hospitality industries by losing jobs or having hours curtailed.[14] Long-existing social norms suggested that women must bear the burden for unpaid labor during the pandemic, caring for elderly parents and grandparents, spouses, and children. The historian Jeanne Boydston's seminal work on the dismissal of women's household labor in the Early Republic remains shockingly relevant today in a myriad of ways. During the pandemic women left the health professions due to risk of exposure and potential infection of multigenerational family members. For many women, the pandemic has resulted in a loss of wages, status, experience, and a temporary halt in their professional advancement.[15]

Professional advancement is a particular issue for Black women scientists, physicians, and researchers who fear the pandemic might have career-long negative consequences. Long-fought battles for the inclusion of Black women and other minorities in the STEM fields have receded during the pandemic with consequences that might not be felt for many years. In the wake of the deaths of George Floyd, Breanna Taylor, and others, Black and minority women have been exhausted by the psychological toll of continued racial and gendered mistreatment in hospitals, clinics, labs, and on the street. Without powerful and thoughtful leadership, one legacy of COVID-19 might include a widening gap of access to STEM fields. Minority women also face more COVID-19–related barriers to advancement in academic medicine in ways that have exacerbated long-standing disparities, including the difficulty of maintaining important networking opportunities and professional virtual spaces that must be negotiated with spouses and the demands of childcare.[16]

Along with economic inequality, domestic violence toward women increased since the start of the pandemic. The reallocation of resources and personnel during the pandemic curtailed access to important sexual and reproductive health services for women in ways that have been threatening to their physical and mental health. The temporary discontinuation of domestic violence and reproductive care services means that women continue to suffer in silence in public and private spaces, where speaking up might lead to even more violence.[17]

Severe Acute Respiratory Syndrome (SARS) caused by a coronavirus (SARS-CoV-2) is the scientific terminology of the specific virus that causes what has been named the novel COVID-19 disease. COVID-19 is a highly transmissible virus that attacks the upper respiratory tract, immune system, and central nervous system. While our understanding of this novel disease continues to evolve, as of the writing of this essay, symptoms occur between two and fourteen days after exposure and include difficulty breathing, cough, fatigue, muscle aches, diarrhea, vomiting, loss of smell, and confusion. This coronavirus, unlike most other coronaviruses, causes short- and long-term disability and extremely high rates of death.[18] It is the first disease to impact every region of the world simultaneously, shutting down the world economy and leading to quarantines in every part of the globe.

The term "novel" belies a more complicated history. Coronaviruses are not unknown to human beings as they serve as the basis of the common cold. Scientists have been studying and analyzing zoonotic coronaviruses in bats and mice and their increasing frequency in human populations since the 1980s. The fear of evolving coronaviruses making the jump from animals to humans and causing a global pandemic animated much of this research. It is telling that even amid the emerging global pandemic of HIV/AIDS of the 1980s, scientists remained committed to the global threat of coronaviruses. COVID-19 is the fourth coronavirus to impact humans since the 1950s, including the 2002 SARS coronavirus and 2012 Middle Eastern Respiratory Syndrome (MERS) coronavirus that has become endemic.[19]

The World Health Organization declared COVID-19 as a Public Health Emergency of International Concern in January 2020 but would not declare it a global pandemic until almost two months later.[20] The COVID-19 pandemic has proven to be historically complicated and messy, resisting a clear beginning, middle, and end. The separation between the "suddenness" of the epidemic is not clearly delineated from the commonness of the endemic or chronic. As Erica Charters and Richard McKay have written, "Although epidemics are captivating moments of drama, they are merely pinpoints in the historical record: the stunning tips of icebergs that too often distract from the powerful mass hidden beneath the surface."[21] The groups suffering the most from COVID-19 have not been surprising; their vulnerability to disasters of all types being historical, structural, and rooted in long-standing public and health policy generations in the making. It is an example of what scholars have termed an "epidemic chronicity" or "pandemicity," a disease or diseases that cause sickness and death over the span of multiple decades or generations.[22]

Polio was the nation's most recognizable epidemic of the early to mid-twentieth century and provides a useful corollary of epidemic disease and long-term disability. Physical and respiratory paralysis and disability impacted millions of children and adults during the nineteenth and early twentieth centuries. Treatment was laborious and often futile, involving ventilation, prophylactics like gamma globulin even after diagnosis, various therapeutics, surgery, physiotherapy, and respiratory technology like the well-known iron lung that provided powerful visual representations of the polio epidemic throughout the world.[23] Curbing polio, however, was not a simple task. After vaccines were marketed in the 1950s led by Jonas Salk and Albert Sabin, the assumption was that suffering from polio had ended. As historian of medicine Dora Vargha has written, for some patients the emergency or urgency of the polio acute period subsided after the 1950s only to be replaced by the permanency of chronic disability.[24] She makes the important point that iron lungs were not simply a symbol of the polio epidemic's acute phase but also would become part of routine and chronic care for weeks, months, and years. While the medical field and public consciousness began to bend toward other diseases and illnesses, survivors of the midcentury polio epidemic might endure respiratory, physical, and emotional complications of their disease for the rest of their lives.

Tuberculosis provides another brief example of a disease that has been both epidemic and endemic in the twentieth century, reflective of racist housing policies, overcrowded cities, and poverty that fueled the infectious disease.[25] Though no longer the feared plague of the early twentieth century, we have never gotten rid of tuberculosis. In 2018 alone, roughly 1.5 million people throughout the world died from tuberculosis and more than 9,000 mostly poor and minority Americans were diagnosed, proving that it is still far from being a disease that we can place in the dustbin of history.[26] In poverty-stricken countries tuberculosis remains a clear and present public health danger. In the United States, the HIV/AIDS epidemic revealed a smoldering upsurge of tuberculosis in immunocompromised patients, and rates of tuberculosis continue to be higher than expected in the twenty-first century.

Diseases like tuberculosis and HIV/AIDS continue to be overlooked and the pain of those sufferers normalized or "othered" in a way as to be made uninteresting even when morbidity and mortality statistics remain exceedingly high.[27] As historians of medicine Jeremy Greene and Dora Vargha write so elegantly about the problem of epidemic endings, "the falling action of an epidemic is perhaps best thought of as asymptotic: never disappearing, but rather fading to the point where signal is lost in the noise of the new normal—and even allowed to be forgotten."[28] The global COVID-19 pandemic is likely to become endemic with the ever-present threat and emergence of variants. The historical record tells us that an eradication of any disease is exceedingly rare. Certain diseases that were epidemic in the past might be unheard of today, like the dietary disease pellagra for instance, but it has not been eradicated and continues to flare up in impoverished spaces throughout the globe. COVID-19 will likely be with us in the future as an endemic disease, meaning that certain segments of the population, including the poor, socioeconomically oppressed, and immunocompromised will never see this epidemic end. Instead, it will become a daily reminder of their unique vulnerability within society.

What happens when a sudden pandemic in COVID-19 meets an old metabolic disease in diabetes? Diabetes is a disease that researchers and clinicians have been defining as epidemic for more than thirty years, yet its presence does not, and perhaps never has, elicited the societal fear and public health response of other diseases. Widely known as one of the nation's most costly chronic diseases, diabetes should be defined as a chronic epidemic. For many people diabetes and the complications represent a daily emergency, wrecking their bodies in the form of elevated blood pressure, nerve damage, kidney destruction, vision loss, amputated limbs, severe headaches, and tooth pain. Those with resources can better manage the disease and protect against emergencies, but others will face a lifetime of daily, weekly, and yearly emergencies—the result of not having adequate access to insulin, medical specialists, and healthy food options.

Today, Type I diabetes is considered a Beta cell autoimmune disease that results in the failure of the body to produce the hormone insulin from pancreatic islet cells in sufficient amount to manage elevated blood glucose levels, resulting in the body becoming external *insulin dependent.* Known as juvenile diabetes because symptoms are often developed in childhood, prior to the discovery of insulin in 1921, premature death was common. Type II diabetes, referred to as adult-onset because symptoms often develop later in life, is the result of a down regulation of insulin in targeted tissues of the body causing *insulin resistance.* Beta cells might produce a normal amount of insulin but will fail to activate receptors in the organs and tissues of the body. Over time, the increased production of pancreatic insulin to compensate for the resistance can result in external *insulin dependence.*[29] The Centers for Disease Control and Prevention (CDC) suggests that roughly thirty-seven million people are diagnosed with diabetes in the United States. The World Health Organization estimates that 430 million people across the globe suffer from diabetes. The CDC and other health organizations frequently make note of the heavier burden of the disease suffered by Blacks, Hispanics/Latinos, American Indians, Alaska Natives, and elderly groups.[30] Diabetes also speaks directly to the history of disability. In her seminal essay "On the Borderland of Medical and Disability History," historian Beth Linker pushed to connect the often-separated research on disability and medical history, arguing that while disability has many forms, "some forms of disability are brought about by disease processes" and are therefore worthy of study by medical and public health scholars.[31]

When talking about diabetes, the complications of blindness, amputation, kidney failure, and diabetic headache that can bring about disability are often ignored. In a widened view of medical disability, these complications take on new form. For example, the United States has one the highest rates of kidney failure in the world, the result of chronic kidney disease, hypertension, diabetes, and End Stage Renal Disease. More than five hundred thousand people in the United States receive dialysis, as do one to two million worldwide.[32] Kidney failure and dialysis also reify health disparities as Black people and Latinos make up the majority of those diagnosed. Chronic dialysis is necessary to sustain life when kidney functioning ceases to filter the blood on its own. Failure to receive dialysis treatment, even during an epidemic, is not an option.[33] Close to 140,000 diabetes-related amputations occur in the United States every year. Black people are four times more likely to endure a diabetes-related amputation. If unchecked, diabetes causes a narrowing of blood vessels and restricted blood flow to the extremities, particularly the legs and feet. The loss of blood to the lower extremities results in foot ulcers, gangrene, and peripheral arterial disease, a circulatory condition of poor blood flow. Amputations can often be avoided with early diagnosis, angiogram screening, and revascularization surgery, which reopens blocked blood vessels. Black people and minorities living in impoverished communities and without adequate medical insurance often do not have access to the valuable resources that might save their limbs and prevent disability. Amputations lead to a reduced quality of life, making it difficult to socialize, work, and move freely in spaces.[34]

Disability among individuals with diabetes is often tied to the lack of access to insulin. The year 2021 marked the centennial of the "Insulin Revolution" that transformed the lives of millions of people with diabetes and transformed diabetes from a deadly disease into a chronic illness. Insulin was one of the world's first "wonder drugs," and while it afforded the opportunity of a longer life, chronic complications and disability now define the disease. In the United States roughly 8.3 million people with Type I and Type II diabetes require insulin to live. Globally the number requiring insulin is thirty to forty million.[35] Insulin remains far out of reach for many Americans due to its high cost, as much as $450 per month for the uninsured. The unaffordability of insulin over the course of a century is a shameful disaster. The global advocacy for generic, biosimilar, and affordable brand-name insulin is critical, especially in moments of disaster (including pandemics) as access to insulin has life-and-death consequences. The lack of generic insulin has helped to fuel the global diabetes pandemic and is part of why vulnerable individuals suffer disproportionately during the COVID-19 crisis.[36] Without proper protections and social policies in place, COVID-19 will impact access and affordability of insulin and thereby make painfully visible the unique vulnerability of those with an ancient affliction to a new disease. For many people suffering from diabetes, the frustration of inaccessible insulin represents a long-standing disaster, a chronic social problem with lasting consequences.

There are more glaring and troublesome connections between the diabetes epidemic and COVID-19. Diabetes is a dangerous COVID-19 comorbidity for social and biological reasons. Finding ways to exercise, eat healthy foods, manage stress and glucose levels, and make routine appointments with diabetes specialists to manage their chronic disease is essential for every individual suffering from diabetes.[37] This level of care is particularly crucial during the COVID-19 epidemic. The necessity of exercising inside or outside is laced with the fear of multigenerational family members who might become infected and the lack of usable green spaces in neglected neighborhoods that makes exercising difficult. Living in a food desert and food insecurity make it difficult to obtain the healthy foods required to manage diabetes; those conditions were (and are) exacerbated during the epidemic.[38] Fears of leaving the home for specialist appointments, cancellation or the delaying of appointments by health centers and physicians for fear of transmission, led to a smoldering epidemic of diabetes and related complications nationwide. The stress of a harsh environment, fear of unemployment and hunger, and the other multidimensional dangers that COVID-19 poses can trigger a potentially dangerous autoimmune response. In May 2020 the WHO warned that numerous parts of the globe were suspending diabetes-related services, which will continue to have longstanding health consequences.[39]

Diabetes and COVID-19 coincide with yet another epidemic: poverty and inequality. Housing insecurity, vulnerability of segregated neighborhoods, low wages, and being uninsured and underinsured add to the dangers. These questions are not new and represent a continuation of the social issues informing the diabetes epidemic. Individuals with diabetes who live below the federal poverty line have long faced the repercussions of not being able to manage their disease and its complications. When factors like where people live, their access to physicians, dentists, grocery stores, pharmacies and parks, and whether they can afford the high costs of insulin strongly influence medical outcomes, the current collision with the COVID-19 disaster becomes particularly dangerous.

The CDC makes note that diabetes is an underlying factor in almost half of those who died of COVID-19 among those under sixty-five years of age (as of the writing of this essay). Diabetes causes nerve damage, hardening of blood vessels, and bodily inflammation that prompts a response from the immune system.[40] Diabetes weakens the immune system to fight viruses and infections, making the presence of COVID-19 a potentially disastrous combination. Particularly for Type II, but also for Type I sufferers, obesity is an added factor that makes a dual diagnosis of diabetes and COVID-19 dangerous. Obesity prompts a continual response from your immune system, or chronic inflammatory status, that can make individuals susceptible to viruses and bacteria. Of the numerous issues that need to be monitored when becoming ill, "You need to be able to breathe. You need to have optimal circulatory function," says one physician. "When we develop obesity, we have excess energy storage and the presence of that fat is inflammatory. And so once we get coronavirus infection, we are less able to mount an appropriate immune response because our immune system is already being set off in an inappropriate manner by the presence of obesity."[41]

There is also early worrisome data that COVID-19 might precipitate new-onset metabolic diabetes. One route that SARS-CoV-2 spike proteins enter cells is binding to angiotensin-converting enzyme 2 (ACE2) receptors expressed in various organs and tissues in the body, among them the pancreas and kidneys. It has been suggested by diabetologists that some people with diabetes produce more ACE2 receptors in tissues and blood vessels, providing more cellular access to the SARS-CoV-2 virus in ways that might damage B cells and cause hyperglycemia and impaired insulin functioning. In an editorial published in the *New England Journal of Medicine*, researchers suggested that, "In the aggregate, these observations provide support for the hypothesis of a potential diabetogenic effect of COVID-19, beyond the well-recognized stress response associated with severe illness."[42] In June 2020 a group of twenty international scholars created a global registry and information database called CoviDIAB. The organization's website suggests the aim of the database is to research diabetes comorbidity risk factors and potential connections between SARS-CoV-2 and novel pathophysiological presentations of diabetes.[43] To be sure, at this moment there are more questions than answers. This is the dilemma of writing history that is currently unfolding before our eyes. Can we predict this correlation between COVID-19 and diabetes with some level of certainty? Is this connection more frequently seen in people suffering from Type I or Type II diabetes (or another clinically recognized manifestation of diabetes like Latent Autoimmune Diabetes in Adults), or does it produce an altogether new pathology of the disease? Does COVID-19 change the pathology of those with preexisting diabetes? These are difficult questions to address amid an ongoing pandemic, yet the answers hold important truths for that difficult question of when an epidemic/pandemic will come to an end. For some, perhaps it will end with the marvelous success of vaccines that have emerged as I write this essay, but for others, the recent troubling observations warrant concern that COVID-19 will become part of a chronic life of disease and disability.

What does the COVID-19 epidemic tell us about disasters? As it turns out, if we think about the long history of COVID-19, it can provide important context. Disasters are rarely the spatially and temporally defined moments we often make them out to be. What is most evident during a disaster was often visible well before the crisis and extends for an undetermined period after the event. Historian Andy Horowitz has written that Hurricane Katrina was a twentieth-century disaster, not simply a summer 2005 crisis. Housing policy decisions made ninety years earlier led to the vulnerability of many New Orleans residents living in lowlands near the Mississippi River. Racism and policy decisions have made it more difficult for Black residents to return to the city and rebuild homes and communities in the decades after the storm. This is the definition of a slow-moving and multigenerational disaster. For many Katrina survivors, the disaster has yet to end.[44] The disasters described in this volume were caused by both natural and social forces. Environmental historian Ted Steinberg wrote twenty years ago that disasters are the "price we pay for living on the planet," though the burden of suffering is not equal.[45] Environmental and biological disasters reveal generational and long-standing societal inequality. It comes as little surprise that some people are unable to quarantine, suffer from lost wages and homelessness, endure mental anguish, continue to experience racism amid a global crisis, and suffer higher rates of death to the current COVID-19 pandemic. The poor and disenfranchised are often the population that suffers the most during a disaster.

Environmental disasters and epidemics can bring important policy and social change, yet the limits of such societal overhauls are evident throughout history. The 1906 San Francisco Earthquake led to some civic improvements and street widening, but the racialization and scapegoating of Asians would continue. The 1927 Mississippi River Flood resulted in a new and improved flood control plan throughout the Mississippi River Valley basin while Black Delta residents continued to suffer vicious economic and physical assaults. Hurricane Katrina in 2005 was supposed to result in a new War on Poverty to address federal, state, and local policies in Gulf Coast states and the country that resulted in vast inequality. The new movement never materialized.[46] The history of disasters suggests that as time passes, and memory fades, our collective engagement with the systematic and structural issues that impact vulnerable populations wanes as society returns to a predisaster norm.

There are remarkably few moments when people are aware that they are living in a historical moment. This will not be the last epidemic/pandemic our society will face, and experts are already suggesting diseases on the horizon may be even more transmissible and deadly then the current COVID-19 virus. Yet we are still dealing with the current diabetes epidemic below the surface. In 2019 almost five million Americans died of diabetes and related complications, which by itself, should be considered a public health disaster. As public health scholar David Jones once stated, "housing policy is health policy."[47] In preparation for the next "Big One," or the ongoing "Big One," the societal factors that influence who is more likely to suffer or not during a crisis must be addressed in policies that remedy systematic racism and infrastructural inequality in every aspect of American society. COVID-19 is the most recent and pressing example of the ways in which disasters reveal the social fabric of our society. Our current crisis will be written about extensively, as much as the HIV/AIDS epidemic of the 1980s, tuberculosis of the nineteenth and twentieth centuries, polio of the twentieth century, and the 1918–19 influenza epidemic, all of which are understood both in terms of science and the broader social and political changes they helped to bring about and, perhaps just as important, failed to materialize universally across society. When the COVID-19 disaster enters the annals of human record, will this moment signal a historical shift in truly transforming American society or yet another lost opportunity?

NOTES

1. George Weisz, *Chronic Disease in the Twentieth Century: A History* (Baltimore: Johns Hopkins University Press, 2014).

2. Erica Charters and Richard McKay, "The History of Science and Medicine in the Context of COVID-19," *Centaurus* 62 (2020): 223–33.

3. Charles Rosenberg, "What Is an Epidemic? AIDS in Historical Perspective," *Daedalus* 118, no. 2 (Spring 1989): 1–17.

4. Rosenberg, "What Is an Epidemic?," 1–17.

5. Charles Rosenberg, *The Cholera Years: The United States in 1832, 1849, and 1866* (Chicago: University of Chicago Press, 1962); Jo Ann Carrigan, *The Saffron Scourge: A History of Yellow Fever in Louisiana, 1796–1905*; Richard McKay, *Patient Zero and the Making of the AIDS Epidemic* (Chicago: University of Chicago Press, 2017).

6. Rosenberg, "What Is an Epidemic?"

7. Mary E. Fissell, Jeremy A. Greene, Randall M. Packard, James A. Schafer Jr., "Special Issue, Reimagining Epidemics," *Bulletin of the History of Medicine* 94, no. 4 (winter 2020).

8. Richard M. Mizelle Jr., *Backwater Blues: The Mississippi Flood of 1927 in the African American Imagination* (Minneapolis: University of Minnesota Press, 2014), 75–101.

9. Mizelle, *Backwater Blues*, 1–25; Theodore Steinberg, *Acts of God: The Unnatural History of Natural Disaster in America* (New York: Oxford University Press, 2000).

10. Eric Klinenberg, *Heat Wave: A Social Autopsy of Disaster in Chicago* (Chicago: University of Chicago Press, 2002), 37–79.

11. Nancy Leys Stepan, *Eradication: Ridding the World of Diseases Forever?* (Ithaca, NY: Cornell University Press, 2015).

12. Doha Madani, "58 Percent of Workers at Tyson Meat Factory in Iowa Test Positive for Coronavirus," May 5, 2020, https://www.nbcnews.com/news/us-news/58-percent-workers-tyson-meat-factory-iowa-test-positive-coronavirus-n1200641.

13. Keith Wailoo, Karen O'Neill, Jeffrey Dowd, and Roland Anglin, *Katrina's Imprint: Race and Vulnerability in America* (New Brunswick, NJ: Rutgers University Press, 2010), 60, 75.

14. Andrew Gregory, "Covid Has Intensified Gender Inequalities, Global Study Finds," *The Guardian*, March 2, 2022.

15. Jeanne Boydston, *Home and Work: Housework, Wages, and the Ideology of Labor in the Early Republic* (New York: Oxford University Press, 1994); Gregory, "Covid Has Intensified Gender Inequalities."

16. Reshma Jagsi, Elena Fuentes-Afflick, and Eve Higginbotham, "Promoting Equity for Women in Medicine—Seizing a Disruptive Opportunity," *New England Journal of Medicine*, June 17, 2021.

17. Senait Fisseha, Gita Sen, et al., *COVID-19: The Turning Point for Gender Equality*, *Lancet*, July 16, 2021.

18. "Symptoms of COVID-19," www.cdc.gov/coronavirus/2019-ncov/symptoms-testing/symptoms.html?utm_campaign=AC_CRNA.

19. Lecture at Vanderbilt University by Dr. Mark Denison, "Preparing for the COVID-19 Pandemic . . . for 36 Years," YouTube, https://youtu.be/HtSXyGMon-U.

20. Monica Green, "Emerging Diseases, Re-Emerging Histories," *Centaurus* 62 (2020): 234–47.

21. Erica Charters and Richard McKay, "The History of Science and Medicine in the Context of COVID-19," *Centaurus* 62 (2020): 225.

22. P. Wenzel Geissler and Ruth Prince, "Layers of Epidemy: Present Pasts during the First Weeks of COVID-19 in Western Kenya," *Centaurus* 62 (2020): 248–56.

23. Naomi Rogers, *Dirt and Disease, Polio before FDR* (New Brunswick, NJ: Rutgers University Press, 1992); David Oshinky, *Polio, An American Story: The Crusade That Mobilized the Nation against the 20th Century's Most Feared Disease* (New York: Oxford University Press, 2006).

24. Dora Vargha, *Polio across the Iron Curtain* (New York: Cambridge University Press, 2018), 180–206.

25. Samuel Roberts, *Infectious Fear: Politics, Disease, and the Health Effects of Segregation* (Chapel Hill: University of North Carolina Press, 2009).

26. Jeremy Greene and Dora Vargha, "How Epidemics End," *Boston Review*, June 30, 2020.

27. Margaret Pelling, "Bosom Vipers: Endemic versus Epidemic Disease," *Centaurus* 62 (2020): 295.

28. Greene and Vargha, "How Epidemics End."

29. Arleen Tuchman, *Diabetes: A History of Race and Disease* (New Haven, CT: Yale University Press, 2020), ix–1.; Matthew Klingle, "Inescapable Paradoxes: Diabetes, Progress, and Ecologies of Inequality," *Environmental History* 20, no. 4 (October 2015): 736–50.

30. Michael Montoya, *Making the Mexican Diabetic: Race, Science, and the Genetics of Inequality* (Berkeley: University of California Press, 2011), 1-40.

31. Beth Linker, "On the Borderland of Medical and Disability History: A Survey of the Fields," *Bulletin of the History of Medicine* 87, no. 4 (winter 2013): 499–535.

32. Caroline Hsu and Daniel Weiner, "COVID-19 in Dialysis Patients: Outlasting and Outsmarting a Pandemic," *Kidney International* 98, no. 6, Commentary (December 2020): 1402–4; National Kidney Foundation, "Kidney Disease: The Basics," www.kidney.org/news/newsroom/factsheets/KidneyDiseaseBasics.

33. Steven J. Peitzman, *Dropsy, Dialysis, Transplant: A Short History of Failing Kidneys* (Baltimore: Johns Hopkins University Press, 2007); Richard M. Mizelle Jr., "Hurricane Katrina, Diabetes, and the Meaning of Resiliency," *ISIS* 111, no. 1 (March 2020).

34. Richard M. Mizelle Jr., "Diabetes, Race, and Amputations," *Lancet* 391, no. 10281 (April 3, 2021): 1256–57.

35. Jing Luo, Gregg Gonsalves, Jeremy Greene, "Insulin for All: Treatment Activism and the Global Diabetes Crisis," *Lancet* 393 (2019).

36. Jeremy Greene and Kevin Riggs, "Why Is There No Generic Insulin? Historical Origins of a Modern Problem," *New England Journal of Medicine* 372, no. 12 (2015).

37. Anthony Hatch, *Blood Sugar: Racial Pharmacology and Food Justice in Black America* (Minneapolis: University of Minnesota Press, 2016), 21–41, 61–77; James Doucet-Battle, *Sweetness in the Blood: Race, Risk, and Type II Diabetes* (Minneapolis: University of Minnesota Press, 2021), 23–51.

38. Hatch, *Blood Sugar*, 23–51.

39. World Health Organization, "COVID-19 Significantly Impacts Health Services for Non-

Communicable Diseases," www.who.int/news/item/01-06-2020-covid-19-significantly-impacts-health-services-for-noncommunicable-diseases.

40. Morbidity and Mortality Weekly Report: U.S. Dept. of Health and Human Services/ Centers for Disease Control and Prevention, "Risk for Newly Diagnosed Diabetes >30 Days after SARS-CoV-2 Infection among Persons Aged <18 Years—United States, March 1, 2020–June 28, 2021," https://www.cdc.gov/mmwr/volumes/71/wr/pdfs/mm7102e2-h.pdf; Chris Feudtner, *Diabetes, Insulin, and the Transformation of Illness* (Chapel Hill: University of North Carolina Press, 2003).

41. Elizabeth Cooney, "Why People with Diabetes Are Being Hit So Hard by COVID-19," *Stat*, October 2020, www.statnews.com/2020/10/01/why-people-with-diabetes-are-being-hit-so-hard-by-covid-19/.

42. Francesco Rubino et al., "New-Onset Diabetes in COVID-19," letter to the editor, *New England Journal of Medicine* 383, no. 8 (August 2020); "COVID-19 and Diabetes: A Co-Conspiracy?," editorial, *Lancet* 8, no. 10 (October 2020): P801.

43. CoviDIAB Registry, http://covidiab.e-dendrite.com.

44. Andy Horowitz, *Katrina: A History, 1915–2015* (Cambridge, MA: Harvard University Press, 2020).

45. Steinberg, *Acts of God*.

46. Steinberg, *Acts of God;* Mizelle, *Backwater Blues;* Keith Wailoo et al., *Katrina's Imprint: Race and Vulnerability in America* (New Brunswick, NJ: Rutgers University Press, 2010).

47. *Unnatural Causes: Is Inequality Making Us Sick?* ("Place Matters" episode), California Newsreel, 2008, https://unnaturalcauses.org/about_the_series.php.

THE MYTH OF THE 100-YEAR FLOOD

THE LANGUAGE OF RISK AND THE 2016 LOUISIANA FLOODS

LIZ SKILTON

The rains poured down on August 11, 2016, dumping steadily in waves for three days across Louisiana. With the ground already saturated from early summer storms, it was clear that it would flood within a few hours. The only question was whether this type of flooding would be similar to the yearly rainfall-induced hourlong events that plagued daily activity or something worse. The rain did not dissipate by the end of the day. It undulated in droves, beat at the roof, and swamped the storm drains, backing up in the streets and up to houses. The water had nowhere to go, and so it stayed.

Three days passed as the flooding worsened. On the news, local meteorologists detailed the flood's impact, throwing terms out like "once-in-a-generation" flood, "100-Year Flood," and "500-Year-Flood" in the same way they would describe a hurricane's "cone of probability" and "impact zone."[1] As floods are the most common disaster experienced globally, using these phrases to describe the 2016 Louisiana Floods emphasized the event's uniqueness, giving gravity to the situation.[2] Cutting to clips of videos of waterlogged vehicles and moments of heroic rescues performed by volunteer boaters known as the "Cajun Navy," news media affirmed the flood's cinematic effect.[3] What was different about this apocalyptic flood, they explained, was that it did not come from likely sources. No rivers broke or overtopped their levees. No storm surge rushed in along coastal zones. And no clear end was in sight.[4]

At the end of the third day, the rain let up, but the state of Louisiana lay underwater. Fifty-six of the sixty-four parishes, or 87 percent of the state, lay inundated due to rains reported to be more than the state experienced during Hurricane Katrina.[5] As damages reached billions, again the phrases "once-in-a-generation flood," "100-Year Flood," "500-Year Flood," and "1,000-Year Flood" circulated along with apocalyptic worries of climate change–induced alterations.[6] The use of these phrases was misleading, though. As reported in local papers like the *Lafayette Daily Advertiser*, many Louisiana residents assumed that a person would experience a 100-Year Flood once in one hundred years, or potentially once in their lifetimes. Or, for a 500-Year Flood, people would experience a flood this size once in five centuries. According to Sherry Romero, a Louisiana native, "I live on a property that my husband's family [has lived on since 1847]. Never, ever, has it ever even come close to flooding like that. [T]hey said that is a 100-Year Flood; no, that was more than a 100-Year Flood."[7]

Some Louisianans even based their homeowner's insurance policy decisions on the perception that they would only experience a sizable flood once in a century, failing to make recommended modifications to their homes and properties to guard against a repeat occurrence or cutting expensive flood coverage after experiencing an event.[8] Dennis Martin stated that his family had two flood experiences, one with flood insurance and one without. "My daughter" and her family, Martin explained, "were covered by flood insurance," but he was not.[9] McKinzie Hall had a similar experience. Before the 2016 Floods, Hall had argued with her spouse over flood insurance. A transplant to the area, Hall stated: "I couldn't imagine not having [flood] insurance [and living] that close to the ocean, [but my spouse] told me repeatedly, 'Lafayette never floods,' . . . even if there's a hurricane, it's not going to flood, . . . and so—[we didn't get insurance]."[10]

As described in nearly every local newspaper within the region, the 100-Year or 500-Year Flood terminology did not mean what the public thought it meant.[11] Instead, the phrases were supposed to help emergency managers and homeowners calculate the risk of extreme flooding based on past flood history. As defined by the 100-Year Flood standard, a flood of a sizable magnitude has a 1 percent statistical probability of occurring each year in a one-hundred-year period. Thus, there was a 1 percent chance a sizable flood would occur each year, or a 26 percent chance that it would occur at least once in the course of a homeowner's thirty-year mortgage.[12]

Despite the common assumption of sizable flood rarity, Louisianans saw historic flooding at least twice within the last one hundred years. In some places, historic flooding occurred five times or more in less than a century.[13] By 2016, the phrases "100-Year Flood" and "500-Year Flood" were used frequently and had been used with increasing regularity since 2005. Twice in the case of recent storms, once in the previous year to describe flooding in the spring, and a few times to reference other significant past events. Overall, on average, Louisianans experienced several 100-Year-Floods and at least one 500-Year Flood in their lifetimes.[14] Which made it all the more puzzling why Louisianans continued to misuse and misunderstand phrases like "100-Year Flood" and "500-Year Flood." With so many historic floods occurring, why were these terms still misunderstood?

To understand the misunderstanding of the terms "100-Year Flood" or "500-Year Flood," it is essential to separate where this terminology first emerged, its intended purpose, how and where it was applied, and how its meaning changed over time. It is also critical to understand how this alteration in meaning has influenced the perception of flood hazards today. The evolution of this disaster terminology showcases how our perception and reaction to floods (and other disasters) has changed historically. It also demonstrates our understanding or misunderstanding of science, our implementation of policy, and our efforts to mitigate impact and prevent or reduce hazards. And while there are many different risk- and hazard-naming systems, the implementation of flood terminology like the "100-Year Flood" or "500-Year Flood" serves as just one example of this that can be used to examine other disaster terminology.

The misunderstanding over the meaning of the 100-Year-Flood and 500-Year-Flood is not unique to Louisiana during the 2016 Floods. The terms have a much longer history of causing confusion as their original meaning was distorted in popular use. Louisianans followed an increasing global trend in using these terms, and globally, this trend has become more common over the past half century in the language used to describe disaster. A review of these terms' publication rate in books available through Google Books' database using the Google Ngram Viewer, a tool developed to chart frequencies of word use in the corpus of books scanned as part of Google Books' digitization initiative, shows that the phrases "100-Year Flood" and "500-Year Flood" grew in widespread use during the 1970s due to their implementation in US flood mitigation policy and have remained part of our popular discourse. It also illustrates that as awareness of global climatic change increased between the 1980s and 2000s, these terms have decreased in use due to repeat extreme flooding incidents but have not disappeared outright[15] (see figure below).

Newspaper databases like ProQuest, NewsBank, and Newspapers.com include thousands of references to these terms to refer to a variety of flood events throughout the United States and elsewhere.[16] Meanwhile, several scholarly publications, government reports, conference proceedings, and even FEMA training manuals reflect on the use of these terms, including attempts to debunk widespread misunderstandings of them.[17]

Before examining how the terms "100-Year Flood" and "500-Year Flood" became part of the public lexicon, it is essential to review how disaster terminology is historically constructed and used to describe hazards and disasters.

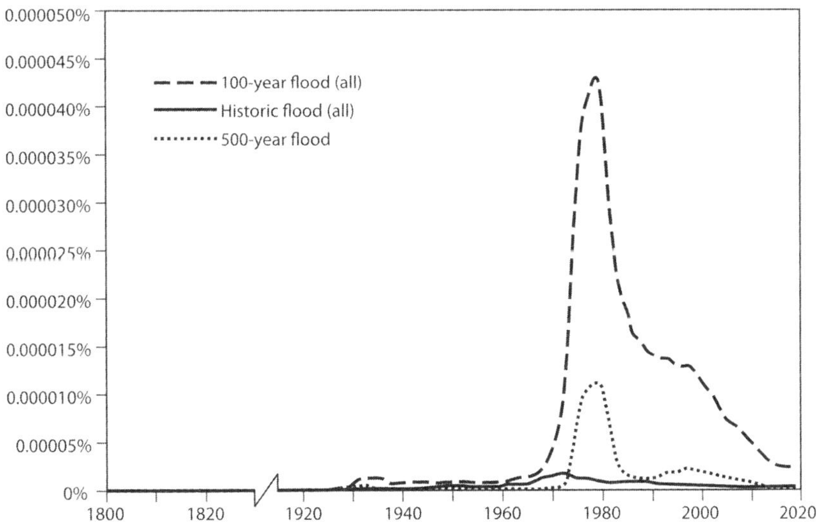

Recreation of Google Books Ngram Viewer Search for Flood Terms. Notice that 100-Year Flood is more common than 500-Year Flood, but both terms increase in use after the 1970s. Map redrawn by Mary Lee Eggart from Google Ngram data on March 2, 2022, using case-insensitive terms "100-Year Flood," "500-Year Flood," and "Historical Flood" for books in Google Books database between 1800 and 2019.

Historians focused on disasters examine the language used to describe such events because disaster language helps us understand a disaster in the scope of others in history. In the language of every disaster, for example, it is possible to find five key components: (1) Risk; (2) Context; (3) Impact; (4) Understanding; and (5) Influence (see figure below).

These five components are often found together or separate within the same description, depending on the type and date of publication or collected material (such as an interview) about the disaster's impact. The components are also often used cyclically, reflecting periods of disaster impact. For example, the first component revealed in disaster language is the perception of risk to a hazard within a population (e.g., potential loss of life, property, or other assets such as information). Since hazards can be both social and natural in origin, but disaster is inherently a social phenomenon (occurring when people are affected by a hazard), risk is frequently expressed using descriptors that emphasize vulnerability to social or natural factors. As individuals describe an impending incident, they indicate their perceived level of risk compared to

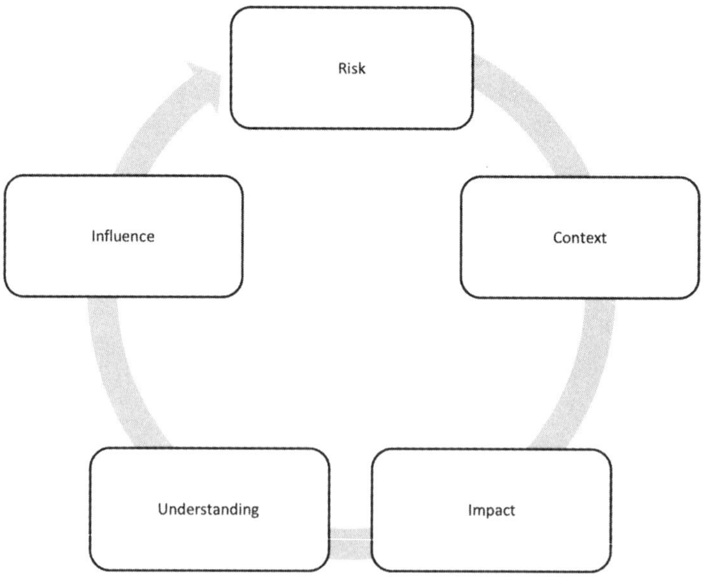

The five key components of language used in descriptions of disaster, and the progressive cycle of use frequently observed. Figure created by author.

other historical events, thus contextualizing the event in culturally transferrable comparisons of vulnerabilities. Disaster language also provides an outline of these events' lived experience that serves as both a reflective marker of experience with all disasters related to this hazard and a chronological account of the current tragedy. In other words, a person experiencing the 2016 Louisiana Floods compared the makeup of the current flood to historic floods of the past like the 1927 Mississippi River Flood with their memories of the impact of previous floods in the 1980s or 1990s in order to gauge their perceived vulnerabilities. This perception of vulnerability helped them judge what actions they needed to take as they responded to the current floods.

While the use of historical events as a marker for calculating perceived vulnerabilities is helpful in succinctly expressing risk to individuals, it does have downsides. First and foremost, disaster risk is not static; it shifts with each incident based on a multitude of factors. For example, if a person misunderstands the complexity of a prior event, is led to believe the current event is not as severe as a prior event, or is not informed of other factors that might change their individual risk to a particular hazard, it can skew the perception of vulnerability during a current incident, increasing risk to individuals and communities. This is why historical and contemporaneous contexts are often reviewed together to help explain vulnerability to populations to minimize any false sense of security afforded through comparisons. Unfortunately, contemporaneous context is often the hardest thing to gauge during an ongoing event, where factors can change quickly as the event unfolds and must be reassessed after the event.

Following the conclusion of a disaster, efforts to understand the disaster's impact are also found in descriptions of the postdisaster efforts to rebuild, restart, or reimagine lives afterward. Attempts to understand the current disaster often rely on perceptions of vulnerability, linking all previous disaster description methods together. For these reasons, disaster language frequently reveals larger understandings of science and cultural influences that play a role in making the disaster. In the 2016 Louisiana Floods case, recent studies to understand the floods' impact led to a review of the cultural decisions to build in flood zones due to increased population expansion near major cities in the state over the last quarter century.

After this rhetorical recapping of disaster impact, the language used with the current incident inaugurates language used for future incidents. For example, new lexicographical descriptions of extreme rain event flooding have entered popular discourse for local populations post-2016 Floods. Locals have constructed new markers for describing future floods, including the specification of their causal factors (extreme rain, regular rain, storm surge, snowmelt).

Overall, the language of disaster keenly illustrates the context and understanding of disasters from perceived threat to postincident analysis. Because of its ties to previous incidents (in building off the language used to describe prior disasters), disaster language can either be used to intentionally embrace the uniqueness of an event (separating from previous histories of disaster) or build upon it (by recognizing that cascading incidents are linked together). Paradoxically, just as historical consciousness can be used to influence how people make sense of disastrous events, it can also be avoided to maintain the perception that one incident is a "fluke" rather than an evolving trend. In this way, disaster language can be used to segment or separate an incident from its links to larger movements to tie repeated disasters to global issues like climatic change, environmental racism, and sustained development.[18] However, it is the vital work of disaster historians to make sure that historical consciousness is recognized in the discussion of disasters of the moment and be aware of the efforts to suppress history from the narrative of incident experience.

Due to its importance in understanding all facets of a disaster and its impact on the perception and reaction to an ongoing incident, several historians focus on disaster language. Some concentrate on the broad definition of a disaster as a way of examining our understanding of it, such as the way a description of a hazard impacts how people react to it or the ways disaster language is used to segment the social and natural components causing the disaster. Others focus on disaster terminology used by emergency managers, academics, politicians, and journalists as "convenience terms" meant to sum up the complexities of a hazard. Meanwhile, a few look more broadly at how we define aspects of disaster risk and reaction, including understanding the development and use of the phrases "vulnerability," "resilience," and "adaptation" currently dominating disaster studies. And finally, some historians look at how disaster language shapes the popular understanding of disaster impact historically. These historians argue that disaster language is a product of its time and reflects how societies explained their understanding of their environments and the hazards that shape them. For example, the terms "global warming" and "climate change" have influenced the perception of these larger issues, often clouding or politicizing related concerns as these terms come with culturally and politically associated meanings. To put it simply, historians are interested in disaster language because it shapes our impressions of both the hazards that initiate disasters and the resulting incidents.[19] Disaster terminology is built on historical understanding and experience with risk, coupled with modern science interpretation, and filtered into widespread use.

Historically, communities or individuals define floods. We know of specific floods because of their documentation in written records or oral tradition or the geological evidence left behind (including geological, chemical, and paleontological residuum). However, comparing size and scope of these floods is much harder as we try to apply modern standards of flood definition to these historical incidents.

Modern efforts to quantify historic floods in the United States emerged from three significant movements: First, from larger governmental efforts to control and modify rivers and streams between the nineteenth and twentieth centuries. Second, from the development of the field of hydrology, a study of the earth's water in relation to land. Third, as part of the development of the private insurance industry for hazards like floods.[20]

Between the nineteenth and twentieth centuries, federal, state, and local governments increasingly sought to regulate water flow through structural alterations by constructing levees, dams, bypass systems, reservoirs, and spillways.[21] Much of the effort to control water flow was directly related to the increased rate of flooding that affected the livelihoods of residents who were increasingly expanding the area of developed lands.[22] Significant floods, such as the 1927 Mississippi River Flood, served as the impetus for federal funding for structural initiatives like levee, dam, and spillway construction.[23] The public reaction to these catastrophic floods also drove policy such as the 1936 Flood Control Act to support flood mitigation efforts as the federal government gradually took on more involvement in disaster prevention, not just relief efforts.[24]

Mitigation efforts to prevent flooding led to increased interest in water movement and the development of the field of hydrology. While practiced since at least 4000 BC, the field of hydrology took on new life in the twentieth century as governments and universities began to fund hydrological research programs.[25] With the introduction of computers, hydrologists' modeling capabilities expanded dramatically, as did their prediction acumen with tools like geographic information system (GIS), leading to further professionalization of the field and its theories.[26]

As efforts to regulate flooding in the United States expanded and prediction methods became more precise, a burgeoning private insurance industry developed around flood hazards. The rise of the private flood insurance industry coalesced with the rise of a bureaucratic language of disaster that emerged with the expanded role of the state in responding to disasters. This created a constructed language, used and understood by the government, insurers, cities, and emergency managers, that simplified historical knowledge of risk. Unfortunately, this language was often misunderstood by the general public. Insurers capitalized on the complexities of understanding the bureaucratic language of floods to justify decisions made in policy payouts. Early insurance policies, for example, relied on the definition of floodplains, studies on the probability of repeat flooding occurrence, and reports by professional hydrologists suggesting meaningful changes to existing structures to mitigate flood effects.[27] By the mid-twentieth century, the federal government also provided insurance based on the assurance of these efforts to control flooding.[28]

Between 1965 and 1968, a flurry of studies on flooding and flood-related insurance programs inspired by recent disasters such as major floods in states like Kansas, Colorado, California, and Michigan, and a multistate flood in the Upper Mississippi River and Hurricane Betsy both in 1965 resulted in an onslaught of publications and reports by groups like the US Army Corps of Engineers, the Water Resources Council, the Department of Housing and Urban Development, the United States Geological Survey, and local and state-subsidized organizations.[29] These publications led to the delineation of flood hazard areas, zoning ordinances, anticipated flood frequency based on past knowledge of flooding, and the recommendation to establish a National Flood Insurance Program (NFIP). A July 1967 report by representatives of twenty-six federal agencies entitled *Proposed Flood Hazard Evaluation Guidelines for Federal Executive Agencies* recommended using a new base standard for flood probability.[30]

Called the 100-Year Flood Standard or the 1 Percent Flood Standard, it relied on previously collected data of flooding in areas around the country and the statistical modeling of predicted flood risk in flood-prone areas.[31] It propagated the level of risk homes in a flood zone had within a year, based on the available local flood rates over one hundred years. This standard built on early iterations of attempts to quantify annual risk of flood and expanded it into a comprehensive policy. Many communities throughout the country used the historical flood of record for their community as the base standard for measuring floods within their region. For example, if floodwaters in Vicksburg, Mississippi, crested at 56.2 feet during the historic 1927 Mississippi River Flood, the standard was used as a base flood rate to construct levees, buildings, and other development thereafter until another flood surpassed it.[32] The US Army Corps of Engineers (USACE) took this one step further by quantifying risk of flooding in major urban areas by delineating it in their Project Design Flood.[33] Project Design Flood estimated the hypothetical worst-case scenario based on peak discharge rates due to rain-based riverine flooding in an area to determine levee height, river dredging schedules, and water control structures. Meanwhile, the Tennessee Valley Authority (TVA) rated a "maximum probable flood," using a fifty-year flooding rate dataset.[34] Later, the NFIP utilized the language of a "base flood" to delineate comparable floods.[35] Thus, this one-hundred-year dataset or 1 percent flood risk rate combined new knowledge with old to create a standard for policy purposes for the NFIP at its inception.[36]

By definition, the 100-Year/1 Percent Flood Standard predicted flooding chances within an area based on available local flood rates, estimating that an individual home in a specified flood zone has a 1 percent chance of flooding in a given year over one hundred years, or a 26 percent chance of flooding at least once during a thirty-year home mortgage.[37] Depending on location, development, and other factors, this risk of flooding might be higher or lower in an area. In keeping with the continuing development of the bureaucratic language of disasters, the definition of the 100-Year/1 Percent Flood Standard was primarily expressed not in human or environmental terms, but in financial (mortgage) ones, again emphasizing the economic impact or risk governmental agencies like NFIP, insurers, and property owners could expect.

Soon after its introduction, the 100-Year/1 Percent Flood Standard was used for regulatory purposes in the National Flood Insurance Act of 1968 for the NFIP.[38] The NFIP led to the acceptance of this standard by other insurance programs, governmental entities, and, in some cases, the American public.[39] However, almost immediately, questions over the application of the 100-Year Flood Standard arose. Between 1968 and 1978, 127 floods equaled or exceeded the 100-Year Flood level in sixty-two counties in the United States, causing two substantial reviews of the standard.

Within the scientific and policy communities, a series of discussions took place in two forums. The first, the US Senate Hearings on the Flood Disaster Protection Act of 1973 concluded that previous methods (e.g., 50-Year Standard, historical flood of record, and a flexible standard) were not as robust in guiding economic development and flood protection and that the 100-Year Standard "is reasonable and consistent with Nationwide standards for flood protection."[40] The second review occurred at the end of the drastic flood growth period when the Government Accountability Office (GAO) recommended a review of this flood standard in March 1979. In 1983, the newly created Federal Emergency Management Agency (FEMA) completed its flood standard review, per the GAO's suggestion, issuing a report stating that the 100-Year Standard and the executive order should be retained. FEMA concluded that the 100-Year Standard "is strongly supported and being applied successfully by all levels of government . . . and no alternatives have been identified that are superior." This standard was soon applied to other flood protection factors, including the accreditation of levee systems at a one-hundred-year level by 1986.[41]

In 1993, the Great Midwest Flood of the Upper Mississippi and Lower Missouri Rivers again tested the use of the 100-Year Standard. Due to the flood's size and scope, affecting 505 counties and nine states with estimated damage at $16 billion (1993 USD), arguments arose in national newspapers about whether a new, higher standard should be applied. One suggestion was to assign different intervals such as 100-Year, 200-Year, and 500-Year flood standards. The concept of a 500-Year Flood event took off in popular media as those in the Midwest looked to describe the devastation caused by the flood as different from a 100-Year event.[42] However, despite the public support of a new 500-Year Flood interval, a review of the flood standard system conducted by Stanley Changnon, author of *The Great Flood of 1993*, found that it would be "hard to show the historic data record [for five hundred years] to base an analysis, changing observation methods, and the difficulty in assigning flow rates and elevations to past historic events."[43] Instead, the only standard used as a policy was the 100-Year/1 Percent Flood Standard, which historical datasets could validate. The terminology of a 500-Year Flood event did not dissipate in popular use in news reports, though, instead remaining as part of the vocabulary used with future historic flood events to delineate them as different or more extreme than a 100-Year Flood.

Despite proposals for alteration, the flood standard continued in use because it was also legally defendable, especially considering other types of environmental language adopted by the end of the twentieth century.[44] For example, as explained by Rutherford H. Platt, the then-director of the Ecological Cities Project at University of Massachusetts, Amherst, in a National Flood Policy Forum review of the 100-Year Flood Standard in 2004, "No Net Loss" in wetlands law and "Best Available Technology" in air quality law are much less precise and difficult to apply than the 100-Year/1 Percent Flood Standard. As such, even with "the ravages of professional misgivings, public criticism, and scientific uncertainty," the 100-Year/1 Percent Flood Standard wrought, the standard, "warts and all, is a durable and useful political compromise between worst-case and routine flood hazards."[45]

At a public level, the 100-Year/1 Percent Standard continued to confuse in the twenty-first century. On the one hand, it positively provided a tangible guideline for building and engineering developers to comply with legal regulations to construct new projects. The flood risk standard is similar to the risk calculations done on other environmental conditions for building design and construction like for fire, hurricanes, wind, snow, earthquakes, and the like, which usually range between 2 percent annual risk (50-Year) and 0.2 percent annual risk (500-Year).[46] For this reason, most building and construction designs factor in this risk, attempting to prevent failure for events up to 0.02 percent annual risk, or 5,000-Year events.[47] It also provided community planners, risk mitigation specialists, and governmental insurance agents tangible guidelines to follow for managing, if not reducing, risk within a region.[48]

For the average homeowner living in a potentially flood-prone zone, however, the 100-Year Flood Standard could be frustrating as prediction does not equal certainty when variables alter over time. For example, variables that can influence flood probability changes include development of communities surrounding a flood-prone area, changes to water quantities, fluctuating climatic conditions, zoning policies (and rezoning policies), structural and nonstructural flood mitigation issues, and even historical bias related to flood control efforts.[49] If a community has never flooded before, their perspective on the risk of flooding to their region likely is that their risk is minimal, despite the probability of a 1 percent annual chance. Additionally, larger climatic factors can influence flood risk.[50] Climatic change and coastal sea-level rise have worsened flood risk throughout the world, enacting a form of "slow violence" that occurs gradually and often invisibly on communities and ecosystems that are already historically vulnerable.[51] For these reasons, modern floods exemplify what historians call "slow disasters," or disasters that stray far from the standard of sudden, discrete events but instead are consequences of a deluge of developmental choices, regulatory policies, and environmental changes that result as much from the poor efficacy of disaster control and prevention as from natural hazards like extreme rainfall, storm surge, or snowmelt.[52]

The misunderstanding of how the flood standard is applied and what it stands for—and education and communication about it—also influenced communities' ability to understand their flood risk. For all of these reasons, the 100-Year Flood Standard or 1 Percent Flood Standard definition was blurred in everyday use, quickly becoming separated in original intent (to calculate and warn of risk) and popular use (to describe uniqueness of an event).[53] While the vague cultural meaning of the 100-Year Standard seems like a minor issue compared to larger mitigation and disaster response issues, it impacts communities experiencing a flooding event, exactly like it did in the case of the 2016 Louisiana Floods.

Within Louisiana, several factors coalesced to create the 2016 Floods disaster. The first was the unique rain event over several days, inundating areas that had not previously flooded and worsening flooding in at-risk areas near watershed outlets.[54] An additional factor influencing this flood event was outdated flood zone maps that inaccurately showed the risk of flooding in recently developed areas.[55] In the impacted region's major cities such as Baton Rouge and Lafayette, for instance, recent development occurred because of longitudinal displacement issues related to prior disasters such as Hurricanes Katrina and Rita and the *Deepwater Horizon* oil spill, as well as economic change that coupled with coastal change pushing people farther inland within the state and into these already swelling city limits.[56] These development alterations impacted watershed capabilities during this incident, leading to greater impact from hazardous rains.[57] While the NFIP requires FEMA to update flood maps every five years, full hydrological studies of underlying shifts to water distribution in these regions often lag. As a result, flood maps can account for some change in population density when calculating risk, but they cannot account for a combination of multiple factors of change. This meant that in grievously impacted areas like East Baton Rouge, Livingston, and Ascension Parishes the hydrological changes in these regions had not been updated in the flood maps since 2005, well before significant alterations to population and development of these regions that came in the post-Katrina period.[58] The problem of outdated flood maps is a concern for other communities, as well. The flood maps in place for New York City during 2012's Superstorm Sandy and areas of Texas during Hurricane Harvey in 2017, for example, had not been significantly updated since 1983.[59] In fact, according to a report by the Department of Homeland Security in September 2017, only 42 percent of FEMA's flood maps "adequately identified the level of flood risk," despite the goal of having 80 percent of its maps up-to-date.[60]

A final factor that exacerbated the disastrous flood results was the misunderstanding of the terminology of "100-Year Flood" and "500-Year Flood" in original intent versus popular use, which, as expressed earlier, drew considerable attention in news of the event. In 163 oral history interviews with flood victims taken at first- and second-year anniversaries of the 2016 Louisiana Floods by myself and student research assistants, many flood victims relayed the details of the floods mentioning factors described above that exacerbated their devastating flood experience. For example, many interviewees expressed their misunderstanding of the risk involved with a flooding incident like the one they experienced in August 2016. Flood victims indicated that they had never flooded before, did not live in delineated flood zones, or did not expect to flood again so soon after prior flooding in the area (assuming that their modification to their homes had brought them up to code and negated their probable risk).

Charles and Barbara White of Lafayette explained that none of their neighbors had flood insurance before the 2016 Floods, and one of their neighbors "directed for an insurance company in Louisiana."[61] James Proctor of Youngsville stated that when he purchased his house before the flood, he was assured it was above the flood line, but "St. Martin Parish had come back like a year or two later and told [him] that they got their surveys wrong and that everybody [in their neighborhood] was below flood." Unsurprisingly, Proctor's house flooded in 2016.[62]

Others expressed their desire to introduce a new flood risk terminology to clarify misunderstandings. Some argued for introducing new warning labels, such as categories of flooding like those used for hurricanes. Others demanded a revision of flood zone maps that they felt were long outdated and did not help them correctly calculate their risk. R. B. Logan of Lafayette said, "[my friend who had just moved from St. Louis before the 2016 Floods asked me]: Did you ever think I would flood? I said not in a million years," just based on his location and the flood maps.[63] Tina Spears of East Baton Rouge worries about repeat incidents: "We flooded again, like not too long ago, and it's just, every time it rains it's scary because I'm on panic mode hoping the water doesn't come back in the house because I don't want to go through that again. . . . I think we need a better template or something" to warn of the risk of floods.[64]

Others wished the 100-Year or 500-Year Flood terminology would disappear from widespread use altogether because of complications in understanding its meaning. "You haven't had an event like this in a thousand years," said John Christ of Denham Springs. Overall, though, those who were flooded hoped they would never experience another flood like it in the future, as this was surely a "once-in-a-lifetime" event, even if statistical probability indicated otherwise.[65]

While the problems creating or exacerbating the risk that caused this flood hazard to develop into a disaster are significant, the 100-Year or 500-Year Flood terminology shaped the perception of this disaster at all stages. It impacted the understanding of risk individuals in Louisiana had to this event. It was used (sometimes inaccurately) to create the context for defining the event before and after its impact. It served as a basis for measuring impact and expressing understanding of what went wrong. And it now sets the tone for describing risk in future flood events in the affected areas. This includes perpetuating the misunderstanding of risk, as well. For these reasons, both the correct understanding of the 100-Year and 500-Year Flood and the incorrect understanding will continue to exist, despite efforts to educate on its true meaning.

Systems of hazardous risk naming are introduced to help understand risk but can confuse, especially as years pass and conditions change. In the case of the 100-Year/1 Percent Flood Standard, developed to abate economic losses and quantify risk at engineering and floodplain management levels, it confused the general public. This is because individuals use it to indicate the severity (historically) and risk of a flood (statistically). In doing so, they blur the line in historical and scientific meaning, not distinguishing their purpose as separate. Knowing the history of the scientific definition of use and its popular use to contextualize historic floods helps us understand why these two meanings of this term continue to exist. Even with repeated explanation and education about its purpose, the popular misconception of its meaning is repeated as part of everyday discourse, creating a "myth" that is not quickly dispelled.

Proposals to alter the system over the years have included the replacement of the confusing standard with a color-coded system of flood insurance risk zones (e.g., those in a red zone are at more risk than those in a yellow or green zone), a recalculated spectrum of risk based on factors influencing the potential for catastrophic or regular flooding, or an expansion of the standard to include adjustable standards ranging from 100-Year, 200-Year, or 500-Year flood risk probabilities.[66] Yet, despite these suggestions and more than a half century of use, no significant change to this system has ensued.

So what can be done to fix this cyclical problem in flood risk terminology? For one thing, it is crucial to recognize how the language used for disaster and the risk associated with it impacts our understanding of it. Knowing the history behind this terminology's introduction and its reasons for use will help utilize it appropriately. And, as historians who understand the power of myths, we should work not to perpetuate them and dispel their use whenever possible as they often lead to damaging results in the future mitigation of disasters. Like other language used to define or delineate hazards or probabilities of them such as "climate change," hurricane categories or names, and even flood standards, the words we use to describe disaster are essential to our understanding of them.

NOTES

1. Elizabeth Crisp and Andrea Gallo, "At One-Week Mark, Louisiana Floods Are Worst Disaster since Hurricane Sandy, Red Cross Says," *Advocate*, August 19, 2016.

2. World Health Organization, "Floods," last accessed January 15, 2021, https://www.who.int/health-topics/floods#tab=tab_1.

3. David Morris, "How the 'Cajun Navy' Is Using Tech to Rescue Flood Victims in Louisiana," *Fortune*, August 23, 2016.

4. Elizabeth Crisp, "Gov. John Bel Edwards Returning from Colorado to Louisiana amid Severe Weather," *Advocate*, August 12, 2016.

5. Jason Samenow, "No-Name Storm Dumped Three Times as Much Rain in Louisiana as Hurricane Katrina," *Washington Post*, August 16, 2016.

6. "Louisiana Flooding Will Cost U.S. Economy More Than $10 Billion," *Advocate*, September 9, 2016.

7. Sherry Romero, interview by Liz Skilton et al., "Memories of the 2016 Floods: Years 1 and 2," August 11, 2018 (hereafter "Memories"), Guilbeau Center for Public History Collection, Part of the Archives of Cajun and Creole Folklore at the Center for Louisiana Studies, Youngsville.

8. Claire Taylor, "Flood Maps from '96 Cause Some Homeowners Big Headaches," *Daily Advertiser*, October 9, 2016.

9. Dennis Martin, interview by Liz Skilton et al., "Memories."

10. McKinzie Hall, interview by Liz Skilton et al., "Memories."

11. Father Jerome Ledoux, "What Is It with These 500-Year Floods?" *Opelousas (LA) Daily World*, September 20, 2016.

12. Note that while one would expect a 30 percent chance of flooding within a thirty-year mortgage at 1 percent rate per year, the statistical probability is actually slightly higher (at 26 percent) because of factors such as the variance of mortgage length, changes to risk levels due to development, and climatic fluctuations (Steve Esak, "Just What Is a '100-Year Flood?,'" *Allentown (PA) Morning Call*, July 9, 2006).

13. Alan Gallagher, "Flood Tested Drainage System, and We Failed," *Monroe (LA) News-Star*, March 27, 2016.

14. Campbell Robertson and Alan Blinder, "As Louisiana Floodwaters Recede, the Scope of Disaster Comes into View," *New York Times*, August 16, 2016.

15. Search by author of Google Ngram Viewer, January 12, 2021.

16. In a January 12, 2021, search on Newspapers.com, "100-Year Flood" populated with 517,897 matches, and the phrase "500-Year Flood" populated with 210,491 matches.

17. Federal Emergency Management Agency Region 10, "The 100 Year Flood Myth," training manual, https://training.fema.gov/hiedu/docs/hazrm/handout%203-5.pdf.

18. Clyde Woods, Development Drowned and Reborn: The Blues and Bourbon Restorations in Post-Katrina New Orleans (Athens: University of Georgia Press, 2017).

19. For examples of scholars who write on the significance of disaster language, see Ilan Kellman, *Disaster by Choice: How Our Actions Turn Natural Hazards into Catastrophes* (Oxford: Oxford

University Press, 2020); Ted Steinberg, *Acts of God: The Unnatural History of Natural Disaster in America* (New York: Oxford University Press, 2000); Ksenia Chmutina and Jason von Meding, "A Dilemma of Language: 'Natural Disasters' in Academic Literature," *International Journal of Disaster Risk Science* 10 (September 2019): 283–92; Greg Bankoff, "Remaking the World in Our Own Image: Vulnerability, Resilience and Adaptation as Historical Discourses," *Disasters* 43, no. 2 (April 2019): 221–39; Liz Skilton, *Tempest: Hurricane Naming and American Culture* (Baton Rouge: Louisiana State University Press, 2019); and Joshua P. Howe, *Behind the Curve: Science and the Politics of Global Warming* (Seattle: University of Washington Press, 2014).

20. For the history of these movements, see Martin Doyle, *The Source: How Rivers Made America and America Remade Its Rivers* (New York: Norton, 2018); Karen O'Neill, *Rivers by Design: State Power and the Origins of U.S. Flood Control* (Durham, NC: Duke University Press, 2006); and Jamie L. Pietruska, *Looking Forward: Prediction and Uncertainty in Modern America* (Chicago: University of Chicago Press, 2017).

21. Michael Hiltzik, *Colossus: The Turbulent, Thrilling Saga of the Building of Hoover Dam* (New York: Simon and Schuster, 2010).

22. John McPhee, *The Control of Nature* (New York: Farrar, Straus and Giroux, 2011).

23. Calvin R. Fremling, *Immortal River: The Upper Mississippi in Ancient and Modern Times* (Madison: University of Wisconsin Press, 2008).

24. Gareth Davies, "The Emergence of a National Politics of Disaster, 1865–1900," *Journal of Policy History* 26, no. 3 (June 2014): 305–26.

25. John E. Gribbin, *Introduction to Hydraulics and Hydrology with Applications for Stormwater Management*, 4th ed. (Clifton Park, NY: Cengage Learning, 2014).

26. June Fabryka-Martin and Jeanne Merz, *Hydrology: The Study of Water and Water Problems: A Challenge for Today and Tomorrow* (Carbondale, IL: Universities Council on Water Resources, 1983).

27. Alice Outwater, *Water: A Natural History* (New York: Basic, 1997).

28. National Academies of Sciences, Engineering, and Medicine National Research Council, *Affordability of National Flood Insurance Program Premiums: Report 1* (Washington, DC: National Academies Press, 2015), https://doi.org/10.17226/21709.

29. Andy Horowitz, *Katrina: A History, 1915–2015* (Cambridge, MA: Harvard University Press, 2020).

30. American Institutes for Research, The Pacific Institute for Research and Evaluation, and Deloitte & Touche LLP, "A Chronology of Major Events Affecting the National Flood Insurance Program" (hereafter "Chronology"), completed for Federal Emergency Management Agency, October 2002, 10.

31. US Water Resources Council, *Flood Hazard Evaluation Guidelines for Federal Executive Agencies*. Washington, DC: US Government Printing Office, 1972.

32. John Barry, *Rising Tide: The Great Mississippi River Flood of 1927 and How It Changed America* (New York: Touchstone, 1997).

33. James F. Barnett, *Beyond Control: The Mississippi River's New Channel to the Gulf of Mexico* (Jackson: University Press of Mississippi, 2017).

34. Matthew L. Downs, *Transforming the South: Federal Development in the Tennessee Valley, 1915–1960* (Baton Rouge: Louisiana State University Press, 2014).

35. Francis V. Reilly, "The 'Base Flood Standard"—Historical Perspective," *Gilbert F. White National Flood Policy Forum 2004 Assembly Reducing Flood Losses: Is the 1% Chance (100-year) Flood Standard Sufficient?* (hereafter *Forum*) (Washington, DC: National Academies Keck Center, 2004), 13–16.

36. Michael F. Robinson, "History of the 1 Percent Chance Flood Standard," in *Forum*, 2.

37. Nicholas Lally, "Flood Insurance and its Relationship to Floodplain Management," unpublished paper prepared for the Federal Emergency Management Agency, 1982, http://65.182.2.246/docum/crid/Marzo2006/CD2/pdf/eng/doc10041/doc10041-contenido.pdf.

38. "National Flood Insurance Act of 1968," Public Law 90–448, Title XII *of* Housing and Urban Development Act of 1968, 82 Stat. 572, 42 U.S.C. 4001–4127.

39. Richard Krimm, "Why the 100 Year Flood Standard," in *Forum*, 11–12.

40. US Senate, *Flood Disaster Protection Act of 1973: Hearings Before the Subcommittee on Housing and Urban Affairs of the Committee on Banking Housing and Urban Affairs, United States Senate . . . on S. 1495 and H.R. 8449*, GPO, October 31, 1973.

41. "Chronology," 28–34.

42. B. Drumond Ayres Jr., "A River Ran through It," *Indianapolis Star*, August 22, 1993.

43. "Chronology," 49.

44. Jon Kusler, "A Legal Perspective on the 100 Year Flood Standard," in *Forum*, 116–18.

45. Rutherford H. Platt, "The Durability of the One %/100-Year Flood Standard Despite Its Many Faults," in *Forum*, 19.

46. Chris Jones, "Building Standards and the 1% Annual Chance Flood Standard," in *Forum*, 85.

47. Jones, "Building Standards and the 1% Annual Chance Flood Standard," 85.

48. Clive Q. Goodwin, "Insurance Alone Is Not Enough—Understanding the Flood Hazard Is the Key," in *Forum*, 122.

49. USGS, "Special Topics: The 100-Year Flood," last accessed December 10, 2020, https://www.usgs.gov/special-topic/water-science-school/science/100-year-flood?qt-science_center_objects=0#qt-science_center_objects.

50. Rebecca Elliott, *Underwater: Loss, Flood Insurance, and the Moral Economy of Climate Change* (New York: Colombia University Press, 2021).

51. Samantha Montano, "The Louisiana Floods Are Devastating, and Climate Change Will Bring More Like Them: We're Not Ready," *Vox*, August 23, 2016; Rob Nixon, *Slow Violence and the Environmentalism of the Poor* (Cambridge, MA: Harvard University Press, 2011), 6–10.

52. Scott Gabriel Knowles, *The Disaster Experts: Mastering Risk in Modern America* (Philadelphia: University of Pennsylvania Press, 2013).

53. Robert Ogle, "Communicating What the 1% Chance Flood Means," in *Forum*, 124.

54. National Weather Service, "August 2016 Flood Summary Page," last accessed January 15, 2021, https://www.weather.gov/lix/August2016flood.

55. Claire Taylor, "Flood Maps from '96 Cause Some Homeowners Big Headaches," *Lafayette (LA) Daily Advertiser*, October 9, 2016.

56. K. van der Wiel, S. B. Kapnick, et al., "Rapid Attribution of the August 2016 Flood-Inducing Extreme Precipitation in South Louisiana to Climate Change," *Hydrological Earth Systems Science Discussions* (2016): 1–40.

57. Louisiana Economic Development, "The Economic Impact of the August 2016 Floods on the State of Louisiana," August 11, 2016, https://gov.louisiana.gov/assets/docs/RestoreLA/SupportingDocs/Meeting-9-28-16/2016-August-Flood-Economic-Impact-Report_09-01-16.pdf.

58. David J. Mitchell, "FEMA Won't Change Maps after Floods: Some Worry of Consequences," *Advocate*, September 24, 2016.

59. Michael Keller et al., "Outdated and Unreliable: FEMA's Faulty Flood Maps Put Homeowners at Risk," *Bloomberg*, October 6, 2017.

60. Quote from Keller et al., 80 percent goal from Office of Inspector General, "FEMA Needs to Improve Management of Its Flood Mapping Programs," Department of Homeland Security, OIG-17-110, September 27, 2017, https://www.documentcloud.org/documents/4066233-OIG-17-110-Sep17.html.

61. Charles and Barbara White, interview by Liz Skilton et al., "Memories."

62. James Proctor, interview by Liz Skilton et al., "Memories."

63. RB Logan, interview by Liz Skilton et al., "Memories."

64. Tina Spears, interview by Liz Skilton et al., "Memories."

65. John Christ, interview by Liz Skilton et al., "Memories."

66. Maggie Koerth, "It's Time to Ditch the Concept of '100-Year Floods,'" *FiveThirtyEight.com*, August 30, 2017.

CONTRIBUTORS

BENJAMIN L. CARP is Daniel M. Lyons Professor of American History at Brooklyn College and teaches at the Graduate Center of the City University of New York. He is the author of *The Great New York Fire of 1776: A Lost Story of the American Revolution* (2023).

ALYSSA TOBY FAHRINGER holds a faculty appointment as the digital scholarship consultant at George Mason University Libraries.

CAROLINE GREGO is a visiting assistant professor of history at Queens University of Charlotte and a historian of labor, race, and environment in the US South. In addition to articles published in the *Journal of Southern History* and the *American Historical Review*, she is the author of *Hurricane Jim Crow: How the Great Sea Island Storm of 1893 Shaped the Lowcountry South* (2022).

JONATHAN TODD HANCOCK is an associate professor of history at Hendrix College, outside Little Rock, Arkansas. A historian of Early America and Native North America, he is the author of *Convulsed States: Earthquakes, Prophecy, and the Remaking of Early America* (2021).

CYNTHIA A. KIERNER is a professor of history at George Mason University, where she teaches courses on early America, disasters, and women's history. She is the author of many books, including *Inventing Disaster: The Culture of Calamity from the Jamestown Colony to the Johnstown Flood* (2019).

SCOTT GABRIEL KNOWLES is a professor in the Graduate School of Science and Technology Policy at the Korea Advanced Institute of Science and Technology (KAIST). He is the author of *The Disaster Experts: Mastering Risk in Modern America* (2011) in addition to other works, including edited collections and the podcast series *COVIDCalls*.

JANE MANNERS is an assistant professor at Temple Beasley School of Law. She received her PhD from Princeton University and her JD from Harvard Law School. Among other topics, her work focuses on the relationship between the legislative and executive branches of government in the nineteenth century, especially in the context of disaster relief. Her articles have appeared in the *Columbia Law Review*, the *Fordham Law Review*, and the *William and Mary Quarterly*.

RICHARD M. MIZELLE JR. is an associate professor of history at the University of Houston. His research focuses on the history of race, medicine, and environment in the twentieth century. He is currently writing a history of race and diabetes.

MATTHEW MULCAHY is a professor of history at Loyola University Maryland. He has written or cowritten several books and articles about natural disasters in colonial British America, including *Hurricanes and Society in the British Greater Caribbean, 1624–1783* (2005) and *Sea and Land: An Environmental History of the Caribbean* (2022).

SARAH E. NARAMORE is an assistant professor of history at Northwest Missouri State University. Her research focuses on the history of the medical profession in the United States in the late eighteenth and early nineteenth centuries. She has published articles in *Social History of Medicine*, *Journal of the History of Medicine and Allied Science*, and *Endeavour*.

ASHLEY ROGERS is the executive director of Whitney Plantation, a museum dedicated to the interpretation of slavery in south Louisiana.

LIZ SKILTON is an associate professor of history and the J. J. Burdin and Helen B. Burdin/Board of Regents Endowed Professor in Louisiana Studies at the University of Louisiana at Lafayette. She is the author of *Tempest: Hurricane Naming and American Culture* (2019) and head of the Recent Louisiana Disasters Oral History Project.

TOM WICKMAN is an associate professor of history and American studies at Trinity College in Hartford, Connecticut. He is author of *Snowshoe Country: An Environmental and Cultural History of Winter in the Early American Northeast* (2018).

INDEX